GETTING TO GRADUATION

GETTING TO GRADUATION

The Completion Agenda in Higher Education

Edited by ANDREW P. KELLY & MARK SCHNEIDER

The Johns Hopkins University Press

Baltimore

© 2012 The Johns Hopkins University Press
All rights reserved. Published 2012
Printed in the United States of America on acid-free paper
9 8 7 6 5 4 3 2 1

The Johns Hopkins University Press
2715 North Charles Street
Baltimore, Maryland 21218-4363
www.press.jhu.edu

Library of Congress Cataloging-in-Publication Data

Getting to graduation : the completion agenda in higher education / edited by Andrew P.
Kelly and Mark Schneider.
     p. cm.
   Includes bibliographical references and index.
     ISBN 978-1-4214-0622-0 (hdbk. : alk. paper) — ISBN 978-1-4214-0693-0 (elec-
tronic) — ISBN 1-4214-0622-5 (hdbk. : alk. paper) — ISBN 1-4214-0693-4 (electronic)
     1. Education, Higher—Aims and objectives—United States.   2. Education and state—
United States.   3. Educational change—United States.   4. Educational attainment—
United States.   5. College graduates—United States.   I. Kelly, Andrew P.   II. Schneider,
Mark, 1946–
   LA227.4.G49 2012
   378.73—dc23   2012000019

A catalog record for this book is available from the British Library.

*Special discounts are available for bulk purchases of this book. For more information,
please contact Special Sales at 410-516-6936 or specialsales@press.jhu.edu.*

The Johns Hopkins University Press uses environmentally friendly book materials, including recycled text paper that is composed of at least 30 percent post-consumer waste,
whenever possible.

CONTENTS

ACKNOWLEDGMENTS

Over the past five years the nation has undergone a fundamental reordering of priorities in higher education policy. Previously concerned primarily with *access* (getting more students through the doors), political rhetoric and policy debates have now shifted to a focus on *completion* (ensuring that more students earn a degree). This rethinking has been pushed by a number of lofty expectations and goals, including President Barack Obama's ambition to produce eight million more degrees by the year 2020. In the wake of this ambitious agenda change, a number of questions have been raised about whether our system of higher education institutions and policies, as currently conceived, is capable of delivering the dramatic increases in productivity necessary to meet these new goals.

To describe and analyze this challenge, we commissioned new research from top researchers and policy analysts. The eleven chapters that resulted present an overview of the new challenges and policy issues facing the nascent "completion agenda" and discuss lessons from several states that have experimented with various reforms. We believe our contributors have provided thought-provoking research and arguments that will help to shape policy debates in the years to come.

The chapters in this volume were initially presented at a research conference at the American Enterprise Institute (AEI) in February 2011. We thank the following discussants for their invaluable feedback from that conference: Dewayne Matthews, vice president for policy and strategy at the Lumina Foundation; Travis Reindl, head of postsecondary education work for the National Governors Association; Sara Goldrick-Rab, assistant professor of educational policy studies and sociology at the University of Wisconsin; Susan Dynarski, associate professor of education and public policy at the University of Michigan; Eduardo Ochoa, assistant secretary for postsecondary education at the U.S. Department of Education; and George Pernsteiner, chancellor of the Oregon University System. Their thoughtful comments and constructive criticism strengthened the volume considerably.

We are grateful for the unwavering support provided by the American Enterprise Institute and its president, Arthur Brooks. The project would not have been possible without the generous financial support of The Bill and Melinda Gates Foundation, and we are deeply indebted to our program officers for their support and guidance throughout.

Thanks also to the staff at AEI, who coordinated the conference and helped complete and edit this volume. In particular, we would like to thank Olivia Meeks and Daniel Lautzenheiser for their diligent efforts, as well as Jenna Talbot and Whitney Downs for their vital assistance. Finally, we are deeply indebted to the terrific team at the Johns Hopkins University Press, most notably executive editor Jacqueline Wehmueller and editorial assistant Sara Cleary, who consistently supported and enriched our efforts to make this volume a reality.

Introduction

ANDREW P. KELLY AND MARK SCHNEIDER

A merican higher education, which has long regarded itself as the best in the world, is in the midst of a dramatic and unprecedented increase in expectations. In his first State of the Union address, in 2010, President Barack Obama issued a bold challenge to America's colleges and universities. "By 2020," the president told a joint session of Congress, "America will once again have the highest proportion of college graduates in the world."[1] The president set an ambitious goal: meeting the challenge will require the production of an additional eight million degrees by the year 2020. Bill Gates, the country's best-known college dropout, set an even more ambitious goal for his foundation, proposing to "double the numbers" of low-income students who earn a college degree. Meanwhile, the Lumina Foundation for Higher Education is pursuing its "Big Goal" of "increasing the share of Americans with high-quality postsecondary degrees and credentials to 60 percent by 2025."[2]

These goals represent more than political talking points or an incremental shift in emphasis: they constitute a fundamental rethinking of priorities in higher education policy. After four decades of a relentless focus on improving college *access*, debates about higher education reform have shifted to questions of student success and degree *completion*. Instead of simply opening the gates to more and more students and then hoping for the best, the new "completion agenda" calls on institutions and policymakers to create policies and practices that improve the rate at which students finish their degrees. These goals have placed newfound emphasis on the idea that institutions of higher education must play a prominent role in promoting student success and institutional productivity, and that federal and state policies should emphasize student retention and completion.

In the process of ratcheting up expectations, however, these ambitious goals have also raised questions about the policy changes necessary to accomplish them and the obstacles that may stand in the way. This volume attempts to take stock of the new higher education agenda, exploring where we stand in the effort to improve student success and which sectors of the postsecondary landscape seem particularly ripe for increases in such success. The contributors suggest that business as usual will not get us to where the president wants us to go and that the challenge goes beyond the incremental and piecemeal reform efforts that have prevailed to this point. Improvements on the scale necessary to meet the nation's completion agenda will require reforms that are more far-reaching and comprehensive, an expansion of what we define as postsecondary education, and a broad and steadfast commitment to raising the productivity of our higher education system.

Where Matters Stand

On many dimensions, America's 40-year commitment to expanding college access is a success story. The proportion of high school graduates who go on to enroll in postsecondary education has risen steadily since the 1970s. In 1980, just about half of the nation's high school graduates immediately enrolled in a two- or four-year college the following fall; by 2008, that percentage had jumped to 69 percent. Although gaps remain between the percentage of white and minority students who enroll in college, as well as between the enrollment patterns of students of high and low socioeconomic status, the percentage of traditionally underrepresented students going on to college has increased dramatically. For example, between 1980 and 2007, the proportion of African American high school completers who went on to participate in postsecondary education went from 44 percent to 56 percent; the gain for Hispanic high school graduates was also 12 percentage points, increasing from about 50 percent in 1980 to 62 percent by 2007.[3] In a relatively short period, American higher education has moved from an elite system designed for the few to a much more accessible mass system of postsecondary options.

While more students than ever are getting a foot in the door, there is little evidence that these gains in access have been accompanied by comparable increases in the rate at which students complete a degree. The percentage of Americans aged 25 to 29 with a bachelor's degree grew impressively between 1950 and 2010, but much of this growth occurred early in the period before flattening out in the most recent decade. For instance, while bachelor's degree attainment among this age group grew from 22 percent to 32 percent between 1975 and 2010, it increased just 2.5 percentage points over the first decade of the 2000s, compared to a gain of more than 7 percentage points in the prior 25 years.[4]

There is a disconnect between expansions in enrollment and sluggish attainment growth, primarily because a consistently large proportion of students who start college fail to finish. Since the federal government began collecting graduation rates for degree programs in the mid-1990s, six-year completion rates for first-time, full-time students at four-year colleges have been stagnant, hovering below 60 percent. The results for two-year colleges are much worse, with around 30 percent of first-time, full-time students completing a two-year degree within three years. The completion rate for sub-baccalaureate programs actually declined slightly between 2002 and 2008, falling to 27.5 percent for the 2005 cohort.[5] Graduation rates in short-term certificate programs are better than those for associate's degrees, but these types of credentials actually don't "count" when the Census calculates attainment rates.

Institutional graduation rates are limited because they don't account for transfer students who go on to graduate elsewhere. Unfortunately, individual-level attainment rates are also mediocre, and the data suggest that completion rates have not improved in recent decades. The latest installment of the Beginning Postsecondary Students (BPS) Longitudinal Study, which tracked incoming students in the 2003–2004 cohort, found that by 2009, 58 percent of students who started at a four-year college had attained a bachelor's degree, 26 percent who started at a two-year college had earned an associate's or above, and about 36 percent were no longer enrolled in any institution.[6] The 1995–96 BPS revealed six-year completion rates that were nearly identical.[7] A rigorous analysis of the National Longitudinal Study of 1972 and the National Education Longitudinal Study of 1988 shows that the percentage of recent high school graduates who completed a degree within eight years of graduation declined by more than five percentage points between the early 1970s and mid-1990s.[8] In short, multiple sources of data collected at different levels of analysis reveal the same pattern: more than half of the students who start postsecondary education fail to finish a degree in six years, and this rate has been relatively stable over time.

Because we are enrolling greater numbers of students, graduating them at the same rate means that degree attainment has grown over the last 15 years, but at a much slower rate than in the past. Our productivity has slowed to the point that other nations have recently caught up and even surpassed our youngest cohort of workers in the international attainment race. According to data collected by the Organisation for Economic Co-operation and Development (OECD), while the United States ranks fourth in overall degree attainment for adults ages 25 to 64, the country ranks twelfth in degree attainment among the youngest cohort (25- to 34-year-olds).[9] Countries like Korea, Poland, and France have made double-digit gains in attainment among their youngest workers since the mid-1990s; in contrast, attainment among 25- to 34-year-olds in the United States increased only 3.5 percentage points between 1997 and 2006.[10] As education secretary Arne Duncan summed it up in August 2010, "We've flat-lined where other countries have passed us by."[11]

These lackluster results, and the bright light shone on them by foundations and policymakers, are at the core of the recent push to boost degree attainment rates by radically revamping higher education. As William "Brit" Kirwan, former chancellor of the University of Maryland system, remarked about the college completion agenda, "The stars are aligning in a way that gives me some hope. . . . This is a problem that has been around for too long. But now there is beginning to emerge a focus of attention and activity that, quite frankly, we haven't had up to now."[12]

No one doubts that there is overwhelming rhetorical support for raising degree attainment. And there is no question that higher education stakeholders are more acutely focused on promoting student retention and completion rates than ever before. But good intentions, lofty rhetoric, and attention to the problem will only carry us so far. Given our current rate of attainment growth, experts estimate that achieving the president's goal of a 60 percent attainment rate by 2020 would require a quadrupling of the historic year-over-year growth rate in attainment. The challenge for community colleges is even larger: to hit the president's target, community colleges will have to produce 33 percent more degrees per year than they do now (approximately 280,000 more degrees per year).[13]

After the speeches, conferences, and blue-ribbon panels conclude, any dramatic improvement in the productivity of our higher education system will require fundamental changes in the way institutions of higher education do business, significant reform of federal and state policies, and an expanded arsenal of cost-effective and proven policy solutions. But our "playbook" of solutions is pretty empty.

What Do We Know about How to Improve?

The short answer to this question: we know little about "what works" when it comes to significantly raising degree completion. However, as the rest of this volume explores at length, we do know that our current set of policy solutions is probably inadequate for making significant progress on the completion agenda and that the tools available to federal policymakers are unlikely to be up to the challenge.

Decades of higher education research have provided us with some unassailable basic findings, but few of these provide clear guidance on how to attack the current challenge. For instance, students who attend more selective colleges are more likely to graduate. This is true even after you hold student characteristics constant. But, as Matthew M. Chingos argues in his chapter, we still know very little about what (if anything) selective colleges actually "do" that promotes student retention and completion more effectively than less selective schools. As a result, there are few lessons about student success that can simply be exported from selective schools with high graduation rates to other campuses.

Data also suggest that students who take a more challenging set of high school classes, particularly students who have taken rigorous high school math courses, are more likely to complete a degree.[14] But does this imply that raising degree completion rates is simply a question of cramming more students into trigonometry and calculus? That's not to say that we haven't tried—more students are taking more rigorous math courses than ever before—but there is little evidence that high school students know any more math or are any more likely to graduate from college.[15]

And though parents and students complain about the cost of college, and dropouts often cite inadequate financial aid as their reason for leaving school, the relationship between financial aid and completion is less straightforward than "more aid equals higher completion rate." As Eric Bettinger argues in this volume, financial aid is a blunt instrument for improving degree completion.

Compounding the problem is the fact that while the federal government has set ambitious goals, it has few tools at its disposal to achieve them. This is true of both federal policy and federal research. On the research side, while federal education research has undergone something of a renaissance since the turn of the twenty-first century, demanding much more by way of scientific rigor and a dogged focus on "what works," higher education has been largely marginalized. At the end of 2010, of the 16 research centers in the Institute of Education Sciences, only one was dedicated to higher education research.[16]

The federal government's role in higher education policy has never been that of the stern taskmaster with an eye on institutional productivity. Instead, the federal government has typically poured money into financial aid programs, required rudimentary data reporting, and set a low bar for staying eligible for Title IV money. On the occasions when federal policymakers have taken a more active interest in promoting higher education accountability and productivity, they have either been rebuffed by the higher education establishment (the Spellings Commission) or become casualties of the budgetary process (Obama's Access and Completion Fund).

The Opportunities

While the country certainly has its work cut out for it, the chapters that follow point out some of the opportunities for making progress. A set of recurring themes stand out. First, we must broaden our definition of what constitutes "postsecondary education" and what "counts" in our measures of degree attainment. Second, we must look to the sub-baccalaureate sector as a place to make gains in the number of students who earn a credential. Third, while experimentation with small-scale interventions is important, we must be sure to emphasize scalability and comprehensive approaches to institutional reform. Finally, we must look to the states, both for examples of policies that have proven successful and to do much of the "real work" in accomplishing attainment goals.

Many of the chapters that follow suggest that our current definition of "college" is far too limited and has led to a portfolio of postsecondary options that does not meet the needs of all students. For one thing, though certificate programs of more than one year have been shown to have a significant labor market payoff, our current method of counting degrees and measuring "degree attainment" does not adequately account for these types of programs. More broadly, less traditional postsecondary activities such as formal, state-recognized apprenticeships are largely ignored as postsecondary options. Instead of narrowing our definition of postsecondary attainment, reaching our attainment goals requires that we expand it, honoring activities that provide labor market skills but are currently excluded from higher education discussions or are under-funded and underemphasized.

Also, while the United States ranks among the world's most educated nations in bachelor's degree attainment, we lag far behind other nations in the production of associate's degrees. This "community college conundrum," as Arthur M. Hauptman puts it, will pose a serious obstacle to making fundamental progress in raising attainment rates. Policymakers must explicitly focus reform energy and attention on sub-baccalaureate programs.

In addition, while a small set of researchers are making strides in developing our understanding of "what works" to promote degree completion, too often these small-bore experiments are not scalable across institutions and are rarely evaluated in terms of their cost-effectiveness. In fact, researchers at the University of Wisconsin have argued that across many higher education policy interventions that are routinely implemented, very few pass a cost-benefit analysis.[17] And even when a single intervention proves successful on a single campus, the vagaries of foundation funding for dissemination and scalability, coupled with skeptical community college cultures, often lead to a dead end.

When interventions of this type prove successful—and there are examples of successful remediation reform, helpful transfer credit arrangements, and the like—the effects are rarely large enough that broad implementation of the strategy will make more than an incremental improvement. Moreover, it is difficult to target policy interventions to the students who will benefit the most from them, and making incremental progress in raising completion rates is often expensive. Targeted interventions are important, but reform-minded policymakers and institutions would also be wise to explore more comprehensive reforms that change the way institutions operate and are organized.

The real opportunities for policy change likely lie with the states. Luckily, there are a handful of pioneering states that policymakers can look to for lessons about how to reform higher education. Ohio has a long tradition of performance-based funding for higher education, a policy that has survived both budget deficits and political turnover. Texas has made great strides in increasing both participation and degree attainment rates across its diverse array of campuses, an effort that was made possible by the state's strong political leadership and commitment to higher education accountability. In both states, the key was to create incentives that emphasize performance while recognizing that different institutions have different missions. Strong and consistent leadership from governors was also essential. The states and higher education institutions themselves are the key players in the attainment challenge; if we are to succeed, they must be the real drivers of significant improvement.

The Way Forward

As the chapters to come point out, our new higher education goals are extremely ambitious; the path to achieving them is anything but clear; and even the opportunities for improvement will require hard work, innovation, and tough choices. But before we can even hope to make progress, policymakers must first wrestle with the thorny questions explored in the rest of this volume.

The eleven chapters that follow are grouped into four sections. Part 1 presents an overview of the challenges facing the country as it tries to improve its postsecondary attainment rates. Part 2 focuses on the performance and potential of sub-baccalaureate programs. Part 3 takes a fresh look at three oft-invoked policy problems and their relationship to raising completion rates: remediation, credit transfer, and financial aid. Finally, part 4 examines lessons from three states, provided by authors who played a central role in each reform effort.

Arthur M. Hauptman, a long-time higher education consultant, leads off in the first chapter with a provocative look at the evolution of national policy goals from increasing access to increasing completion. His chapter looks at trends in participation, completion, and attainment, and describes and clarifies the goals set by President Barack Obama and others. Hauptman pays particular attention to the need to distinguish between efforts to increase completion rates and efforts to increase the number of graduates produced. With a broad sweep, the chapter considers historical trends of postsecondary attainment in the United States and examines whether international data, often used to create a sense of crisis in American higher education, are valid for comparing the United States with other advanced industrial countries. Using these data, Hauptman explores whether the nation's new completion targets are realistic and identifies the rhetorical and statistical pitfalls to avoid in pursuing attainment goals.

In the second chapter, Matthew M. Chingos of the Brookings Institution focuses on what we know and what we need to know about graduation rates in our universities. Chingos's analysis explores the "playbook" the nation can draw on as it tries to rise to the challenges inherent in the completion agenda. One of the most controversial arguments in the chapter is his discussion of the effect that placing more qualified students in seats at highly selective campuses will have on the overall attainment rate. The analysis suggests that combating "undermatch"—the central problem highlighted in Chingos's previous book, *Crossing the Finish Line: Completing College at America's Public Universities*—is unlikely to significantly boost the national bachelor's degree attainment rate. Chingos also reviews the small number of other interventions that have been rigorously studied and concludes that the research base is still in its infancy. He argues that researchers should increasingly turn their energies to topics like instructor quality, student learning, and online delivery.

When people think of postsecondary education, the image that most likely pops up is an ivy-covered campus where students start in the fall of one year and walk out with a bachelor's degree four years later. But there is definitive evidence that the nation needs to pay far more attention to its sub-baccalaureate degree and certificate programs. The three chapters of part 2 focus on these programs.

Thomas Bailey, a professor at Teachers College, Columbia University, who is one of the nation's leading authorities on community colleges, looks at the extent to which these institutions can achieve the lofty graduation goals that must be met if the nation is to reach its attainment targets. Bailey begins by noting just how much attention the Obama administration has focused on community colleges as a key to American competitiveness. He explores the likelihood that community colleges, as they are currently constituted, can achieve these ambitious goals. Given the low graduation rate of public community college students, Bailey explores what it would take to increase the number of degree and certificate completers to hit the president's targets. The chapter assesses whether the optimism surrounding the potential for improving graduation rates among community college students is well founded, given realities, and what reforms must be in place to achieve the ambitious goals set for these institutions.

Next, Brian Bosworth, of FutureWorks, explores the importance of certificates as pathways to postsecondary success and good jobs. Again, most people think about postsecondary education success in terms of the production of degrees. But Bosworth argues that certificate programs have become an increasingly important piece of the postsecondary landscape, especially for minority and low-income youth and for midcareer adults. Bosworth argues that we still do not know much about which types of certificate programs are particularly successful, with regard to both completion rates and economic returns, or what policies are conducive to a productive system of certificate programs. His analysis reviews how these programs have grown in importance, which varieties of programs are most promising, and the extent to which they are an efficient way to improve our attainment rates. Bosworth concludes with recommendations for action at the national, state, and institutional levels to increase high-value certificate programs and make those programs more accessible to those who need them most.

While certificate programs have begun to attract attention, Diane Auer Jones, of the Career Education Corporation and a former assistant secretary of education, looks at the promise of apprenticeship programs, a postsecondary path to success that has been neglected in the United States even as it has become a highly successful pathway to careers in other countries. Jones argues that apprenticeship programs, which include on-the-job training and coordinated instruction, are an effective and efficient way for individuals to gain academic skills while also preparing for meaningful careers. Jones looks at the barriers that stand in the way of expanding apprenticeship programs and identifies the aspects of international apprenticeship programs that could be adopted to strengthen our offerings and prepare more individuals for the jobs they seek.

Part 3 considers some of the most common policy levers that are viewed as means of increasing completion. Stanford economist Eric Bettinger leads off the section with an analysis of student financial aid, which he describes as a blunt instrument for increasing degree attainment. Bettinger explores the cost-effectiveness of existing aid policies and explores the extent to which state and federal financial aid policies can improve retention and completion rates. Given how much money the nation spends on student aid, his conclusions are sobering. Bettinger concludes his chapter with an analysis of innovative financial aid policies that are emerging in some states and explores the extent to which these new, more cost-effective policies might be replicated.

The Harvard Graduate School of Education's Bridget Terry Long studies another widely used, very expensive, and less than successful approach to improving student success: academic remediation for underprepared college students. She shows that while upwards of 60 percent of incoming community college students and around 30 percent of incoming students at four-year institutions are in need of remedial or developmental courses, these students are more likely to drop out and less likely to complete a degree or credential even after enrolling in remedial programs. These disappointing results are particularly noteworthy given the high costs of remediation to both students and taxpayers. Long's chapter ends with a discussion of how we may go about improving remediation.

In chapter 8, Josipa Roksa, of the University of Virginia, looks at credit transfer and portability. This policy question has attracted less public attention than financial aid and remediation, but many higher education analysts believe that lack of credit portability drives down completion rates by erecting barriers to the increasing number of students who wish to transfer from one institution to another. Roksa maintains that even as policymakers increasingly focus on the issue of credit transfer and as calls for articulation agreements become louder, there is no empirical evidence to suggest that streamlining credit transfer will increase degree attainment. She argues that though streamlining credit transfer is a useful enterprise, it is of limited utility when it comes to increasing degree completion rates.

Part 4 recognizes that though much of the debate about increasing postsecondary completion rates has been spurred on at the federal level by President Obama, it is the states that have most of the levers to drive change in higher education. A handful of states have already been experimenting with a "completion agenda" of their own, providing lessons for reformers across the rest of the country. The chapters in part 4 profile three of those states: Colorado, Texas, and Ohio.

Elaine DeLott Baker's case study of three Colorado community college initiatives explores why reforms that prove successful on one campus are often difficult to export to other places. Baker, of the Community College of Denver, argues that the traditional methods of "disseminating" promising reforms—via research reports and conference presentations— are not likely to lead to the successful adoption of those reforms on other campuses. What is needed, she argues, is a more proactive approach to replication, and state policies and foundation funding cycles that reflect these demands. Geri Hockfield Malandra of Kaplan University provides a detailed look at higher education reform in Texas, a state that is often held up as a model for how to improve accountability and performance. According to Malandra, a decade ago Texas embarked on a targeted strategy to improve the diversity, quality, and productivity of higher education. Malandra shows that the efforts of higher education reformers, coupled with strategic initiatives and investments, led to enrollment growth, improved persistence and completion rates, and increased degree production. She concludes by discussing the lessons that policymakers can learn from the Texas experience that are replicable and scalable elsewhere. Lastly, Richard Petrick, recently retired from the Ohio Board of Regents, looks at the Ohio experience with outcomes-based funding. Petrick describes where the push for performance-based funding came from, how the funding policies were structured and implemented, the extent to which they achieved their goals, and what their longer-term impact has been. He also explains the major factors that contributed to the success of the funding policies and, by implication, provides tentative lessons for other state systems.

Together, the contributors to this volume acknowledge that we have entered a new era of higher education. Expectations are higher, funding levels are likely to decline, and answers about what works are not necessarily easy to come by. In short, while the imperative to improve is clear, the path to doing so is anything but.

The authors' conclusions are often sobering, but they also point out many useful lessons about where to focus our reform energy and the opportunities for creating a more highly educated workforce. Whether American higher education can capitalize on those opportunities and rise to the president's challenge is an open question, one that we leave to future work. Whatever your degree of optimism or pessimism about the prospects for the completion agenda, we can all agree that before policymakers can hope to make progress, they must first have a clear-eyed assessment of where we stand, where we need to go, and the potential ways to get there. The chapters that follow take up this task, and they will help to inform policy debates in this new era of higher education reform.

NOTES

1. Barack Obama, "Remarks by the President in the State of the Union Address," Washington, DC, The White House, 2010.

2. The Lumina Foundation, "Goal 2025: Aims for 60% College Attainment Rate, Relevant Degrees," Jan. 2010, www.luminafoundation.org/newsroom/news letter/archives/2010-01.html

3. S. Aud, M. Fox, and A. Kewal Ramani, *Status and Trends in the Education of Racial and Ethnic Groups*, NCES 2010-015 (Washington, DC: National Center for Education Statistics, 2010).

4. S. Aud et al., *The Condition of Education, 2011*, NCES 2011-033 (Washington, DC: National Center for Education Statistics, 2011), Indicator 24.

5. T. D. Snyder and S. A. Dillow, *Digest of Education Statistics, 2010*, NCES 2011-015 (Washington, DC: National Center for Education Statistics, 2011), table 341.

6. A. W. Radford et al., *Persistence and Attainment of 2003–04 Beginning Postsecondary Students: After Six Years*, NCES 2011-151 (Washington, DC: National Center for Education Statistics, 2010).

7. L. Berkner, S. He, and E. F. Cataldi, *Descriptive Summary of 1995–96 Beginning Postsecondary Students: Six Years Later*, NCES 2003-151 (Washington, DC: National Center for Education Statistics, 2002), table 2.0-A.

8. John Bound, Michael Lovenheim, and Sarah Turner, *Understanding the Decrease in College Completion Rates and the Increased Time to the Baccalaureate Degree*, University of Michigan Population Studies Center Research Report 07-626 (Ann Arbor: University of Michigan, 2007).

9. Organisation for Economic Co-operation and Development, *Education at a Glance, 2010* (Paris: OECD, 2010), available at www.oecd.org/dataoecd/45/39/45926093.pdf.

10. Organisation for Economic Co-operation and Development, *OECD Factbook 2009: Economics, Environmental and Social Statistics* (Paris: OECD, 2009).

11. Arne Duncan, quoted in Janet Adamy, "Obama to Tout Education Efforts," *Wall Street Journal*, Aug. 9, 2010.

12. William Kirwan, quoted in Tamar Lewin, "Once a Leader, the U.S. Lags in College Degrees," *New York Times*, July 23, 2010, p. A11.

13. Thomas Bailey and Davis Jenkins, "How Community Colleges Can Reach Obama's Goals," *Inside Higher Education*, Oct. 13, 2009.

14. See, for instance, Heather Rose and Julian Betts, *Math Matters: The Links between High School Curriculum, College Graduation, and Earnings* (San Francisco: Public Policy Institute of California, 2001).

15. Mark Schneider, "Math in American High Schools: The Delusion of Rigor," American Enterprise Institute *AEI Education Outlook*, no. 10 (Oct. 2009).

16. That center, the Center for Postsecondary Research, was not continued in the 2011 competition, but a new center on postsecondary education and employment will be funded, leaving the investment in postsecondary R&D disproportionately small.

17. Douglas Harris and Sara Goldrick-Rab, *The (Un)Productivity of American Higher Education: From "Cost Disease" to Cost-Effectiveness*, La Follette Working Paper no. 2010-023 (Madison: Robert M. La Follette School of Public Affairs, University of Wisconsin, 2010).

PART ONE

The Challenges

CHAPTER ONE

Increasing Higher Education Attainment in the United States

Challenges and Opportunities

ARTHUR M. HAUPTMAN

Over the past decade, the traditional policy focus on increasing access to higher education has been supplemented with much greater attention to improving the chances that students complete their degree—the completion rate. Even more heartening, debates in the United States and many other countries now place heightened emphasis on increasing the proportion of adult workers with a degree—the attainment rate.

This overview examines issues arising from this shift in policy and pays particular attention to the challenge of increasing degree attainment in the United States by

- describing three measures of higher education—participation, completion, and attainment—and how the United States stacks up against other industrialized countries on these measures;
- tracing the evolution of the goals that have been set forth by President Obama and others for improving degree completion and attainment rates;
- considering whether the president's attainment goal is realistic and how effective any increases in attainment are likely to be in meeting projected labor force needs; and
- suggesting eight rules for the road to increase degree attainment in the future.

Examining the Relationship: Participation, Completion, and Attainment

A natural place to start the process of understanding recent debates is to recognize the interconnection between and the differences in the three key indicators that define the scope and performance of any higher education system—participation, completion, and attainment—defined as follows:

1. Participation rate is the percentage of a population who enroll in higher education.
2. Completion rate is the percentage of entering students who earn a degree.
3. Attainment rate is the percentage of the working population who earn a degree.

Examining the Higher Education Attainment Pipeline

While the three rates differ from each other in important ways, higher education attainment rates may be best understood as a pipeline in which these measures relate to each other in a specific way, as indicated in figure 1.1 and the equation below:

High school attainment × Higher education participation × Higher education completion = Higher education attainment

Figure 1.1 underscores the fact that society can increase higher education attainment at three junctures on the pipeline:

1. by increasing the number of high school graduates, preferably those who are ready to do college-level work;
2. by increasing the number of students who enroll in college, in the belief that enough of these students will complete their education to lift attainment rates; and
3. by improving the rate at which entering students complete their education.

The figure also summarizes where the United States stands among OECD countries on these different pipeline measures.

High school attainment rates are the culmination of elementary and secondary education and thus represent the first leg of the higher education attainment pipeline. With its long commitment to compulsory education, the United States ranks at or near the top in terms of high school attainment rates among OECD countries. This contrasts with high school graduation rates, where the United States does not rank as high among members of the OECD. That a large number of Americans

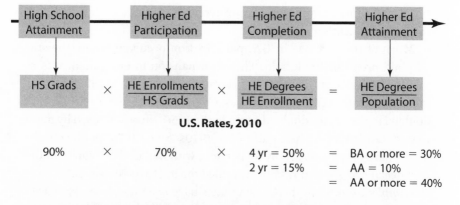

FIGURE 1.1. The higher education attainment pipeline.

earn their high school degrees or the equivalent (such as the GED) later in life may help explain why we rank higher on high school attainment among OECD countries than on high school graduation.

Participation rates are the most traditional way of measuring the scope of a higher education system. Since the end of the Second World War, the United States has transformed itself from an elite to a mass system and then to a universal system of higher education.[1]

In the United States we tend to measure participation as the share of high school graduates who enroll in college within the next year, in part because reliable trend data exist for this rate. It stood at 45 percent in 1960 after the first two waves of the GI Bill and grew to 50 percent in 1965, when the Higher Education Act (HEA) was enacted. By 1990 the rate was 60 percent, and it recently reached 70 percent.[2] Even though many OECD countries have since become mass or universal systems, the United States still has one of the highest participation rates.[3]

The high U.S. participation rates also are a function of the size of the country's community colleges. If these two-year schools were not considered part of American higher education, U.S. higher education participation rates and enrollment figures would be much lower and more in line with data reported by many other countries, where further education and technical training programs typically are not counted as part of the higher education sector.

Much of the increase in U.S. participation occurred before the student aid programs took hold. The big expansion in enrollment was in the third quarter of the twentieth century, primarily in public four-year institutions and community colleges. Overall, public sector enrollments doubled in the 1950s, doubled again in the 1960s, and increased by more than one-third in the first half of the 1970s. Since 1975, public enrollments have only increased by 50 percent, with half of that growth in the past decade, as student numbers swelled during two recessions.[4]

Completion rates in the United States have been mediocre compared with other industrialized countries for many decades, but OECD published figures are not at all helpful in making these comparisons because of how they are calculated.[5] Although reports vary, it seems roughly half of U.S. students enrolling in four-year institutions graduate within six years, and fewer than one-fifth of community college students complete their program within three years; among those enrolling full-time the percentage is probably higher.[6]

These mediocre degree completion rates are largely the result of the United States' becoming a mass or universal system long before most other countries, as elite systems tend to have higher completion rates. But the fact that U.S. completion rates have been mediocre for decades seems lost in many recent debates. Speakers or writers assert that we must regain our global leadership in college completion rates when we never exhibited such leadership, at least not since we became a mass system of higher education in the 1950s and 1960s.[7] Either they are confusing college completion with attainment—a distressingly frequent error—or they are failing to acknowledge the inherent tension between our commitment to opening the doors of higher education wider than most other countries and how that may contribute to our lower completion rates.[8] In either case, the persistent confusion between completion and attainment rates often distracts us from having an honest debate on the real issues.

Attainment rates were not extensively used in higher education debates until a decade ago, but their recent use has enhanced the quality of the debate for several reasons. First, attainment rates by definition include indices of both access and success and thereby broaden the scope of the debate. Attainment rate data also allow for comparisons by age of workers, giving some sense of trends over time in attainment, although this feature has been misused in many recent debates. In addition, the use of attainment rates allows for a differentiation between bachelor's and sub-bachelor's programs in various countries, whereas participation rate measures tend not to allow for such comparisons.

How our attainment rates compare with those in other countries has played a large role in recent debates about higher education reform. Given the prominence of these arguments, it is worth examining the source data in greater detail. It is particularly important to consider how and why attainment rates may differ by type of degree earned and the age of workers, and to what extent these rates have changed over time.

Looking at Different Measures of Attainment

Table 1.1 shows how four educational attainment rates compare to those in OECD countries for different age groups and different types of degrees. The key observation is that for each type of degree, the U.S. ranking among OECD countries for the oldest age group is higher (i.e., better) than the rankings of the younger age groups. It is fair to say that the principal concern that led to the basic theme of this book—that we are losing our edge in the global marketplace—is predicated on the fact that the attainment rates of our youngest workers lag behind those in an increasing number of OECD countries.

But as in so many public policy issues, the data need to be looked at more carefully to get the full story. One consideration is that many countries with higher attainment rates among their younger workers have undergone radical changes in their higher education systems arising from a variety of factors, including fighting wars on their own soil and policy decisions to expand from elite to mass or universal systems.[9]

In addition, a large number of European countries now conform to Bologna process requirements such as moving from the traditional five-year bachelor's degree to degrees of three or four years' duration.[10] But unless we think that three-year bachelor's degrees are the answer to our attainment challenge, it makes little sense to tie our reform agenda to European developments, especially since many features of the Bologna process (such as transferring credits across borders) represent Europe's attempts to emulate us.

We also ought to understand the underlying demographics and immigration patterns. Many of the countries overtaking us in attainment among younger adult workers have declining numbers of traditional

TABLE 1.1. U.S. international ranking among OECD countries in attainment, by age of workers, 2008

Educational attainment	Ranking by age of workers				
	25–64	25–34	35–44	45–54	55–64
High school	3rd	8th (tied)	7th	2nd	1st
Sub-bachelor's	9th (tied)	14th	13th (tied)	8th (tied)	7th (tied)
Sub-bachelor's or more	3rd	8th (tied)	4th (tied)	3rd	2nd (tied)
Bachelor's or more	2nd	7th (tied)	2nd	1st	1st

SOURCE: OECD, *Education at a Glance, 2010: OECD Indicators* (Paris: OECD, 2010), tables A1.2a and A1.3a.

college-age youth because of low birth rates and net outmigration, while in the United States the number of younger adult workers is growing because of higher birth rates and net immigration of workers. Thus, many of the countries with the highest attainment rates are educating an increasing share of a declining base of young adults, while the United States faces the task of educating a growing base of young adults. These countries may well be outpacing us on attainment rates, but they may have a devil of a time filling all their jobs in the future.[11]

Immigration patterns also lead to attainment rate comparisons that can be deceiving because the United States has had much more rapid increases in immigration than most other OECD countries. To the extent that our immigrants tend to be less well educated than our resident population, this reduces our attainment rates.

Also apparent from table 1.1 is the similarity in the rankings for U.S. attainment for secondary and postsecondary degrees. This striking similarity has been little remarked upon in recent debates. The data in this table strongly suggest that the factors which have contributed to the decline in the rankings for the youngest group of workers in postsecondary education are also at work when it comes to our high schools. The slowing increase in high school attainment rates was one of the premises of *A Nation at Risk* when it was released a quarter century ago.[12] This issue of declining high school performance has not been fully addressed and has now spread to higher education as well, at least as it applies to the younger workers.

Solving the Community College Conundrum

While contextual factors like demographics and immigration patterns are an important part of the story, one fact is clear: a primary cause of the United States' middling attainment rates is the relatively low attainment rate among workers who attended community colleges. Table 1.1 confirms large differences in where the United States ranks by type of postsecondary degree held; the U.S. rank for bachelor's degrees is much higher for every age group than it is for sub-bachelor's degrees.

The poor ranking of the United States when it comes to sub-bachelor's degrees raises an interesting issue, one that I refer to as the "community college conundrum." Associate's degree attainment rates have been relatively flat for many years in the United States despite the fact that associate's degrees are the fastest growing type of degree awarded, as figure 1.2 indicates. From 1970 to 2005, the number of associate's degrees awarded annually grew at an average annual rate of 3 percent per year, twice that of bachelor's degrees and slightly faster than master's degrees. Interestingly enough, the annual growth in the number of bachelor's and associate's degrees awarded exactly mirrors the growth of enrollments in these two sectors. Yet despite the rapid annual growth in associate's degrees awarded, the attainment rate for workers holding them remains in the middle for OECD countries.

How can this be so? One reason is that our associate's degrees are often not terminal ones; one estimate is that 17 percent of those earning a bachelor's degree have previously earned an associate's degree.[13] In contrast, technical training programs in other countries often lead to terminal degrees, so that those receiving these degrees do not eventually show up as bachelor's degree holders nearly as often as in the United States. Although data are sketchy, a reasonable estimate is that as many as 10 percent of those earning associate's degrees in the United States already have bachelor's degrees and are coming to community colleges for retraining. They, too, show up in the data as bachelor's degree holders.

What other countries require of their students also can make a difference. For example, Canada has the highest combined attainment rate in the world because it has the highest sub-bachelor's rate. One reason that Canada's sub-bachelor's rate is so high, though, is that Quebec, one of the largest provinces, requires all its students to attend intermediate two-year degree programs between high school and college. The degrees earned in these intermediate programs pump up Canada's overall attainment rate.[14]

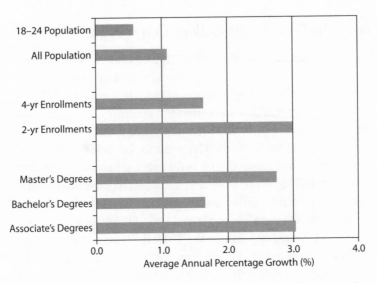

FIGURE 1.2. Average annual growth in population, enrollments, and degrees awarded, 1970 to 2005.

Attainment Rates: Separating Fact from Fiction

A frequent assertion in recent debates and a premise of President Obama's initiative is that we need to regain our historical position as number one in attainment. But the source data cast doubt on this assertion, as it is not provably true that we were ever first on the combined attainment rate. The first year for which I can find combined attainment rate data for enough countries to be meaningful is 1991, when the United States already ranked third behind Canada and Finland.[15] Even then, this ranking was entirely because our sub-bachelor's rate was so mediocre that it offset our long-standing hegemony on the proportion of the population with a bachelor's degree or higher.

In warning us about the consequences of losing our global lead in attainment, many observers have argued that the U.S. standing on attainment has declined over time because our attainment rates have been flat for decades. Two prominent examples of these statements, by the Lumina Foundation for Education and the White House, respectively:

> College attainment rates are rising in almost every industrialized
> country in the world, except for the U.S. Today roughly 39 percent of
> American adults hold a two- or four-year degree. That attainment rate,

which has held steady for four decades, led all other nations for much of the postwar period.[16]

Today, only 40 percent of young adults have a college degree—a lower percentage than eleven other countries and no higher than a generation ago.[17]

Tables 1.2 and 1.3 indicate why these two statements and similar ones about stagnant attainment are simply incorrect. Table 1.2 shows the attainment rates for sub-bachelor's degrees or more from 1991 to 2008 in the United States and the average for OECD countries.[18] This table makes clear that U.S. attainment rates have steadily increased over the past two decades and have at least kept pace with the average for OECD countries, for both younger workers and across all age groups. Table 1.3 indicates how bachelor's degree attainment rates have grown since 1950. It makes clear that bachelor's degree attainment rates in this country have been growing at a healthy rate for more than a half century.

This notion of stagnant attainment is one of the more counterproductive aspects of our current national debate. It has led a broad range of policymakers and opinion leaders to assert that a problem is at hand when it is not. But why are so many saying that our attainment has been flat when the source data make it clear that attainment rates have continued to increase steadily even after we have moved to a mass or universal system? The basic problem seems to be that officials from OECD, the Lumina Foundation, and others are using a mistaken assumption to come to an incorrect conclusion, and then others are picking up on the incorrect assertion.[19]

TABLE 1.2. Attainment rates in the United States and OECD countries: percentage of workers with sub-bachelor's degree or more, by age of workers, 1991–2008

Age group	1991	1995	2000	2005	2008
25–34					
U.S.	30	34	38	39	42
OECD	20	22	26	32	35
25–64					
U.S.	30	33	36	39	41
OECD	18	19	22	26	28

SOURCES: OECD, *Education at a Glance, 2004: OECD Indicators* (Paris: OECD, 2004), tables A3.4a and A3.4b; OECD, *Education at a Glance, 2010*, tables A1.3a and A1.4.

TABLE 1.3. U.S. attainment rates: percentage of workers with college and high school education, by age of worker, 1950–2009

Age group	1950	1960	1970	1980	1990	2000	2009
			4 or more years of college				
≥ 25	6	8	11	17	21	26	30
25–34	5	11	16	24	24	29	32
≥ 55	4	5	8	10	15	19	26
			4 or more years of high school				
≥ 25	34	41	55	69	78	84	87
25–34	47	58	73	85	86	88	88
≥ 55	19	23	36	50	62	74	83

SOURCES: U.S. Census, Educational Attainment, Historical Tables: Table A-1, Years of School Completed by People 25 Years and Older, by Age and Sex, Selected Years 1940–2009; T. D. Snyder and S. A. Dillow, *Digest of Education Statistics, 2009* (Washington, DC: National Center for Education Statistics, 2010), table 8; *Digest of Education Statistics, 1995* (Washington, DC: NCES, 1995), table 11.

The source of the analytic problem is the assumption that the lack of difference in attainment rates between the youngest and oldest workers in the United States means that our attainment rates have not grown over time. This inference also has led many groups to suggest that our younger workers now have lower attainment rates than the older workers for the first time in our history.[20] This latter suggestion also seems without merit or foundation. As the data in tables 1.2 and 1.3 show, over time the attainment rate for 25- to 34-years-olds has consistently been higher than the rates for older workers. That continues to be the case.

These incorrect assertions reflect a fundamental misunderstanding of attainment rates. These rates are cumulative measures that track an age cohort over time. Therefore, the rate of attainment for a cohort of workers will increase as the workers age. For example, if 20 out of 100 workers have earned a bachelor's degree by the time they are 25 years old, that cohort's attainment rate is 20 percent. If 10 more members earn a degree over the next 30 years, then the attainment rate for the cohort (now 55 years old) is 30 percent (30 out of 100).

Is it a bad sign that the younger and older age groups have similar attainment rates? No. On the contrary, we should be celebrating if the attainment rate for a given age cohort grows over time because it means workers are seeking more education and training throughout their careers. Table 1.3 makes it clear that growth is occurring in two ways. First, the attainment rate for the 25- to 34-years-olds today is significantly higher than it was for this cohort 10, 20, 30, or 40 years ago. In addition, the rates for those older than 55 years of age are substantially higher than the rates for those 25 years and older 30 years before (these are the same people). From both perspectives, then, attainment rates in the United States are growing, not declining or stagnant, as is so often stated in recent debates.

Setting the Goals for Achieving Greater Attainment or Degree Completion

In response to reports decrying low completion rates and declines in how our attainment rates rank relative to other countries, a number of national organizations have set goals for improving these two measures of higher education performance. Initially, the goals were set principally in relation to increasing the number of degrees earned and improving attainment rates; more recently, the goals have been more tied to improving college completion rates. Table 1.4 summarizes some of the organizations and their goals.

Goals for Improving Attainment

The most prominent voice declaring goals for higher education has been President Obama. In his first speech to Congress in February 2009 he declared that "by 2020, America will once again have the highest proportion of college graduates in the world."[21] This statement eventually was translated into a more precise statement that 60 percent of our workers ages 25 to 34 should have a degree by the year 2020, so that we would have the highest combined rate among OECD countries.

But goal-setting along these lines began much earlier in the decade, and it is worth examining how the debate has evolved over time. This history might start with work done in the early 2000s by Jobs for the Future (JFF) under the direction of its president, Hilary Pennington, now a senior official with the Bill and Melinda Gates Foundation. In October 2003, JFF sponsored a conference that resulted in an edited volume of papers entitled *Double the Numbers*.[22] As the title suggests, the theme

TABLE 1.4. Stated educational attainment and completion goals of different groups

Group	Stated goal
	Attainment
Jobs for the Future (2003)	Double number of low-income college graduates
Lumina Foundation (2008)	Achieve 60% attainment rate for ages 25–64 by 2025
College Board (2008)	Achieve 55% attainment rate for ages 25–64 by 2025
Obama administration (2009)	Achieve 60% attainment rate for ages 25–34 by 2020
Gates Foundation (2010)	Double number of degrees and certificates awarded
	Completion
Community college associations (2010)	Increase community college completion rates by 50% over next decade[a]
McKinsey and Co./Gates Foundation (2010)	Increase annual number of college graduates by 1 million over next decade
College Board (2009)	Dramatically increase college completion rates
National Governors Association (2010)	Increase degree and certificate completion rate so that 8 million more college students graduate by 2020

[a]Proclamation goal is to "double the numbers of quality degrees and certificates awarded by 2020."

of the conference and the volume was to identify policies and practices that would lead to doubling the number of low-income students gaining quality postsecondary degrees and credentials.

The *Double the Numbers* effort was significant in several regards. It was one of the first national higher education efforts in which the goal was to increase the number of students from disadvantaged circumstances who graduated rather than the number of students who enrolled. It thus shifted the focus from the middle of the attainment pipeline to the end result of graduates entering the work force. It also represented an effort to bring officials from K–12 and higher education together to work toward a common goal, not typical in education policy. And although most of the focus was on the traditional means of using student aid and better alignment between K–12 and higher education to achieve the goal, at least two papers in the volume discussed what could be done to encourage institutions to graduate more of these targeted groups of students.[23] This represented one of the first steps in shifting discussions of performance-based funding in higher education in this country from setting aside funds to building performance measures into funding formulas.

Much of the groundwork underlying *Double the Numbers* and other related efforts was done by Dennis Jones and his colleagues at the National Center for Higher Education Management Systems (NCHEMS). It was built on their innovative approach of using attainment rates rather than the more traditional participation rates to compare states and OECD countries in measuring the scope of their higher education systems.[24] This NCHEMS analysis was critical in translating the initial JFF goal of increasing the number of degrees awarded to improving the attainment rate in the United States so that we could once again be a leader among OECD countries.

The analysis of Jones and his colleagues also led a number of groups to examine this issue further and publish the results of their examination. In a policy brief published by JFF in 2007 entitled *Hitting Home*, Travis Reindl reported how the United States was falling behind many other countries in attainment rate on the basis of the OECD data.[25] It also showed how states differed in the proportion of 25- to 34-year-olds with postsecondary degrees and how most states were far behind Canada's combined attainment rate of 55 percent. On the basis of this data, the report argued the United States needed to increase its attainment rates substantially if we as a nation were to maintain our ability to compete globally.

The Lumina Foundation for Education was the next organization to throw its hat into the attainment rate ring. Jamie Merisotis was one of a group of higher education analysts who had identified increasing higher education attainment as a key variable in determining America's future economic success. When he became president of the foundation in 2008, Merisotis convinced its board to embrace a "big goal"—"to increase the percentage of Americans with high quality degrees and credentials from 39 percent to 60 percent by the year 2025."[26] The College Board also got into the act in 2008 when its Commission on Access, Admissions and Success in Higher Education declared that the United States should have a goal that 55 percent of 25- to 64-year-olds should hold an associate's degree or higher by 2025.[27] In 2010, the Gates Foundation clarified its primary postsecondary goal as doubling the numbers of degrees and certificates awarded.[28]

These various calls for more attainment were clearly influential in convincing the Obama administration when it took office to adopt a similar goal as the keystone of its very aggressive higher education agenda. What is less clear is how these figures, years, and targets were chosen in each case. One wonders, for example, why the administration picked the youngest group of workers while Lumina focused on improving attainment among all workers, or why the administration selected 2020 versus Lumina's and the College Board's 2025 (since either was beyond the president's possible term of office). Whatever the targeted group and year, it is clear that each organization was sincerely motivated to restore the United States to prominence in higher education attainment as a vehicle for the nation to become more economically competitive.

What is also clear, though, is that setting specific goals can lead to problems as to what may or may not be included in the goal. For example, the goals described above, as well as those set by other organizations, have tended to focus on increasing the attainment rate for those holding associate's degrees or higher, meaning that these goals do not differentiate between the number of people holding associate's degrees and the number with a bachelor's degree.

This tendency not to differentiate between bachelor's and sub-bachelor's degrees is one of the more problematic aspects of the attainment debate. Given that we continue to be among the countries with the highest bachelor's degree attainment rate while we are consistently average to below average when it comes to sub-bachelor's degree attainment, recommendations for improving the combined rate are likely to be less effective than if the problem is broken into its two respective parts. *Combining these two rates into one obscures too much information to be helpful in deciding which strategies are most worth pursuing in the push to increase attainment rates.*

One particular concern is that we might adopt strategies that are of less relevance for community colleges even though the data show that they are the biggest problem for the United States in increasing our attainment rates. The lack of differentiation in goals could very well lead to a lack of differentiation in strategy as well, giving rise to reforms and initiatives that do not focus enough on the very low rates of completion and the mediocre international standing of the United States when it comes to attainment of sub-bachelor's degrees.

Another problem with being too specific about the goal is that certain key groups of people or certain types of activity may be excluded. For example, the administration's decision to focus on increasing the attainment rate for the youngest group of workers excludes two critical groups: the millions of individuals who are older than 34 years of age and those who hold certificates for the training they receive. Though older workers would clearly benefit from additional education and training, any progress we make on increasing the educational attainment of workers older than 34 will not be recorded in the list of the president's achievements. The same goes for students who enroll in certificate and degree programs that are less than two years in duration or those individuals who become apprentices, because these activities do not qualify as degrees under the traditional U.S. or OECD definition of attainment.

The Shifting Focus to Completion Rates

The more recent trend in goal setting related to higher education has been to emphasize increases in degree completion rates as the primary path to increasing attainment rates. In *Hitting Home*, Reindl in 2007 attributed much of the reason for the decline in U.S. attainment to low completion rates: "We are losing ground to other nations largely because of relatively low college completion rates. Although the United States still ranks in the top five in the proportion of young people who attend college, it ranks 16th in the proportion who actually finish, according to the National Center on Public Policy and Higher Education's *Measuring Up 2006*'s report."[29]

This shift in focus to improving completion rates as the principal means for improving our attainment rate has gained considerable steam in recent years. For example, six major community college associations in 2010 agreed that student completion rates should be increased by 50 percent over the next decade (though the proclamation itself reads that they commit to "produce 50 percent more students with high quality degrees and certificates by 2020").[30] Also in 2010, the College Board augmented its attainment rate goal with a much more vague declaration that completion rates must be dramatically increased.[31] And the National Governors Association (NGA) selected "Complete to Compete" as its major policy theme for 2010–11; it exhorts states to increase degree completion rates so that President Obama's goal of increasing the number of college graduates by eight million over the next decade can be reached.[32]

The Obama administration also seems to have shifted its focus to completion rates. In a November 2010 speech, Deputy Secretary of Education Tony Miller focused almost exclusively on the need to increase completion rates as the means to reach the president's goal of increasing attainment rates.[33] Deputy Secretary Miller's emphasis reflects a growing tendency within the administration and elsewhere that equates increasing degree completion rates with increasing attainment in what many now refer to as the "college completion agenda."

The growing emphasis on completion rates as the principal vehicle for increasing attainment rates poses two problems. First, it ignores the fact that increasing participation rates must be a key part of the solution for increasing attainment. Second, this emphasis fails to recognize that increased completion rates could be achieved by reductions in quality or increases in selectivity, both of which would be detrimental to the larger goal of increasing the share of adults with a credential that has real labor market value.

On the first point, the shift towards completion rates largely ignores the arithmetic fact that increasing attainment rates substantially will require very large increases in both the completion rate and the participation rate. A 2010 report prepared by McKinsey and Company for the Gates Foundation underscores this fact by displaying a chart which shows how much each rate must be increased to achieve the kinds of increases in attainment rates called for by the Obama administration and others.[34] The McKinsey figures indicate that to reach the goal of a 60 percent attainment rate, it would be necessary to have participation and completion rates in excess of 80 percent. And the McKinsey analysis, if anything, understates the effort needed, since raising the rates for the entire cohort means that the rates for the new entrants must be even higher to offset the lower rates for the majority of workers who are already through the system.

The second concern with the growing emphasis on raising completion rates is that it fails to recognize that increasing these rates is not always a good thing to do. In football parlance, when someone throws a forward pass, two of the three things that could happen are bad—an interception or an incomplete pass; only a completed pass is good. In terms of increasing higher education completion rates, two things that could happen are bad: standards could be lowered or selectivity could be increased. (While more selectivity is good in many respects, it would tend to lead to lower attainment rates because fewer students would finish.)

A related problem in using higher completion rates as the primary goal is that efforts to increase these rates could be portrayed as improving attainment when they may really serve another purpose. Take the case of Louisiana, where the passage of legislation in 2010 was based on the promise that more funding would be provided to universities that raised their graduation rates. The stated purpose is to increase both numbers of graduates and the degree completion rate by seven percentage points over six years.[35] This Louisiana program has been lauded by the Gates Foundation and others working with the foundation for moving its higher education funding scheme to a performance basis.

Closer examination, however, reveals that this program has a different purpose. Those involved with the effort admit that Louisiana is using the goal of higher graduation rates to encourage the state's universities to raise their admissions standards for entering students because many officials (apparently rightly) believe the current standards are too lax. Another underlying purpose is to move more students into the chronically underutilized community college sector. These are certainly reasonable goals, but the effort should be labeled for what it is and not lauded as a way of improving attainment, which it may well not accomplish.

The Louisiana effort is also a good example of what I consider to be a broader problem: using rates as a policy goal when numbers will do a better job. In Louisiana and some other states that have built completion rates into the funding mechanism, there are generic problems associated with using rates as goals because it is almost always hard to define the denominator without controversy. In the specific case of completion rates, establishing the denominator includes these considerations: How does one count students who transfer from your school to another school and complete their degree there? How does one count students who transfer into your school and then graduate? Are part-time students counted the same as full-time students, differently, or not at all?

This is of concern with regard to any initiative advocating for large-scale increases in completion rates. Imagine that the president of a college sits down with the dean and says, "We will be getting more funding if we can increase our graduation rates." The light bulb goes on the dean's head, who figures out that if they can get rid of all those students taking remedial courses, they can make the faculty happier by eliminating headaches, improving quality, and getting more funding to boot. They will also be able to cut their student loan default rates because poorly prepared students won't be adding to the list of defaulters. One of the only reasons not to go this route may be if officials are unwilling to forgo the tuition revenues paid by poorly prepared students.

Tying policies to completion rate goals could also negatively affect access for low-income and minority students, as schools acting strategically will choose to become more selective in order to enroll students with the best chance of completing. It is also difficult to design a policy using completion rates that targets high-priority fields of study such as science and engineering—or education, for that matter. By contrast, policies tied to increasing the *numbers* of low-income and minority students who graduate, or policies that encourage more students to earn degrees in high-priority fields, would reward institutions to recruit these students rather than exclude them, as a graduation rate goal might do.

To be sure, setting goals that aim to increase the number of graduates still raises the issue of ensuring that quality is not reduced in the rush to reach the goals, but that's a problem with using graduation rates as well. In general, quality assurance should be key to any of these initiatives, but I think that many of those calling for increased completion rates have paid too little attention to it in their calls for action. At least, tying goals to the number of graduates doesn't raise the selectivity and quality debasement issues simultaneously.

The argument for adequate quality control also applies to efforts that seek to increase attainment rates, which is a tricky business for the reasons described above. Increasing the number of degrees awarded each year or increasing the numbers of workers with degrees is much more straightforward. To the extent that the population is changing in a predictable way, increasing the numbers also increases the proportionality.

The early goals laid out by JFF for doubling the numbers of low-income students obtaining degrees made good sense. That is why I have argued for rewarding states and institutions on the basis the *number* of Pell Grant recipients who graduate rather than graduation rates. While this goal still raises concerns about quality and growing debt burdens, that would be a more understandable focus that would produce better results than the current emphasis on increasing completion rates and attainment rates for all students as the key policy goals.

Assessing the President's Goal: Is It Realistic? Will the Effort Be Effective?

The origin of the president's attainment initiative seems straightforward. When he came into office in January 2009, officials in his administration picked up on a drumbeat that had been building for several years: America was falling behind many other OECD countries in the proportion of its workers who had a college degree. This spelled trouble for our capacity to compete in the global marketplace because other countries would have more highly trained workers, in contrast to earlier decades when we were first in the world on this key education statistic. For the new administration with a heavy Democratic majority in both houses of Congress, this meant that a huge challenge—making the United States more globally competitive—could be addressed and, it was hoped, solved by improving the performance of the nation's higher education system.

The administration's interest in higher education also fit well with the president's intent to shake up the K–12 educational establishment. Recent discussions about the decline in American higher education mirror a much longer and larger discussion about how U.S. elementary and secondary school students have fallen behind in the basic skills of math and science and what that portends for U.S. global competitiveness. Many now draw a comparison between the mediocre math and science performance of the United States in primary and secondary education and declines in U.S. attainment rates in higher education.

I think this analogy between mediocre U.S. rankings in high school test scores and higher education attainment rates is flawed in several respects, including the fact that one discussion is about what students know and the other is about how many people graduate, which may or may not be related positively to student quality.

But to see the problems in setting ambitious and unrealistic goals, one only need examine the track record of K–12 education in this country in recent decades. The Goals 2000 set out in 1989 included the goals that "all children in America will start school ready to learn" and that American students would be first in the world in math and science by 2000. These goals were not met by 2000, nor are we closer to reaching them now. The proficiency goals for math and reading set forth in the No Child Left Behind (NCLB) legislation are no more realistic or reasonable than those laid out in Goals 2000; a good case can be made that both efforts have contributed more to a watering down in standards and have heightened gaming of the system.[36]

Is the President's Goal Realistic?

One relevant question here is whether the Obama initiative in higher education is any more realistic than the national goals set in K–12 education over the past several decades. The simple answer is that the Obama goal is equally unrealistic. Figure 1.3, which displays the increase in attainment rates over the last four decades, indicates how unrealistic the

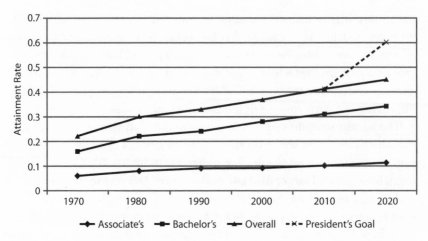

FIGURE 1.3. Attainment rates for sub-bachelor's degree or more, workers 25 to 34 years old, 1970 to 2020 (projected).

goal is.[37] As the figure shows, far from being flat, the bachelor's degree attainment rate has been increasing at a remarkably stable rate of roughly 0.5 percent per year for the past 40 years, and table 1.2 confirms that the combined attainment rate has been increasing at about that same pace in the two decades since it has been regularly recorded. What figure 1.3 also clearly shows is that this rate of increase would have to accelerate dramatically—quadruple, in fact, to 2 percent per year for the entire decade—to reach 60 percent by the end of the decade.

An irony here is that many officials in the Obama administration have bought into the argument that attainment has been flat for a generation or more. But if this were in fact true, reaching the president's goal would be even harder to achieve because the rate would have to increase at remarkably rapid rates after having stood still for decades. To make another sports analogy, this is like trying to set the broad jump record from a standing start. It will be hard enough to achieve the president's goal of 60 percent attainment rate by 2020 assuming we have a running start of steady growth in attainment over time, but proposing to increase the current attainment rate by 50 percent over a decade from a standing start is totally unrealistic.

As a general matter, then, the likelihood of achieving a 60 percent attainment rate by 2020, or even 2025, is close to nil. The only way that these goals could be reached is for a lot more money to be spent on higher education in this country, something on the order of shifting from 3 percent of GDP to 4 percent of GDP, or for federal and state policies to be sharply revised to reflect the heightened commitment to increasing attainment. So far there is little evidence of either of these shifts happening.

Another possibility, though, is to redefine the goal. For example, if one were to look at all workers 25 to 64 years old, we are much closer to being number one now among OECD countries; and thus, we are closer to regaining our number one status by 2020. But it also would be more difficult to increase attainment rates for all workers because most of the current adult population has already finished their education. A definitional change that would produce greater success would be to include workers who hold certificates and other nondegree credentials which are not currently counted in the figures reported by OECD.

It appears that NGA and Complete College America are two organizations who realize this point, as they have redefined their goals for increasing attainment and completion rates to include certificates as well as degrees awarded. While this change is reasonable, it will complicate future rate comparisons if we do not make clear that we will be measuring future rates differently than when the goals for improvement were first established.[38]

Comparing Results with Past National Mobilizations

One way of judging the realism of President Obama's initiative is to examine how much attainment grew during previous national mobilizations involving higher education, including the GI Bill, the National Defense Education Act of 1958, and the Higher Education Act of 1965. Each was related to a major global event or a compelling national concern that motivated politicians and the public to unite in recognizing that something needed to be done. It is worth noting that none of these earlier mobilization efforts set specific goals, in contrast to the current initiative for increasing completion and attainment rates.

To judge the impact of these national efforts on attainment, we can examine the data in table 1.3 on the U.S. attainment rate for bachelor's degrees or more from 1950 to 2009 by decade for all workers, the youngest group of workers, and the oldest group of workers. These data show that the rates for each age group have consistently increased over the past half century.

But since 1950, there have been only two decades—the 1950s and the

1970s—when the attainment rate grew by at least 50 percent, the percentage growth in the overall attainment rate needed to reach President Obama's goal by 2020. In the 1950s, the underlying data confirm that attainment growth for the youngest workers was a function of the GI Bill's opening opportunities for veterans from the Second World War and the Korean War. The number of males aged 25 to 34 with four years of college or more increased by 60 percent from 1950 to 1960 while the number of female workers of that age group earning college degrees grew by 20 percent.

The attainment rate for all workers and younger workers also grew by at least 50 percent in the 1970s. But rather than being the result of Vietnam-era GI Bill recipients going to college, the data show the attainment increase was larger for females than males. The number of younger males holding bachelor's degrees doubled during the 1970s, but the number of younger females holding at least a bachelor's degree grew by 150 percent; the number of the youngest groups of workers of both genders increased 25 percent.[39] It would certainly be worth further exploration why this growth in attainment among younger female workers occurred in the 1970s and whether similar efforts might spur greater degree attainment among younger male workers in the future.

Will the Effort Be Effective?

Ultimately, judging whether the president's initiative will be effective requires asking whether the number of new graduates produced will fully meet projected labor force needs so that we can become more globally competitive in the future. Unfortunately, there is no clear answer to this question, which may be why the current initiative is not nearly as compelling as earlier national mobilization efforts in higher education. Estimates of new degrees needed to meet labor force needs are all over the lot, and they often are not clearly stated. The administration has talked about eight million new graduates, but it is not clear to me how this figure relates to projections of new graduates in the absence of its initiative.

To provide some perspective, we can look at the flow and stock of the population with a college education. Roughly 700,000 students now receive an associate's degree annually, while 1.7 million students earn a bachelor's degree, for a total of 2.4 million.[40] In terms of the "stock" of degree holders, currently there are about 60 million individuals with at least a bachelor's degree (four years or college or more) and roughly 50 million with one to three years of college, of which one-third or more hold an associate's degree.[41]

So how many more degree holders does the economy require to meet future labor force needs? Here is where estimates and projections sharply diverge. Those supporting the administration's view, such as Tony Carnevale and his colleagues at Georgetown University's Center on Education and the Workforce, have produced a series of reports indicating that the economy will require many millions of new college graduates over the next decade and beyond to keep us globally competitive.[42] The Gates Foundation and others report that by 2018 more than 6 in 10 jobs will require workers with some sort of postsecondary education.[43] The previously cited McKinsey report estimates that we must produce one million more graduates per year over the next decade—an increase of 40 percent over the current annual volume—to meet future labor force demand.[44]

The opposite view is well expressed in a 2010 report produced by Richard Vedder and colleagues at the Center for College Affordability and Productivity.[45] It begins by saying that "colleges and universities are turning out graduates faster than America's labor markets are creating jobs that traditionally have been reserved for those with degrees." This leads the authors to conclude that we are over-investing public funds in colleges and universities, which echoes and reinforces the recent work of Charles Murray and others.[46]

A related issue is how many additional certificate holders are needed to meet the need for well-trained non-college graduates for the many vocationally oriented positions that will require filling as well. A number of recent analyses do not address this issue, but a recent report entitled *Certificates Count* makes this point well: it estimates the number of certificates annually provided and argues that individuals gaining shorter-term certificates or becoming apprentices can make a real difference in meeting our future job force needs.[47]

Eight Rules of the Road for Increasing Attainment in the Future

This chapter has examined the data on participation, completion, and attainment to put the current higher education debate in perspective. To summarize the results of this statistical tour, the data suggest the president's goal for increasing degree attainment would be almost impossible to achieve in the best of circumstances. And we know these are hardly the best of circumstances.

But we also know that it makes sense for us as a nation to improve the preparedness of students and the quality of postsecondary education and training students receive to help us remain globally competitive. To achieve this goal, this concluding section lays out eight rules for the road that could help us meet our future national and regional labor force needs.

1. *Get the facts straight.* In nearly 40 years working around higher education policy debates, I can't remember another time when the facts were so mangled in the effort to make the case for needed changes or improvement. Arguing that attainment rates have been flat when they have grown steadily is one example. Another is the frequent conflation of completion and attainment rates or the assertion that we must regain our international lead in completion rates when we haven't had it in decades, if ever. These errors detract from the quality of the debate and can lead to misspecification of goals.

2. *Refrain from setting unrealistic national goals.* The higher education debate increasingly seems to be following the path that has dominated the K–12 debate in this country for the past several decades—setting unrealistic national goals as well as proposing to have the government become much more involved in academic issues. This seems unwise given that our K–12 education system is generally regarded as mediocre by international standards, while U.S. universities dominate the global rankings and American higher education is still viewed by most observers as the best in the world. The solutions to the very real challenges facing higher education should respect its great diversity and its traditional independence from government involvement in academic matters.

3. *Address all facets of the higher education attainment pipeline.* The recent focus on raising completion rates as the primary means to lift attainment is counterproductive, in my opinion. To make real strides in improving attainment, we must address all facets of the higher education attainment pipeline. Probably the single most important thing we can do to increase higher education attainment in this country is to improve the preparation of students

coming out of high school. Not only would this help with degree attainment, but it would also improve the job readiness of the millions of students who do not continue their education after high school while saving billions in other societal costs.

Another problem with the growing emphasis on increasing completion rates is that it diverts attention from increasing enrollments as an effective strategy for increasing attainment. The most frequent response to state funding cutbacks has been to raise public sector tuitions. A seemingly unrecognized reality, though, is that increasing enrollments without raising prices is the most direct way to improve productivity in higher education while promoting greater access. Institutional officials should therefore try to find ways to expand at current prices by growing enrollments in those academic units where capacity utilization is low as measured by faculty teaching loads and student-faculty ratios.[48]

4. *Depend more on innovative policies to meet goals.* For all of the rhetoric devoted to the president's initiative, the reality is that policies enacted thus far are unlikely to increase attainment rates. The principal higher education achievements during the 111th Congress were a total shift to Direct Loans and a huge increase in funding in Pell Grants as part of the economic stimulus legislation. Whatever their merits, neither of these policies is likely to produce cost-effective improvements in completion or attainment rates or even lead to big increases in the number of degrees awarded.

To be fair, President Obama did propose some bolder higher education initiatives such as an access and completion fund that would pay states and institutions based on their performance and a substantial community college initiative. But these proposals did not make it through Congress, and significant funding for them never materialized. In this regard, one is reminded of Rick Hess's recent criticism of K–12 education, when he writes that calls for reform have been brash but remedies have been bashful and notable for their timidity.[49] That seems to be the case for the higher education as well.

5. *Understand why other countries are succeeding.* The recent preoccupation with where we rank on attainment compared to other OECD countries sometimes obscures the real value of interna-

tional comparisons—to identify what strategies countries are using to achieve the desired result of higher attainment rates. I co-wrote a report for JFF in 2009 on cost, commitment, and attainment in higher education which identified eight successful strategies that OECD countries have used to achieve high rates of attainment. These included expanding sub-bachelor's programs, reducing time-to-degree, and relying more on the private sector to accommodate bulging demand.[50] As in other policy areas, learning from others can be a key to our future success in improving our attainment rates.

6. *Aim to increase the numbers of degrees awarded, not the rates of graduation.* Setting policies in terms of increasing completion or attainment rates is problematic because of the difficulties associated with defining the denominator. For this reason, it would be better to set institutional and national goals in terms of increasing the number of degrees awarded than to focus on increasing rates of completion or attainment. Setting numerical goals allows for a better connection to chronic equity concerns, since the goals can be set more easily for different groups of students. Goals for degrees awarded also makes for a better connection to relevance because they can easily be tied to degrees awarded in different fields of study.

7. *Tailor policies by type of degree or credential.* By setting broad overall objectives, the administration and others engaged in the debate have not differentiated enough between bachelor's degrees and associate's degrees in identifying problems or in proposing solutions. To be successful in substantially increasing attainment and numbers of degrees awarded, we need to target policies on where attainment rates are lowest, principally associate's degrees. We also need to examine carefully how to increase the number of certificates and apprenticeships, which are equally critical in meeting future labor force needs but do not count in traditional measures of attainment rates.

8. *Ensure that quality is maintained or improved.* One of the greatest concerns about the rush to increase rates and numbers of degrees is that quality will be sacrificed. Yes, the goal of increasing attainment and completion rates is typically stated in terms of providing quality credentials, but it seems fair to say that main-

taining or improving quality has been the junior partner in the general push for improving completion and attainment rates. This underemphasis on quality needs to be reversed if the drive for greater completion and attainment is ultimately to be successful in meeting the needs of employers and other higher education stakeholders.

Conclusion

This book represents an opportunity to reassess recent efforts in this country to increase attainment. That reassessment should include setting more realistic goals for increasing the number of different types of degrees and certificates, with a special emphasis on improving the situation of low-income and minority students and focusing on fields of study deemed to be of particularly high priority. Policies need to be designed to meet those goals, a characteristic also lacking in the current debate. As importantly, we need to be more aware of possible unintended adverse consequences of policies and practices and try very hard to avoid them. That is a map for the road we should be taking.

NOTES

1. In the 1960s and 1970s, Martin Trow developed a typology based on participation rates to distinguish among elite, mass, and universal higher education systems that is still used today. See, for example, Trow, "From Mass Higher Education to Universal Access: The American Advantage," in *In Defense of American Higher Education,* ed. Philip G. Altbach, Patricia I. Gumport, and D. Bruce Johnstone (Baltimore, MD: Johns Hopkins University Press, 2001).

2. T. D. Snyder and S. A. Dillow, *Digest of Education Statistics, 2009,* NCES 2010-013 (Washington, DC: National Center for Education Statistics, 2010), table 200.

3. Comparing U.S. participation with that in other countries is difficult because OECD measures participation rates differently than looking at the progression of high school graduates. The OECD enrollment ratio uses population figures in its denominator and counts only students currently enrolled (excluding those in the age group who have graduated or are no longer enrolled); it also includes international students in the numerator but not the denominator (although this is being addressed in recent data sets). See discussion on enrollment ratios in Organisation for Economic Co-operation and Development, *Education at a Glance, 2010: OECD Indicators* (Paris: OECD, 2010), pp. 292–303.

4. Snyder and Dillow, *Digest of Educational Statistics, 2009*, table 180.

5. OECD publishes two measures relating to how many students complete a higher education degree. Both are poor ways to compare degree completion among countries. One—graduation rates—is a synthetic measure that divides the number of graduates in a given year by the population of the relevant age group in that year. It is really more a bad measure of attainment than of degree completion and should not be relied upon for international comparisons. The other OECD measure—completion rates—compares the results of longitudinal surveys conducted in various OECD countries. On this measure, the United States ranks slightly below average among OECD countries. For more detail, see OECD, *Education at a Glance, 2010*, pp. 58–80. For concerns about this rate, see Clifford Adelman, *Spaces between the Numbers* (Washington, DC: Institute for Higher Education Policy, 2009).

6. See, for example, NCES *Persistence and Attainment of 2003–04 Beginning Postsecondary Students: After Three Years* (Washington, DC: NCES, 2007) (for U.S. figures); or OECD, *Education at a Glance, 2010*, pp. 72–80 (for international figures).

7. For example, Gov. Chris Gregoire of Washington State writes in the introduction to National Governors Association, *Complete to Compete: Common College Completion Metrics* (June 2010), that the initiative seeks to "enlist the help of all governors to make our nation a global leader in college completion." This brochure is available online at www.subnet.nga.org/ci/1011.

8. For example, the August 9, 2010, White House briefing document "Restoring America's Leadership in Higher Education" states that America must raise its "college completion rate" from 40% to 60% when it should have said "attainment rate."

9. See Adelman, *Spaces between the Numbers*, pp. 14–35, for a discussion of the various factors that affect attainment and graduation rates.

10. Information on the Bologna process can be found at its official website, www.ehea.org.

11. Clifford Adelman has been particularly forceful in calling attention to the importance of demographics in explaining trends in attainment and completion rate. See *Spaces between the Numbers*, pp. 22–25.

12. As described in Diane Ravitch, *The Death and Life of the Great American School System* (New York: Basic Books, 2010), p. 24.

13. Anthony Carnevale, Nicole Smith, and Jeff Strohl, *Help Wanted: Projections of Jobs and Education Requirements through 2018* (Washington, DC: Georgetown University, Center on Education and the Workforce, 2010), p. 17.

14. Canada's high ranking for sub-bachelor's degree attainment may also be a function of how its labor force surveys are conducted, since the surveys may count some short-term certificate holders as sub-bachelor's degree recipients; U.S. labor force surveys do not count certificate holders as having degrees. If the U.S. surveys were conducted in the same manner as Canada's, the gap between American and Canadian attainment rates would narrow, perhaps considerably.

15. See NCES, *International Education Indicators: A Time Series Perspective*,

1985–1995 (Washington, DC: NCES, 2000), and OECD, *Education at a Glance, 2004: OECD Indicators* (Paris: OECD, 2004), table A3.4B.

16. Lumina Foundation, *A Stronger Nation through Higher Education* (Indianapolis: Lumina, 2009), p. 1.

17. White House, "Restoring America's Leadership in Higher Education," Press Release, Aug. 9, 2010.

18. Systematic collection of data on attainment rates for sub-bachelor's degrees did not begin until 1990 in both the United States and many OECD countries; therefore, I present historical trends in the attainment rates of sub-bachelor's degrees and above only since 1990.

19. OECD documents and presentations use the difference in attainment rates by age group as an indicator of growth in attainment rates. See, for example, the discussion in OECD, *Education at a Glance, 2010*, p. 26.

20. Two recent examples of this assertion can be found in NGA, *Complete to Compete*, www.subnet.nga.org/ci/1011, and Complete College America, "The Completion Shortfall," http://completecollege.org/completion_shortfall.

21. President Barack Obama, Speech to Congress, Feb. 24, 2009.

22. Richard Kazis, Joel Vargas, and Nancy Hoffman, eds., *Double the Numbers* (Cambridge: Harvard Education Press, 2004).

23. One of the two supply-side chapters was written by David Longanecker, who examined the different strategies states were taking or could take to increase institutional incentives. I wrote the other supply-side chapter and argued, among other things, that at least a portion of state and federal funding should be allocated to higher education institutions based on the number of low-income students who graduated from them each year. Both of these chapters to some extent grew out of a series of conversations in the late 1990s between higher education leaders and analysts in the United Kingdom and the United States, most especially a session in Colorado Springs in 1999 that focused on funding mechanisms. See David Longanecker, "Financing Tied to Postsecondary Outcomes: Examples of States," pp. 113–22, and Arthur M. Hauptman, "Using Institutional Incentives to Improve Student Performance," pp. 123–33, both in Kazis, Vargas, and Hoffman, *Double the Numbers*.

24. NCHEMS has provided statistical support to a number of organizations on the issues of participation, completion, and attainment patterns in the states. A recent example of this kind of analysis is Dennis Jones, "Defining Attainment and Policy Responses to Improve Performance" (paper presented to a joint meeting of the Miller Center of Public Affairs, Association of Governing Boards of Universities and Colleges, National Conference of State Legislatures, and National Governors Association, Charlottesville, VA, Dec. 6, 2010, www.nchems.org/pubs/docs).

25. Travis Reindl, *Hitting Home* (Boston: Jobs for the Future, 2007).

26. Lumina Foundation, *A Stronger Nation through Higher Education*, p. 3.

27. College Board, *Coming to Our Senses: Education and the American Future* (New York: College Board Advocacy and Policy Center, 2008).

28. Bill and Melinda Gates Foundation, "Why College Completion?" www
.gatesfoundation.org/postsecondaryeducation/Pages/why-college-completion
.aspx.

29. National Center for Public Policy and Higher Education, *Measuring Up: The National Report Card on Higher Education* (San Jose, CA: National Center for Public Policy and Higher Education, 2008).

30. American Association of Community Colleges, "Democracy's Colleges Call to Action," April 2010, www.aacc.nche.org/about/documents/calltoaction.

31. John Michael Lee, Jr., and Anita Rawls, *The College Completion Agenda: 2010 Progress Report* (Washington, DC: College Board, 2010), p. 12.

32. National Governors Association, *Complete to Compete* (Washington, DC: National Governors Association, 2010).

33. The Miller speech to financial aid administrators relied extensively on a report by Byron G. Auguste et al., *Winning by Degrees: The Strategies of Highly Productive Higher-Education Institutions* (New York: McKinsey, 2010). The speech text is available at www.ed.gov.

34. Auguste et al., *Winning by Degrees*, p. 26.

35. Details of the Louisiana program can be found at www.regents.state.la.us.

36. For further discussion of the adverse effects of K–12 goal setting, see Ravitch, *Death and Life of the Great American School System*, pp. 31 and 102, where she writes that "the most toxic flaw in NCLB was its legislative command that all students in every school must be proficient in reading and mathematics by 2014."

37. Figure 1.3 uses an estimate of sub-bachelor's rates for the years preceding 1990 when the statistic was not regularly kept. The estimate is based on the number of workers with one to three years of college, information that has been collected regularly by the Bureau of the Census since the 1950s. U.S. Census Bureau, "Current Population Survey Data on Educational Attainment," table A-1 for select years, available at www.census.gov/hhes/socdemo/education/data/cps.

38. See National Governors Association, *Complete to Compete*, p. 7, and Complete College America, *Essential Steps and Model Policies*, available online at www.completecollege.org.

39. U.S. Census Bureau, "Current Population Survey Data on Educational Attainment," table A-1 for select years, www.census.gov/hhes/socdemo/education/data/cps.

40. NCES, *Digest of Education Statistics, 2009*, table 188.

41. U.S. Census Bureau, Current Population Reports, www.census.gov/cps.

42. Carnevale, Smith, and Strohl, *Help Wanted*. In a January 2011 opinion piece, Carnevale makes a spirited defense of the need for more college graduates in the future while citing problems with some government forecasts; see Anthony Carnevale, "College Is Still Worth It," *Inside Higher Education*, Jan. 14, 2011.

43. Gates Foundation, "Why College Completion?"

44. Auguste et al., *Winning by Degrees*, p. 7.

45. *"From Wall Street to Wal-Mart: Why College Graduates Are Not Getting Good Jobs"* (Policy Paper, Center for College Affordability and Productivity, Washington, DC, Dec. 16, 2010).

46. Charles Murray, *Real Education: Four Simple Truths for Bringing America's Schools Back to Reality* (New York: Crown Forum, 2008).

47. Complete College America, *Certificates Count: An Analysis of Subbaccalaureate Certificates* (Dec. 2010), www.completecollege.org.

48. For a further elaboration of this point, see Arthur Hauptman and Philip Nolan, "Four Budget Balancing Strategies in Higher Education" (paper prepared for OECD/IMHE Conference, Sept. 2010).

49. Frederick M. Hess, "Doing the Same Thing Over and Over Again," *AEI Education Outlook*, no. 11, p. 2.

50. Arthur M. Hauptman and Young Kim, *Cost, Commitment, and Attainment: An International Comparison* (Washington, DC: Jobs for the Future, May 2009), p. 19, table 8.

CHAPTER TWO

Graduation Rates at America's Universities

What We Know and What We Need to Know

MATTHEW M. CHINGOS

At first glance, it may seem relatively straightforward to meet President Obama's goal that "by 2020, America will once again have the highest proportion of college graduates in the world."[1] After all, the United States led the world in educational attainment for generations. According to the most recent figures, 55- to 64-year-olds in the United States are more educated than their counterparts in every other OECD country, with a postsecondary attainment rate six points higher than the next-place countries (30% vs. 24%).[2] But this dominance slowly eroded over time. Americans in the 45 to 54 age group were also the most educated, but only two points ahead of the Netherlands and Norway. The next youngest Americans, those ages 35 to 44, lagged only behind the Norwegians in terms of postsecondary attainment, though only by a percentage point (34% vs. 33%).

The current generation of young Americans—those ages 25 to 34— are in a three-way tie for seventh place among the OECD countries, with an attainment rate fully ten percentage points behind Norway, the world leader (31% vs. 41%). Five countries have attainment rates only one or two points lower than the United States; all of them have made substantial gains in recent years. Most notable is Poland, which in less than a generation increased the share of its population with a college education from 18 to 30 percent. The United States is one of only 2 out of the 30 OECD countries that has fewer college graduates among its 25- to 34-year-olds than among the 35 to 44 age group.

Not only has the United States lost its dominant position in the world; our stagnation coupled with the rapid progress being made by other countries means that we are quickly slipping towards the bottom

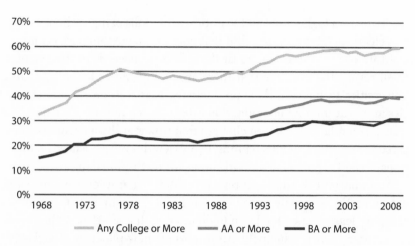

FIGURE 2.1. Educational attainment of 25- to 29-year-olds, 1968–2009.
Source: Current Population Survey

of the list. In order to meet President Obama's goal, in a single decade the United States would need to reverse the current trend and increase the share of young people that earn college degrees by at least one-third and perhaps by one-half or more, from its current level of 31 percent.[3] Such an increase is not unprecedented: bachelor's degree attainment increased by approximately this amount from the late 1960s to the late 1970s, although on a substantially smaller initial rate of 15–20 percent, as shown in figure 2.1.[4] There were also steady (albeit more modest) gains from the late 1980s to the late 1990s, when bachelor's degree attainment rose from 22 percent to its current level of about 30 percent.

As can be seen in the figure, only about half of Americans ages 25 to 29 who start college earn a bachelor's degree (another 15% earn an associate's degree), a ratio that has remained more or less unchanged for decades. The 30 percent of Americans who start college but never finish are an obvious pool of candidates who might be converted to college graduates. The main purpose of this chapter is to review what is known— and what is not known—about how institutions of higher learning might increase their graduation rates.

Colleges and universities are certainly not the only important players in efforts to increase educational attainment. The college enrollment rate in the United States lags behind that of several other countries, and there is surely great progress to be made in the academic preparation of students in elementary and secondary schools.[5] Efforts to graduate more students from high school and to improve the skills of high school graduates clearly need to continue, but that does not mean that postsecondary institutions get a free pass until those efforts succeed. In this chapter I will review the evidence that there are opportunities for colleges and universities to increase their productivity. Research on specific strategies aimed at improving graduation rates is much more limited and has focused on relatively modest changes that tinker at the margins as compared to more fundamental reforms. In my view this reflects a need for more research and not a lack of opportunities for institutional improvement.

An important theme I will return to later is that improvements cannot be costly, especially in the current fiscal environment. Institutions of higher learning need to learn to do more with less—that is, they need to increase their productivity. An important new paper by Douglas N. Harris and Sara Goldrick-Rab makes the argument that proposed policies and programs need to be considered in terms of both their costs and their benefits.[6] These two authors carefully summarize a large number of studies and estimate cost-benefit ratios for each one, an exercise that I will not repeat here but one that should be conducted in every study and not left for readers to try to sort out on their own.

The primary aim of this chapter is to review the lessons learned from the relatively small number of high-quality studies of the factors that shape college graduation rates and discuss some promising areas for future research. I focus mostly on institution-level factors—those that are (theoretically, at least) within the control of the institution. However, I begin with a related but distinct question: could overall attainment be substantially improved by improving the "match" quality between students and the colleges they attend? If the answer is "no"—that is, if moving some students to more selective colleges and others to less selective colleges does not improve overall attainment—should we expect colleges to be able to do better with the existing stock of students? In recent years there have been calls to base the funding of public universities at least in part on the number of students they graduate (rather than solely on enrollment), but do we even know how institutions could improve their performance in response to such incentives?

Institutional Selectivity and Student-College Match

There is consistent, strong evidence that institutional selectivity is strongly correlated with—and causally linked to—graduation rates. Stu-

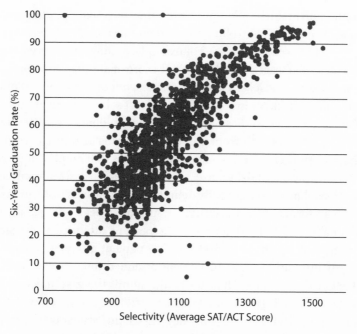

FIGURE 2.2. Graduation rates versus selectivity (*N* = 1,219).
Source: IPEDS

dents who attend more selective institutions are more likely to graduate than students who attend less selective institutions. The simple (unadjusted) relationship between graduation rates and selectivity (as measured by average SAT/ACT scores) is depicted in figure 2.2.[7] On average, a 100-point increase in average SAT/ACT score is associated with a six-year graduation rate that is 11 points higher. Additionally, there is not a large amount of variation in graduation rates among institutions with similar SAT scores (that is, the data points in fig. 2.2 are fairly tightly clustered around a line). There simply are not many unselective institutions with high graduation rates or highly selective institutions with low graduation rates.

Of course, college and university students with higher average test scores are better prepared academically (on average) and thus are more likely to graduate regardless of where they go to college. It is not possible to compare the graduation rates of students with similar test scores at different institutions using institution-level data such as the Integrated Postsecondary Education Data System (IPEDS) data on which figure 2.2 is based, but in a previous study my coauthors and I were able to do exactly that using student-level data in a study of graduation rates at public universities.[8] We found the same selectivity-graduation relationship, even after controlling for students' academic preparation (test scores and high school grades). For example, among students with a high school GPA of at least 3.5 and SAT/ACT score of at least 1200, 89 percent graduated at the most selective universities, but only 59 percent of these well-qualified students graduated at the least selective universities.[9]

Numerous other studies have shown that students who attend more selective schools benefit from doing so—in terms of future earnings, in addition to graduation rates—including studies that employ more rigorous quasi-experimental designs.[10] Of course, selectivity varies only across institutions that are selective. By definition, open-access institutions cannot vary in terms of their selectivity.[11] Among college-going students in a nationally representative survey, 38 percent attended two-year colleges (most of which are nonselective), 5 percent attended nonselective four-year institutions, and 10 percent attended four-year colleges that are technically "selective" but in practice admit the vast majority of applicants.[12] It certainly matters whether a student starts at a two-year or a four-year institution: bachelor's-degree-seeking students who start out at two-year institutions are substantially less likely to earn that degree (or any degree, including an associate's, for that matter) than similarly qualified students that start out at a four-year institution (even one that is not very selective).[13] This finding holds even among students with the weakest academic credentials, who might be expected to benefit from the less demanding environment of a community college.[14]

An important implication of the institutional effects literature is that where a student goes to college has enormous consequences for his or her chances of earning a degree. Recent evidence that academically talented students from low-income and less-educated families are much less likely to attend a more selective college than their more advantaged peers partly explains the troubling gaps in educational attainment by socioeconomic status (SES) that are so pervasive in the United States.[15] Efforts to mitigate disparities in the college choices of similarly prepared high school graduates are clearly warranted on equity grounds alone, but what impact could such programs and policies have on the overall bachelor's degree attainment rate?

In order for policies aimed at improving college match quality to have a positive impact on overall attainment while holding the number of places at each institution constant, it would have to be the case that low-

SES students benefit more from attending a more selective college than high-SES students. This is because encouraging well-qualified students who would otherwise attend less selective institutions to attend more selective universities means that students who would otherwise have attended the more selective universities will be displaced and have to attend less selective institutions.

The evidence on this point is limited, but University of Washington economist Mark C. Long presents evidence that low-SES students benefit disproportionately from attending a higher-quality college in terms of the likelihood that they will earn a bachelor's degree. Specifically, using data from the National Education Longitudinal Study (NELS) he finds that a one standard deviation increase in a college quality index is associated with increases in bachelor's degree attainment of 4, 10, and 15 percentage points for high-, middle-, and low-SES students, respectively.[16]

This finding suggests that a modest reshuffling of the college choice deck could improve overall attainment, but by how much? To get a rough sense of the answer to this question, I performed a simple simulation using the NELS data. First, I classified the first postsecondary institution each student attended into the following selectivity categories from Barron's College Admissions Selector Ratings: most or highly competitive, very competitive, competitive, less competitive, and noncompetitive.[17] These categories apply only to four-year institutions, so I created a separate category for students who first attended a two-year institution. Second, I sorted students according to a measure of their academic preparation and then assigned them to the type of college that they would have attended if college choices were made solely on the basis of this measure and if the share of students attending each type of college remained exactly the same.[18] For example, 7.7 percent of college entrants attended a four-year college in the most or highly competitive category, so in the simulation I assigned the 7.7 percent of students with the highest values of the academic preparation index to this category.

Third, I estimated the relationship between bachelor's degree attainment rates and the category of college attended, controlling for high school GPA and the standardized test score. I estimated this relationship separately for low-, middle-, and high-SES students in order to allow the college selectivity effect to vary.[19] Finally, I predicted each student's probability of earning a bachelor's degree *if they had attended a college in the selectivity category determined only by their academic qualifications.*[20]

The average of this probability is the simulated bachelor's degree attainment rate in a world where students' college-going decisions are affected only by their academic qualifications.

The results of the simulation show, as we would expect, a modest drop in disparities in bachelor's degree attainment rates. The adjusted gap (controlling for test scores and grades) between low- and middle-SES students falls from 8 to 6 percentage points, and the gap between high- and low-SES students falls from 27 to 21 points. But the overall bachelor's degree attainment rate barely budges at all: the simulation indicates an increase of just 0.2 percentage points, from 32.8 to 33.0 percent. This small change probably results from the fact that low-SES students are disproportionately unlikely to go to college at all and even less likely to have the qualifications necessary for admission to a selective university. So while improvements can and should be made in the college choices of talented low-SES students, the pool is just not large enough to have much of an impact on the overall attainment rate.[21]

This simulation is admittedly crude, but because my estimate of the simulated change in the overall attainment rate is so small, even quadrupling it (from 0.2 to 0.8 percentage points) would still yield a similar conclusion: desirable as it is to improve college match quality (particularly among disadvantaged students), this strategy is not likely to yield payoffs in terms of the overall bachelor's degree attainment rate. The numbers of affected students simply are not large enough.[22]

Given that improving student-college matches appears unlikely to significantly boost the national bachelor's degree attainment rate, a natural question to turn to is whether institutions can improve the graduation rates of the students that they are already enrolling. Is there room for institutions to educate students better, rather than just trying to recruit better students? How much (or little) is known about strategies that boost graduation rates?

Institutional Characteristics and Policies

One interpretation of figure 2.2 is that individual institutions do not have much control over their graduation rates if the characteristics of the student body are taken as fixed (and graduation requirements are not relaxed). After all, 71 percent of the variation in six-year graduation rates is explained by a single variable: the average SAT/ACT score of the entering freshmen class. Add into the mix student gender, race/ethnicity, and age and whether the university is public or private, and that statistic jumps to 82 percent.[23]

This view—that institutions are doing about as well as could be expected given their student bodies—is probably incorrect for two main reasons. First, there is still a fair amount of variability in graduation rates even after controlling for these variables—the standard deviation of institutions' divergence from their predicted graduation rates is seven percentage points.[24] Second, interpreting the data in this way is probably misleading because measures of student body quality such as average SAT/ACT scores are strongly correlated with other institutional characteristics. For example, average test scores and instructional expenditures per full-time equivalent (FTE) student are positively correlated ($r = 0.84$), meaning that it is not just the average quality of the student body that explains so much of the variation in graduation rates in figure 2.2. Variation in how much institutions spend on student services could also shape graduation rates. Higher average SAT/ACT scores are also associated with higher expenditures per FTE on student services ($r = 0.37$) and academic support ($r = 0.48$). These are factors that are clearly within the control of the institution (or the legislative body overseeing it, as in the case of many public universities).

The conundrum is that while we know that the average student is best off going to the most selective college that will admit him or her, the research tells us nothing about *why* a student is more likely to graduate from a more selective university. Is it because the other students are highly qualified and there are high expectations that students will graduate? Or is it because more selective universities also tend to spend more educating their undergraduates? Or is it yet some other factor that is associated with both selectivity and graduation rates?

This gap in our knowledge is partly rooted in how difficult it is to document the causal effect of a given policy or institutional characteristic with existing observational data. For instance, although it is straightforward to estimate the relationship between graduation rates and factors such as spending in various categories while holding student characteristics constant, the fact that these variables are associated with both each other and the student characteristics (not to mention unobserved differences across institutions) means that it is difficult to tease out their various *causal* effects. The bottom line is that it is difficult, if not impossible, to make credible inferences about the causal effects of institutional policies using traditional cross-sectional methods.

This does not mean that analyses of institution-level datasets such as IPEDS are not worthwhile. For example, a recent study used IPEDS data to examine whether certain categories of spending are more strongly associated with graduation rates than are other categories.[25] The authors found that, on average, marginal changes in student service expenditures were more strongly associated with graduation rates than were similar marginal changes in instructional expenditures, especially at less selective institutions. It is not clear that these results should be interpreted as causal, given that they are based mainly on comparisons across institutions that may differ in other (unobserved) ways.[26] However, these results raise several interesting questions, such as, what types of student service spending are particularly productive and what instructional expenditures are less productive? They also suggest that future research on the potential for productivity gains in higher education might benefit from focusing on less selective institutions.

One topic where studies with different methodologies have produced different results is the effectiveness of full- and part-time faculty. Two studies using institution-level data found that employing a greater share of part-time, adjunct, or non-tenure-track faculty is associated with lower graduation rates at both four-year colleges and community colleges.[27] However, another study that used student-level data from Ohio and exploited variation in the composition of departments' faculty over time found an apparently opposing result: adjuncts often have a small positive effect on the number of courses the student takes in a given subject, particularly in fields tied to particular occupations.[28] These studies differ in several ways besides methodology that might explain the divergent results, including context, the level of aggregation of the data, and the outcome measures examined. But the broader point is that using methods that do not allow for strong causal inferences coupled with data at a high level of aggregation make it difficult to make specific policy recommendations. For example, the results of the Ohio study might justify hiring more adjuncts in certain fields, but such a precise course of action could not be drawn from either of the two studies that used institution-level data.

There are a handful of rigorous (experimental or quasi-experimental) studies on three general types of policies that might affect graduation rates: pricing and financial aid, student support services, and remediation. I will briefly review some of the key lessons that emerge from these studies, without any presumption of being comprehensive. Two of these topics are covered in detail elsewhere in this volume: Eric Bettinger's chapter on financial aid and Bridget Terry Long's chapter on remediation. Additionally, by limiting this review to experimental and quasi-experimental studies I necessarily leave out a large number of observational studies.[29] Such studies often provide useful descriptive information and generate questions worthy of further research but for the most part do not yield the kind of *causal* evidence that would be needed to support policy recommendations.

It is not surprising that increasing grant aid (that is, reducing the cost of college) causes more students, particularly those from low-income families, to enroll in and complete college.[30] But marginal changes in costs are just one part of the college dropout story, and not a large one, perhaps due to existing aid programs such as Federal Pell Grants. Even programs that make college free have no more than a modest impact on graduation rates.[31] A less obvious lesson than "money matters, but not enough to solve the dropout problem" is that the way aid is provided can matter just as much as, if not more than, the amount that is provided. A recent randomized experiment showed that helping lower-income families complete the Free Application for Federal Student Aid (FAFSA) increased the odds that their children would enroll in college the following fall, suggesting that the sheer difficulty of filling out the FAFSA was an impediment to families eligible for need-based aid.[32] An evaluation of West Virginia's PROMISE scholarship program, which provides aid to students only as long as they maintain a full-time course load, found that this policy not only increased bachelor's degree attainment but also decreased time-to-degree.[33]

Studies of student support services have found that these programs often are most effective when coupled with financial incentives. A large Canadian university offered students support services or financial incentives for earning a target GPA, or a combination of both as part of a randomized experiment (which also included a control group). Neither the support services nor the financial incentives had consistently positive effects in isolation, but the combined treatment had a positive effect on the academic outcomes of women (but not men).[34]

Elements of this program were also part of MDRC's Opening Doors initiative, a randomized experiment conducted at six community colleges. On top of receiving services and additional financial aid (which was often tied to behaviors such as making use of services or earning a certain GPA), students were part of "learning communities"—small groups of entering students that took classes together. The results from many of the campuses were promising. For example, program participants in New Orleans (who, in addition to participating in learning communities, were offered $1,000 per semester if they enrolled at least half-time and maintained a C average) were 18 percentage points more likely to remain enrolled the following semester.[35]

The final area with multiple high-quality studies is remediation, whereby students deemed academically underprepared for college are encouraged or required to take supplementary courses (without receiving college credit) before they begin college-level work. Two studies, one of community colleges in Florida and the other of both two- and four-year colleges in Texas, measure the causal effect of remediation by comparing students right around the cut score in the exam used to place students in remedial courses.[36] It is more or less random which students score just above the cutoff (and thus are not placed in remedial courses) and which students score just below the cutoff (and are placed in remedial courses as a result). As a result, the causal effect of remediation can be calculated as the average difference in college outcomes between students just above and just below the cutoff. Both studies find few benefits of remediation and some evidence of negative effects (perhaps resulting from students being discouraged by having to take remedial courses).[37]

What We Need to Know

So what do we know about successful strategies for improving graduation rates? A relatively small number of high-quality studies yield credible evidence about the effectiveness of a handful of policies, such as financial aid, student support services, and remediation. More generous aid that is better targeted (and tied to academic progress) has positive effects, as do student support services coupled with financial incentives. Remediation probably has few positive effects, and may have some negative effects, despite being quite costly.

On the basis of this evidence, a university might reallocate some resources away from remediation and toward incentive-based aid and student services. Such an approach might well make a difference, but it is hard to imagine that tinkering at the margins is going to result in substantial increases in graduation rates. And costly policies that require an increase in overall spending are going to be extremely difficult to pursue in the near future, as institutions continue to weather the recent economic recession. In the words of Harvard education professor and Gates Foundation official Thomas J. Kane, "Public higher education must learn to do more with less. . . . We must fundamentally rethink the function, pricing, and operation of public colleges."[38]

It seems obvious that fundamental reform is needed, but of exactly what type should it take? The disappointing conclusion of this chapter is that we don't really know, but that does not mean that there aren't ideas worthy of further investigation. In the remainder of this chapter, I will discuss some promising possibilities, focusing on strategies aimed at improving the quality of instruction. It seems reasonable to expect that improvements in the quality of undergraduate education will lead to students' persisting and graduating at higher rates, and strategies focused on quality have the added benefit of mitigating concerns that pressure to increase graduation rates will lead universities to lower their standards in order to graduate more students (but without a commensurate increase in what students have actually learned).

One of the most promising strategies to increase productivity in higher education is to leverage recent advances in information technology to deliver higher-quality instruction at a lower cost. There is a certainly a great deal of variation in the quality of computer-based courses, so this is an area where attention to quality is particularly important. Simply taking existing course materials and putting them online is unlikely to increase productivity, and one recent randomized experiment demonstrated that such a crude form of online instruction may be less effective than traditional modes of instruction.[39]

But a sophisticated course that is primarily computer-based can have substantial advantages. Each student can learn at her own pace, and built-in feedback loops can identify the areas where the student is proficient as well as areas where she needs additional help. This information can be instantaneously provided to both the student as he goes through the course and to instructors, most of whom previously had little information about how well their students were learning the course material until after the first exam. Studies of the sophisticated courses developed by the Open Learning Initiative at Carnegie Mellon University have found these courses to produce outcomes at least as good as traditional face-to-face learning, although more evidence is needed before such courses can be taken to scale.[40] It is relatively straightforward (albeit logistically challenging) to test the effectiveness of specific online courses by randomly assigning students to either the face-to-face or the online version of the same course and then comparing their learning outcomes (such as scores on a common final exam). It is also important to collect data on the relative costs of the two modes of instruction, as a reduction in costs would imply an increase in productivity even in the absence of an increase in learning.

The greatest productivity gains can be realized from computer-based learning only if the substantial cost of developing high-quality courses is shared by many institutions. A campus-by-campus approach is unlikely to yield real cost savings, especially in the short run. An added benefit to standardizing certain large introductory courses across campuses (particularly within large state systems) is the reduction of barriers to transferring between campuses, as many students do. This issue is particularly salient at community colleges, where the use of computer-based courses that are also used at four-year institutions would smooth the transition between sectors for students who are seeking bachelor's degrees but start at two-year schools. Online courses also have obvious appeal for use as part of remediation programs that could be made available to students *before* they arrive on campus for their first year of college.

This potential innovation has obvious applications at traditional brick-and-mortar colleges and universities, which could replace some traditional face-to-face large lecture courses with high-quality computer-based versions that are offered online. Such online courses would be taught in a substantially different way from other courses at the same institution, but they would still be part of the same credit-hour-based system and could have a face-to-face component such as weekly course meetings with a teaching assistant. Online courses without an in-person component could be offered to students who did not live near the institution, but those students would still need to earn a certain number of credit hours in order to graduate with a degree.

But one can also imagine a more radical shift in which progress towards a degree would be measured by knowledge acquired by the student rather than the number of credit hours a student completed. In theory, such a self-paced, competency-based system could be applied at residential or commuter campuses, but it has the most obvious appeal for degrees that are offered entirely online, for which the credit hour (historically roughly based on the amount of time a student spent in class) doesn't make much sense.[41] Students who need twice the normal amount of time to successfully complete a course would not be lost in a class that moved too quickly, and students who can learn the material in half the normal time could breeze through and move on to more advanced courses. Self-pacing would be particularly advantageous for older students trying to balance their studies with work and family responsibilities (in 2007–8, 40 percent of undergraduates in the United States were 24 or older, with more than half of these students age 30 or above).[42]

Quality control would be crucial to the success of this idea, as is made clear by the existence of "diploma mills" that promise degrees in exchange for evidence of life experience (and tuition payments!). It would also be important to have some way of ensuring that the person completing the online courses is the same person awarded the degree. Clearly, much more evidence is needed before such a fundamental shift should be pursued on a large scale. For example, researchers might examine the completion rates of students in entirely online programs and the economic returns for degrees earned in this way. An important task for researchers is to identify the most promising versions of this innovation and then rigorously evaluate how well they work, so that they might be replicated if found successful. Identifying programs that appear ill-conceived from the outset and then showing that they are ineffective is much less useful.

Instruction that is primarily computer-based may well make sense for certain courses or even entire degree programs—but what about courses that are best taught in the traditional face-to-face manner? Presumably students would benefit from an increase in the quality of their instructors, but is such an increase possible? Currently very little systematic direct evidence is available as to the quality of undergraduate instruction. There is some research on the relative quality of different types of instructors, such as adjuncts compared to tenure-track faculty (as discussed above), but there could well be enormous variation in quality among instructors of each type. There is an obvious parallel to elementary and secondary education, where research has found that there are few differences in average quality between teachers with different observable characteristics (such as whether and how they were certified), but large differences among teachers with similar characteristics.[43]

Large differences in instructor quality in higher education, if they exist, would imply there were opportunities to improve undergraduate instruction by selectively retaining the superior instructors or improving the quality of the inferior teachers. Measuring instructor quality would be a challenge, as it would require access to student-instructor matched data with consistent outcome data for students taught by different instructors. However, data constraints may relax as state-level longitudinal systems proliferate. Currently, the most rigorous study of postsecondary instructor quality uses data from the U.S. Air Force Academy, an atypical institution in American higher education.[44]

If there are opportunities to improve undergraduate education by increasing the quality of instruction, would the incentives currently embedded in the higher education system permit the realization of such gains? Or would the dual mission of many institutions to both teach and produce research complicate any such efforts? Once again, the possibility of competing interests of students and employees echoes debates in K–12 education. Might some of the ideas embedded in reforms currently being tried within the nation's public K–12 schools also hold promise for higher education? For example, one might compare commentators who blame low college graduation rates on poorly prepared students with those who blame the poor academic performance of elementary and secondary students on their families and larger social problems. Of course, educational institutions at all levels are affected by forces larger than themselves, but the important question is whether they can do better even in the face of factors beyond their control. The stellar performance of some "no excuses" charter elementary and secondary schools suggests that they can.[45] One might well imagine the creation of an undergraduate college aimed at taking underprepared students and providing them with a high-quality education—making up for past deficiencies if need be.

These types of questions clearly cannot be adequately covered in a single brief review piece such as the present one. And there are certainly many other proposals worthy of consideration, such as creating stronger incentives for students to finish college in four years (rather than five or six) and tying the funding of public institutions to the number of graduates produced instead of the number of students enrolled. My primary aim in this section is not to cover every one of these proposals, but rather to illustrate the types of larger questions that institutions and their critical friends in the research community need to consider if real progress is going to be made on the graduation rate issue.

One general principle worth keeping in mind is that different contexts call for different programs and policies. The steps a flagship public university should take to improve its graduation rate should not necessarily be pursued by the nearby community college. As obvious as this may seem, one often sees common practices across higher education that should not be so common. For example, the SAT was created at the behest of a 1930s-era Harvard president with the goal of identifying promising candidates for admission to Harvard. To this day, students' scores on the SAT remain a reasonable predictor (in combination with other factors) of how well they will do at places like Harvard. But SAT and ACT scores are a poor predictor of graduation rates at institutions outside of the most elite publics and privates—that is, the institutions attended by most students in this country.[46] Why, then, are SAT and ACT scores used at so many places where they appear to add so little value?

Are there other policies and practices of the small number of elite research-intensive institutions—faculty tenure and the importance of research productivity in the faculty hiring and tenure review process, to name two candidates—that have trickled down, perhaps to ill effect, to the institutions whose primary mission is to educate undergraduates? Returning briefly to the question of instructor quality, does it make sense for less selective institutions to hire the cast-off PhDs of the more elite institutions instead of recruiting individuals who are passionate about teaching undergraduates?

Public and private nonprofit colleges and universities might also consider whether there are any lessons that can be learned from for-profit institutions, the fastest-growing sector in higher education.[47] In theory, relatively new for-profit providers are not as affected by the type of historical baggage that weighs down older institutions thus enjoy greater flexibility to innovate. The for-profits enroll disproportionately large shares of at-risk students—the kinds of students least likely to be adequately served by traditional institutions—and claim to serve these students as well as or better than traditional institutions.[48] However, this is a contested proposition that has not been satisfactorily resolved, largely because of a lack of publicly available data covering the for-profits. If any lessons are to be learned from the practices of this rapidly growing sector, researchers will need much greater access to their data. Given the for-profits' fiduciary interest in not releasing any data that may damage their reputation, compelling the release of such data seems like an obvious role for government regulators.

Clearly there is no shortage of questions for researchers to tackle, even if many of the most important questions are also the most challenging. Additionally, the urgency that many feel to improve educational attainment will not wait for the results of carefully conducted studies, so lessons may be learned from steps (or missteps) taken in the absence of hard evidence. For this to happen, individual institutions and state higher education systems must be willing to allow researchers to track student outcomes. Several state systems already have longitudinal databases that allow for such research, including the incredibly detailed data system in Ohio that has been used in several important studies by economists Eric Bettinger and Bridget Terry Long.

The federal government as well as its counterparts in the states can help sustain this trend by funding (if not mandating) the development and maintenance of such databases, the best of which link records from postsecondary institutions to other sources such as the state's K–12 education database, the National Student Clearinghouse (to track transfer to private and out-of-state institutions), state unemployment insurance records (to track the subsequent earnings of college graduates and dropouts), and other sources of data on students' later-life outcomes.

The federal Department of Education also plays an important role in the support of research by providing funding through its Institute of Education Sciences (IES). However, of its 15 research grant programs, only one is devoted specifically to postsecondary education. (Several others are aimed solely at K–12 education.)[49] Likewise, higher education is not included in the "What Works Clearinghouse," an IES-created effort to identify rigorous education research and make the results readily available to educators, policymakers, and the public.[50]

In addition to increased commitments to higher education research through its current programs, the federal government might also play a more active role in postsecondary R&D by funding experimentation at individual campuses. In a recent paper, Dominic Brewer and William Tierney propose a competitive proposal process designed to encourage "traditional higher education institutions to develop and test operational innovations."[51] Successful innovations that confer a competitive advantage on the institutions that adopt them might then spread on their own to other campuses (perhaps including previously recalcitrant ones).

Conclusion

America's institutions of higher learning cannot drastically increase the level of educational attainment in the country on their own. College students need to arrive on campus better prepared academically, and more students need to graduate high school with the skills needed to attend college at all. But the poor preparation of many entering college students should not be used as an excuse for poor graduation rates. At many institutions, even students with impressive high school grades and test scores graduate at mediocre rates. Data points like this one make it clear that institutions can do better with their current students, without lowering academic standards. The research community has a vital role to play in identifying promising strategies for improvement and evaluating the efforts of institutions seeking to better fulfill their mission of educating undergraduates.

NOTES

1. Barack Obama, "Remarks of President Barack Obama—Address to Joint Session of Congress," text of a speech released by the White House Press Office, Feb. 24, 2009.

2. The statistics reported in this paragraph and the next are drawn from Organisation for Economic Co-operation and Development, *Education at a Glance, 2010: OECD Indicators* (Paris: OECD, 2010), table A1.3a, columns labeled "Tertiary-type A and Advanced research programmes." According to the OECD glossary, "Tertiary-type A programmes have a minimum cumulative theoretical duration (at tertiary level) of three years' full-time equivalent, although they typically last four or more years." This glossary is available at http://stats.oecd .org/glossary/detail.asp?ID=5440.

3. If Norway stagnates at 41%, then the United States needs to increase attainment by about one-third. If Norway increases its attainment rate to 45%, the United States needs to increase attainment by about half.

4. The largest recorded 10-year increase in both relative and absolute terms was 1968–78, when the bachelor's attainment rate increased by 9 percentage points, from 15% to 23% (a 58% increase).

5. Whereas the United States tied for 7th place among OECD countries in postsecondary attainment, it ranks 12th in terms of college access rates; see OECD, *Education at a Glance, 2010*, table A2.3. Countries where more than 64% (the U.S. rate) of citizens enroll in college include Norway (71%) and Poland (83%). For a recent international comparison of student achievement, see Eric A. Hanushek, Paul E. Peterson, and Ludger Woessmann, *U.S. Math Performance in Global Perspective: How Well Does Each State Do at Producing High-Achieving Students?* Program on Education Policy and Governance Report no. 10-19 (Cambridge: Harvard University, 2010).

6. Douglas N. Harris and Sara Goldrick-Rab, *The (Un)Productivity of American Higher Education: From "Cost Disease" to Cost-Effectiveness*, La Follette Working Paper no. 2010-023 (Madison: Robert M. La Follette School of Public Affairs, University of Wisconsin, 2010).

7. This figure, which is based on Integrated Postsecondary Education Data System (IPEDS) data from 2007–8 compiled by the Delta Cost Project, includes

only four-year colleges and universities that reported both six-year graduation rates and average SAT/ACT scores and enrolled at least 100 first-time full-time freshmen. Average SAT/ACT score is calculated on the basis of the test taken by the greatest share of students (averaging the 25th and 75th percentiles), with ACT scores converted to the SAT scale. Institutions where fewer than 50% of students took the SAT or the ACT are excluded.

8. William G. Bowen, Matthew M. Chingos, and Michael S. McPherson, *Crossing the Finish Line: Completing College at America's Public Universities* (Princeton, NJ: Princeton University Press, 2009), chap. 10.

9. Reported in David Leonhardt, "Colleges Are Failing in Graduation Rates," *New York Times*, Sept. 9, 2009. This information, though not included in the book *Crossing the Finish Line*, was a part of our findings and was provided to Leonhardt for his article. The most selective universities had average SAT/ACT scores greater than 1,200; the least selective universities had average scores below 1,000. More detailed regression analyses yielded similar results.

10. See Caroline M. Hoxby, "The Changing Selectivity of American Colleges," *Journal of Economic Perspectives* 23, no. 4 (Fall 2009), for a brief summary of some of these studies. The one often-cited exception is a study that compared the earnings of students who were accepted by a similar set of schools but attended different schools; the study found no selectivity effect (except among low-income students). See Stacy Berg Dale and Alan B. Krueger, "Estimating the Payoff to Attending a More Selective College: An Application of Selection on Observables and Unobservables," *Quarterly Journal of Economics* 117, no. 4 (Nov. 2002). However, the range of selectivity of the institutions included in that study is extremely limited, and the results are based only on students who applied to a similar set of schools and thus do not reflect the large amount of variation in college choices that results from student decisions about where to apply.

11. Nonselective institutions can vary in terms of the average quality of their students. However, it is often difficult to measure such variation, since most nonselective institutions do not require or record admissions data such as students' SAT/ACT scores.

12. Author's calculations from the National Education Longitudinal Study (NELS) using the Barron's College Admissions selectivity ratings.

13. See, for example, Bowen, Chingos, and McPherson, *Crossing the Finish Line*, chap. 7; Curtis Lockwood Reynolds, "Where to Attend? Estimating the Effects of Beginning College at a Two-Year Institution" (working paper, Kent State University, Kent, OH, 2009); and Bridget Terry Long and Michal Kurlaender, "Do Community Colleges Provide a Viable Pathway to a Baccalaureate Degree?" *Educational Evaluation and Policy Analysis* 31, no. 1 (Mar. 2009).

14. Bowen, Chingos, and McPherson, *Crossing the Finish Line*, chap. 7.

15. Melissa Roderick, Jenny Nagaoka, Vanessa Coca, and Eliza Moeller, *From High School to the Future: Making Hard Work Pay Off* (Chicago: Consortium on Chicago School Research, 2008); and Bowen, Chingos, and McPherson, *Crossing the Finish Line*, chap. 5.

16. Mark C. Long, "Changes in the Returns to Education and College Quality," *Economics of Education Review* 29, no. 3 (June 2010), table 4.

17. I did not classify students who attended a four-year institution for which the Barron's rating was not available or an institution in the "special" category.

18. Specifically, I estimated an academic preparation index for each student based on his or her high school GPA and score on a standardized test administered in the 12th grade as part of the NELS study as the linear predictions from an ordered probit regression of the college category variable on high school GPA and the standardized test score. I used the standardized test score instead of SAT/ACT scores because the SAT/ACT is taken only by a self-selected sample of students. For students for whom a 12th-grade standardized test score was not available, I predicted a score using the results from a similar test administered in the 10th grade. All analyses using the NELS data are weighted using the appropriate survey weights.

19. I estimated these relationship using probit regressions. I defined low-SES students as those from families in the bottom half of the income distribution where neither parent earned a college degree, high-SES students as those from families in the top half of the income distribution where at least one parent earned a college degree, and middle-SES students as all other students. I also estimated this relationship separately for students for whom data on SES are missing.

20. Students who did not attend any college (or attended a college that was not included in one of the selectivity categories) were assigned their actual bachelor's degree attainment.

21. This simulation admittedly makes a number of potentially faulty assumptions. A simple regression analysis is unlikely to yield accurate estimates of the causal relationship between college selectivity and bachelor's degree attainment. The college selectivity categories probably miss a fair amount of variation in college characteristics within each of these categories. And there may well be general equilibrium effects from resorting large numbers of students; these would not be reflected in my analysis.

22. It could well be that a more ambitious reengineering of the college match process (for example, one that gave admission preferences to low-SES students at selective universities) could boost overall attainment rates, but such a thought experiment is beyond the scope of this chapter. I did run an additional simulation in which I increased the shares of students attending most, highly, and very competitive colleges by 20%; kept the shares of students attending noncompetitive and two-year colleges the same; and allocated the remaining students to competitive and less-competitive colleges in proportion to the original shares in those categories. In other words, I simulated an increase in the number of available spaces at the more selective colleges and a decrease in the number of spaces at less selective (but not open-enrollment) four-year colleges. Students were still assigned to colleges on the basis of their grades and test scores. This reallocation of spaces increased the simulated bachelor's degree attainment rate only by an additional 0.2 percentage points, to 33.2%.

23. These statistics are r-squared values from linear regressions that are weighted by student full-time equivalent (FTE) enrollment. The unweighted statistics are 65% and 73%.

24. This figure is based only on four-year institutions that report average SAT/ACT scores. The variation among two-year and nonselective four-year institutions could be larger or smaller.

25. Douglas A. Webber and Ronald G. Ehrenberg, "Do Expenditures Other than Instructional Expenditures Affect Graduation and Persistence Rates in American Higher Education?" *Economics of Education Review* 29, no. 6 (Dec. 2010).

26. Technically, the authors use panel data, but they do not take advantage of the panel structure of the data using methods such as fixed effects because, they argue, there is not enough variation in spending within institutions over the four cohorts covered by their panel.

27. The study of four-year colleges is Ronald G. Ehrenberg and Liang Zhang, "Do Tenured and Tenure-Track Faculty Matter?" (National Bureau of Economic Research Working Paper 10695, Cambridge, MA, 2004), and the study of community colleges is Daniel Jacoby, "Effects of Part-Time Faculty Employment on Community College Graduation Rates," *Journal of Higher Education* 77, no. 6 (Nov./Dec. 2006).

28. Eric P. Bettinger and Bridget Terry Long, "Does Cheaper Mean Better? The Impact of Using Adjunct Instructors on Student Outcomes," *Review of Economics and Statistics* 92, no. 3 (Aug. 2010).

29. See, for example, Clifford Adelman, *The Toolbox Revisited: Paths to Degree Completion from High School through College* (Washington, DC: U.S. Department of Education, 2006), and the many studies cited therein.

30. For a review of this literature, see Bowen, Chingos, and McPherson, *Crossing the Finish Line*, chap. 8; and David Deming and Susan Dynarski, "Into College, Out of Poverty? Policies to Increase the Postsecondary Attainment of the Poor" (National Bureau of Economic Research Working Paper 15387, Cambridge, MA, 2009).

31. Susan Dynarski, "Building the Stock of College-Educated Labor," *Journal of Human Resources* 43, no. 3 (Summer 2008); and Ralph Stinebrickner and Todd R. Stinebrickner, "Understanding Educational Outcomes of Students from Low-Income Families: Evidence from a Liberal Arts College with a Full Tuition Subsidy Program," *Journal of Human Resources* 38, no. 3 (Summer 2003).

32. Eric P. Bettinger et al., "The Role of Simplification and Information in College Decisions: Results from the H&R Block FAFSA Experiment" (National Bureau of Economic Research Working Paper 15361, Cambridge, MA, 2009).

33. Judith Scott-Clayton, "On Money and Motivation: A Quasi-Experimental Analysis of Financial Incentives for College Achievement," *Journal of Human Resources* 46, no. 3 (Summer 2011).

34. Joshua Angrist, Daniel Lang, and Philip Oreopoulos, "Incentives and Services for College Achievement: Evidence from a Randomized Trial," *American Economic Journal: Applied Economics* 1, no. 1 (Jan. 2009).

35. An excellent summary of the Opening Doors demonstrations (with citations to the original studies) is contained in David Deming and Susan Dynarski, "Into College, Out of Poverty? Policies to Increase the Postsecondary Attainment of the Poor" (National Bureau of Economic Research Working Paper 15387, Cambridge, MA, 2009).

36. The Florida study is Juan Carlos Calcagno and Bridget Terry Long, "The Impact of Postsecondary Remediation Using a Regression Discontinuity Approach: Addressing Endogenous Sorting and Noncompliance" (National Bureau of Economic Research Working Paper 14194, Cambridge, MA, 2008); the Texas study is Paco Martorell and Isaac McFarlin Jr., "Help or Hindrance? The Effects of College Remediation on Academic and Labor Market Outcomes" (working paper, RAND and the University of Michigan, 2010).

37. Another reasonably high-quality study, by Eric P. Bettinger and Bridget Terry Long, "Addressing the Needs of Underprepared Students in Higher Education: Does College Remediation Work?" *Journal of Human Resources* 44, no. 3 (Summer 2009), finds evidence that students in remediation have higher persistence rates than non-remediated students. However, the identifying assumption made in this paper (that distance to the nearest college only affects student outcomes through the remediation policies at that college) is a stronger assumption than the assumption made by the regression discontinuity analyses.

38. Quote from back cover (endorsements) of Bowen, Chingos, and McPherson, *Crossing the Finish Line*.

39. David N. Figlio, Mark Rush, and Lu Yin, "Is It Live or Is It Internet? Experimental Estimates of the Effects of Online Instruction on Student Learning" (National Bureau of Economic Research Working Paper 16089, Cambridge, MA, 2010).

40. See, for example, Marsha Lovett, Oded Meyer, and Candace Thille, "The Open Learning Initiative: Measuring the Effectiveness of the OLI Statistics Course in Accelerating Student Learning," *Journal of Interactive Media in Education*, special issue (May 2008).

41. One example of such a competency-based, entirely online university is Western Governor's University, which was founded by the governors of 19 states. More information is available at the university's website, www.wgu.edu.

42. "Who Are the Undergraduates?" *Chronicle of Higher Education*, Dec. 12, 2010.

43. See, for example, Thomas J. Kane, Jonah E. Rockoff, and Douglas O. Stagier, "What Does Certification Tell Us about Teacher Effectiveness? Evidence from New York City," *Economics of Education Review* 27, no. 6 (Dec. 2008).

44. Scott E. Carrell and James E. West, "Does Professor Quality Matter? Evidence from Random Assignment of Students to Professors," *Journal of Political Economy* 118, no. 3 (June 2010).

45. See, for example, Caroline M. Hoxby, Sonali Murarka, and Jenny Kang, *How New York City's Charter Schools Affect Achievement* (Cambridge, MA: New York City Charter Schools Evaluation Project, 2009).

46. Bowen, Chingos, and McPherson, *Crossing the Finish Line*, chap. 6.

47. William G. Tierney and Guilbert C. Hentschke, *Making It Happen: Increasing College Access and Participation in California Higher Education* (La Jolla, CA: National University System Institute for Policy Research, 2011).

48. See, e.g., Kaplan University, *Academic Report: The Year in Review, 2009–2010* (Chicago: Kaplan Higher Education Corporation, 2011).

49. A list of grant programs (with links to their descriptions) is available at the Institute for Education Sciences website, at http://ies.ed.gov/funding/ncer_progs.asp.

50. For a list of "What Works Clearinghouse" topic areas available, see the IES website, at http://ies.ed.gov/ncee/wwc/reports.

51. Dominic J. Brewer and William G. Tierney, "Barriers to Innovation in U.S. Higher Education" (American Enterprise Institute conference paper, Washington, DC, June 2010).

PART TWO

The Performance and Potential of Sub-Baccalaureate Programs

CHAPTER THREE

Can Community Colleges Achieve Ambitious Graduation Goals?

THOMAS BAILEY

Over the past decade, the completion agenda has swept through the world of higher education policy and practice. According to this agenda, access to and opportunity for enrollment are no longer adequate: not only must colleges give students a chance to enroll, but students should also graduate or complete a degree. It is hard to overstate the extent to which this represents a change. The education reform agendas of the 1990s were not focused on higher education, and affirmative action was probably the most controversial and widely discussed higher education policy issue—a topic that concerned admission to selective colleges. Indeed, until the late 1990s, when the U.S. Department of Education began to publish graduation rates for all colleges whose students were eligible to receive federal financial aid, there were no consistent and nationally comparable data on the completion rates of individual colleges.

College graduation is now the focus of much of the higher education reform discussion. Since 2008, the Obama administration and the major private foundations involved in higher education reform have set ambitious targets to increase the number of college graduates and the share of the population with a college degree. And in another break from the past, community colleges are now at the center of most discussions of higher education reform.

In this chapter, I first review the degree attainment goals set by the Obama administration, the Bill and Melinda Gates Foundation, and Lumina Foundation for Education and explain why the goals were set where they are; I also describe and explain the prominent role that community colleges play in this discussion. For the most part, the goals have been set for the sum of associate's degrees and bachelor's degrees, based on projections of total degree production and population growth. But the derivation of degree goals for community college degrees (and indeed what would count as a community college "degree") is less clear.

Next, I discuss the extent of the increase in degree production that would be necessary to meet the goals, reviewing what we know about the ability of the most common reforms and strategies to produce those increases. Indeed, the goals are extremely ambitious, and past reform efforts have not resulted in improvements anywhere near the level that will be necessary to meet these goals. Meeting the articulated goals will thus require ambitious and comprehensive reforms involving fundamental changes in the way colleges operate and in incentives for both institutions and students. I conclude with some discussion about what colleges might need to do to significantly increase their degree production.

Although this chapter is about community colleges, in several sections I make reference to for-profit institutions. The for-profits have experienced even faster growth than the public community college sector, and I discuss how they might contribute to the attainment of completion goals. Moreover, the rapid growth of the for-profits suggests that there might be lessons for community colleges in the operations and methods of the for-profits. The chapter also reviews these possibilities.

Graduation Goals

Americans have been proud of their system of higher education for several decades now. U.S. universities have always dominated lists of the top world-class institutions. Even in an era of trade deficits, higher education has consistently been a strong export industry: foreign students have chosen to enroll in American colleges and universities, not only filling classrooms—often paying full tuition—but also providing a rich source of skilled human resources, as international graduates have often remained in the United States to work. International data indicated that the United States used to lead the world in the share of its population with postsecondary credentials.

However, this enthusiastic confidence in American higher education has weakened over the last ten years. There are many reasons for this shift, but data from OECD showing the distribution of educational attainment have played a fundamental role in the policy discussion and debate.[1] These data indicate that in 2008, 39 percent of the young adult population (25–34 years old) in the United States had a postsecondary credential (these include bachelor's and associate's degrees, or equivalents, and certificates that require at least two years of instruction). That share exceeded 50 percent in some other countries.[2] There are, to be sure, criticisms of the meaning and validity of these international comparisons, as discussed by Arthur Hauptman in chapter 1.[3] Nevertheless, the Obama administration and prominent foundations have used the gap between the 39 percent in the United States and the 50-plus percent elsewhere to develop the goal that 60 percent of the young U.S. adult population should have a postsecondary degree by 2020. The derivation of that goal is simple: since the leading countries are likely to continue to increase the share of their population with a postsecondary education, the United States needs to set a goal that substantially exceeds the current percentage in the leading country. A 60 percent share for the United States will result in restored U.S. leadership even if the countries that are currently at the top in educational attainment continue to increase their shares.

The National Center for Higher Education Management Systems (NCHEMS) has calculated that in order to meet the 60 percent goal, the U.S. higher education system would have to produce by 2020 an additional 8.2 million individuals between the ages of 25 to 34 with associate's or bachelor's degrees—more than the system is projected to produce given past trends.[4]

The Obama administration has adopted the 8 million degrees goal. The Lumina and Gates Foundations have established similar goals. Lumina has called for an additional 23 million graduates between the ages of 25 to 64 with high-quality degrees and credentials by 2025; according to the foundation's calculations, that will require an increase of 150,000 graduates a year.[5] The Gates Foundation set a target to double the number of low-income students who earn a postsecondary degree or credential with genuine value in the workplace by age 26. Reaching this completion target would require an increase of approximately 250,000 additional graduates each year.[6]

Forecasts of the supply and demand of college graduates have also been used to support recommendations for increasing the number of college graduates. Projections by the Georgetown Center on Education and Work imply a shortfall in college-educated labor by 2018 of about three million people.[7]

The goals discussed so far have concerned aggregations of postsecondary degrees. But community colleges in particular play an important role in the attainment goals of the administration and the foundations. Analysts have not produced formal forecasts of the contribution of community college degrees to these overall goals. A logical assumption would be to expect the increase in community college degrees to be proportional to their share of the total. In 2009, twice as many bachelor's degrees as associate's degrees were conferred (and only about two-thirds of the associate's degrees were conferred by community colleges). This would suggest that the most of the increase should be expected to come from bachelor's degrees. However, most organizations setting these goals, especially the Obama administration and the Gates Foundation, have emphasized the role of community colleges to a greater degree than a proportionate forecast would suggest. For example, in conjunction with the goal of 8.2 million postsecondary degrees, the administration has also called for an additional 5 million community college graduates by 2020.[8] The Gates Foundation programs, designed to help the higher education system achieve the foundation's ambitious degree goals, are primarily focused on community colleges.

Whatever the specific derivation of the community college degree goals, they do represent a conviction that community colleges must play a disproportionate role in any significant increase in postsecondary attainment. There are several reasons for this emphasis.

First, the lag in the U.S. share of young adults with postsecondary degrees is almost entirely due to the deficiency in sub-baccalaureate degree completion and attainment. The United States continues to be among the leaders in attainment of bachelor's degrees.[9]

Second, there are millions of students in community colleges who do not graduate. In seeking to increase the number of graduates, trying to get students already in college over the finish line seems like an easier goal than trying to increase the number of graduates by recruiting new students. According to data from the National Education Longitudinal Study (NELS), which tracked students for eight years after their scheduled entry into a community college, about 15 percent of community college entrants left with between 30 and 59 credits, and another 8 or 9 percent left with between 20 and 29 credits. Clearly, the goal of a degree or certificate is much closer for these recipients of "some college" than it is for new enrollees.

Third, a rapid increase in two-year degrees is more feasible and economically realistic than an equivalent increase in four-year degrees. Moreover, certificate programs, which take less than two years, could play a major role in making progress on completion goals.

Fourth, low-income students, first-generation college students, immigrants, and minorities, especially Hispanics, are overrepresented in community colleges; and any increase in college attainment will have to involve these groups. Upper-middle-class and wealthy white people already have high college attainment rates. By emphasizing the improved performance of community colleges, the policy would presumably have a disproportionate effect on traditionally underrepresented groups and would therefore have an additional benefit in terms of equity.

The Gates Foundation summed up its emphasis on community colleges in this way: "We are focusing our efforts on helping community colleges improve their completion rates because they are flexible, affordable, and accessible institutions that enroll the largest number of low-income students."[10]

Community College Growth Implied by Attainment Targets

Are the community college goals set by the foundations and the administration attainable? Despite the emphasis on community colleges, in most cases specific community college goals are not well defined. Moreover, there are important differences among the goals: some have a target date of 2020 and others, 2025; the Gates goals include only degrees with "genuine labor market value" for individuals up to 26 years old; the administration's goals refer to 25- to 34-year-olds, and Lumina's, to 25- to 64-year-olds. The Obama administration's goal of 5 million additional community college degrees is the best defined, although complications still arise concerning the definitions of "additional" and "degrees." Although I know of no formal statement, in practice, members of the administration have suggested that certificates of one year or more would count toward the 5 million. The emphasis on one-year-or-more certificates is supported by data that suggest that many of these awards have a good labor market payoff, while there is little payoff to certificates that can be attained in less than one year.[11]

To give an illustration of the size of the increase in attainment implied by the goals, I will take the 5 million goal and include both associate's degrees and one-year-or-more certificates.[12] I will define "additional" as the number of completed degrees above the number implied by an extrapolation to 2020 of degree and certificate trends between 2000 and 2009.

Table 3.1 displays the number of bachelor's and associate's degrees and certificates conferred by Title IV–eligible institutions in two time periods. Between July 1, 2008, and June 30, 2009, public community col-

TABLE 3.1.   Bachelor's and associate's degrees and certificates conferred by Title IV–eligible institutions in two time periods: July 1, 1999, to June 30, 2000, and July 1, 2008, to June 30, 2009

Educational institution	Bachelor's degrees	Associate's degrees	Certificates		
			1 year or more	Less than 1 year	All certificates
			2000 Completions		
4-year and above college					
Public	810,855	36,813	4,915	5,169	10,084
Private not-for-profit	406,968	30,764	6,562	1,794	8,356
Private for-profit	20,062	22,102	3,184	1,784	4,968
2-year school					
Public		411,633	116,962	101,763	218,725
Private not-for-profit		15,580	6,714	7,399	14,113
Private for-profit		48,111	45,316	25,936	71,252
Less-than-2-year school					
Public			29,193	37,046	66,239
Private not-for-profit		9	3,408	2,703	6,111
Private for-profit		45	66,856	91,561	158,417
2000 total	1,237,885	565,057	283,110	275,155	558,265
			2009 Completions		
4-year and above college					
Public	1,060,898	87,485	10,303	17,185	27,488
Private not-for-profit	537,700	40,632	6,189	3,802	9,991
Private for-profit	84,830	86,119	13,552	7,341	20,893
2-year school					
Public		509,615	147,161	218,476	365,637
Private not-for-profit	0	6,383	6,578	2,392	8,970
Private for-profit	1	58,453	86,367	57,712	144,079
Less-than-2-year school					
Public			18,277	17,325	35,602
Private not-for-profit			4,268	8,796	13,064
Private for-profit		22	83,420	96,611	180,031
2009 total	1,683,429	788,709	376,115	429,640	805,755

SOURCE: Calculated using data from Integrated Postsecondary Education Data System (IPEDS).

leges granted about 510,000 associate's degrees and 147,000 one-year-or-more certificates, for a total of 657,000 awards. Data from nine years earlier—June 30, 1999, through July 1, 2000—show a total of 529,000 awards (412,000 associate's degrees and 117,000 certificates of one year or more). Thus, over those nine years, the number of awards grew by about 24 percent, or at an annual rate of about 2.5 percent.[13]

How much growth would be necessary to generate 5 million additional community college degree holders by 2020? Assuming that "normal" growth continues at an annual rate of 2.5 percent, then that growth would generate 1.6 million new graduates between 2010 and 2020. Therefore, to generate 5 million new graduates, community colleges would need to increase the total number of graduates by 6.6 million over the decade, requiring an annual growth rate of 8.5 percent, or an incremental growth rate of 6 percent (8.5%–2.5%).

The estimates presented above assume that the completion goals refer specifically to community college associate's degrees and certificates. But in 2009, community colleges conferred only about 65 percent of the associate's degrees and 39 percent of the certificates of at least one year (table 3.1). Moreover, while the community colleges maintained their share of certificates during the first decade of the century, other sectors were growing faster in the production of associate's degrees. Growth was particularly rapid for the for-profit institutions, although they started from a low base. Including all institutions allows the attainment of the target with a slightly lower incremental growth rate of 5.5 percent, instead of 6 percent.[14]

Calculating the required increases in community college awards for the other goals that do not differentiate between associate's and bachelor's degrees is more difficult. Assuming a somewhat disproportionate role for community college degrees and making reasonable assumptions about the definition of "additional" degrees still yields required incremental growth rates of 5 to 7 percent.[15]

Achieving Ambitious Goals

In the following sections I consider three strategies to increase the total number of graduates: increase overall enrollment, shift enrollment to sectors or degree programs with higher graduation rates, or increase graduation rates (including reducing time to degree).

Increasing Enrollment

Though the discussion about college has shifted from access to success, many students still do not enroll in college. Moreover, low socioeconomic status (SES) remains a major determinant of college enrollment. Data from NELS suggest that about one-half of the students who had not enrolled in any college eight years after their scheduled high school graduation come from the lowest SES quartile.[16] Therefore, from the point of view of equity, increased enrollment for lower-income students remains an important goal. Nevertheless, increasing enrollment as a strategy to increase attainment has serious limitations, especially for community colleges.

First, as it is, the types of students who have not been enrolled in the past face significant barriers and have the least financial and social capital, meaning that they would likely require the most help and resources to graduate. Although I have not focused on cost here, it is reasonable to conclude that directing resources toward these types of students would be would be a very costly approach to increasing completions.

Second, given low completion rates (discussed in more detail below), increasing completions by boosting enrollment would require huge increases in enrollment. Roughly speaking, an additional 500,000 graduates from an entering cohort would require an increase in that cohort of 1.5 million community college students—and all of the entering cohorts would have to be increased. Put another way, in 2009, over 10 million students enrolled in public community colleges at some point during the year. During that year, the colleges awarded 510,000 associate's degrees and 147,000 one-year-or-greater certificates. These data suggest that currently, graduation totals sit atop a pyramid with an immense base of enrollments. Moreover, in 2011, community colleges in many states already had no room for additional students, so a significant increase in graduation primarily through expanding enrollment would require inconceivable increases in capacity.

Online education has the potential to expand enrollments, and therefore completions, without large increases in physical capacity. Online education is already growing rapidly and will be an important component of any strategy to achieve dramatic increases in the number of graduates. But much of the growth in online instruction involves hybrid courses that combine distance and face-to-face instruction. The capacity savings for hybrid instruction are more doubtful. Moreover, research suggests that fully online instruction has lower course completion rates than face-to-face instruction, especially for the low-income students and students with weak academic skills who would have to be enrolled in much greater numbers to meet the various goals.[17]

To be sure, increasing access to college remains an important policy goal. Working to reduce the continued inequality in access by race and SES is by itself an adequate motivation for continuing to work on the access agenda. But given the large numbers of students already in college who do not finish a degree, increasing completion rates for those students is a more logical first step. This would require a smaller increase in capacity and a lower increase in total credits conferred because students in this group have already earned credits.

Shifting Enrollments to Sectors with Higher Completion Rates

Some colleges have much higher completion rates than others. In the 2008–9 academic year, the Tennessee Technology Center at McKenzie had a 99.1 percent graduation rate (this is a graduation rate for the cohort of full-time students entering college in 2005 after they have been tracked 150 percent of the time it would take a full-time student to complete), but 135 public two-year institutions reported graduation rates of less than 10 percent. If all colleges could perform like the Tech Center at McKenzie, then all of the ambitious goals would be more than surpassed.[18] The most striking feature of McKenzie is that it does not grant associate's degrees. Indeed, of the 50 two-year institutions with the highest graduation rates as reported by the Integrated Postsecondary Education Data System (IPEDS), only 13 granted any associate's degrees. Similarly, public institutions classified as "less-than-two-year institutions" (the highest degrees conferred by these institutions are certificates taking less than two years) had an average graduation rate of 71.2 percent for 150 percent of normal program completion time. Shifting enrollments to certificate programs (if that can be done) would increase completions.

Are certificates the answer to the completion problem? Recent studies on certificates, or shorter-term credentials awarded by community colleges that are usually more specific to certain careers and technical skills, have shown that they increase earnings relative to the economic benefit of a high school degree and can offer students a relatively quick path to employment. Using longitudinal data from Florida, Louis Jacobson and Christine Mokher show that students with certificates in health care earn significantly more than students in academic concentrations. Brian Bosworth reviewed the empirical literature on the value of certificates and concluded from studies using both national data and state administrative data that certificates in some fields—primarily health care (but also in some vocational fields) and primarily for men—have good economic returns, in some cases rivaling returns for associate's degrees.[19]

Thus, if certificates in some fields represent solid economic opportunities for some students, they may be underutilized and, given the high completion rates for students in certificate programs, probably do represent an opportunity to increase overall completion of postsecondary degrees with reasonable labor market payoffs. Moreover, earning a certificate has higher returns than accumulating an equivalent number of credits.[20] At the very least, students should be informed about these programs (for-profit institutions have certainly been successful in convincing many students that certificates make sense for them); and educators, policymakers, and researchers should pay more attention to them. Recent reports and activities by major foundations indicate that this is already happening.[21]

On the other hand, there are disadvantages to relying too heavily on certificates to meet the current ambitious goals. Even if certificate programs have higher completion rates, those rates may reflect the nature of the students now attracted to certificates rather than the characteristics of the programs themselves.[22] Many students wish to maintain the possibility of continuing their education, and students who earn certificates rarely continue on to complete additional degrees. In many cases, other institutions do not recognize credits earned in certificate programs as counting toward other types of awards, although this is something that might be corrected if certificates are elevated as increasingly important elements of educational attainment. One-year certificates, which even the certificate advocates acknowledge have uncertain economic payoffs, are growing faster than the more-than-one-year certificates. Moreover, it is only in some fields that even the longer-term certificates have good returns. Occupational forecasts have not isolated the potential demand for certificates, so while wage data suggest that the labor market could absorb some additional certificates (assuming that the recession ends), an increase by one million in high-return fields seems optimistic.

Finally, while there may be many reasons to promote an increase in certificate attainment, regaining the lead in the OECD statistics is not one of them. The OECD data that have catalyzed much of the drive to increase completion do not recognize certificates of less than two years. Thus, while certificates will count toward the Obama administration's goal of 5 million additional community college graduates, they will not count toward the overall goal of 8.2 million associate's and bachelor's degrees.

Some analysts have argued that the for-profit colleges are more successful at getting students through to completion than the public community colleges.[23] If this is true, then a shift of enrollments from community colleges towards for-profits would increase graduation rates without necessarily increasing initial enrollments. Published graduation rates seem to bear this out. In 2008–9 the two-year for-profits had a 61.2 percent graduation rate, and the public community colleges had an average rate of 22 percent. But this comparison is also distorted by the differences in the share of certificates within overall awards. Fifty-seven percent of the for-profit institutions listed in IPEDS in the two-year sector awarded no associate's degrees, compared with 12 percent for public community colleges. Thus, the comparison between for-profits and community colleges suffers from the same distortion as the comparison between the Tennessee Technology Centers and the state's community colleges: certificate programs have much higher completion rates than associate degree programs, so an institution that emphasizes certificates may have a higher graduation rate than an associate's degree–heavy college, even though the programs at the two colleges are identical.

Given the varied mix of programs represented by the IPEDS graduation rates, comparison of these rates thus presents a misleading contrast between the two types of colleges. More sophisticated analyses could be carried out with longitudinal unit record data that track individual students. Although such data are now widely available for public community colleges through state data systems, for-profit institutions have not allowed research using their administrative data. As a result, despite the very active and controversial debate about the quality of the for-profits, there is almost no research using individual longitudinal data comparing student outcomes in the two types of institutions.

The one study that did use longitudinal data to control for confounding student characteristics or program enrollments used the National Education Longitudinal Study of students who were in eighth grade in 1988. These students were tracked until 2000. The study found a positive effect for private colleges compared with publics, but there were so few students in for-profits in the sample (only 70) that the authors had to combine those students with students in private not-for profit institutions in order to get a statistically significant result. Thus, as we shall see later, while there are some reasons to think that some of the processes and policies at for-profits lead to comparatively good completion rates, it is fair to say that the empirical evidence showing that conclusion is extremely weak. The data at this point do not suggest that a shift from enrollments in community colleges to enrollments in the same program areas and majors in for-profits would lead to significant increase in completions.

Increasing Graduation Rates

Any realistic strategy to increase significantly the number of community college graduates must involve increasing graduation rates. These rates at community colleges are frequently criticized for being too low. The Department of Education publishes graduation rates for community colleges based on tracking an entering cohort of first-time full-time students for three years (for an associate's degree), or 150 percent of the time that it would normally take a full-time student to complete the program in which they were enrolled. A crucial issue here, though, is that these rates only track students through the college in which they first enrolled, therefore counting students who did not complete an associate's degree but transferred to a four-year college (or even a two-year college) as noncompleters. The latest data show a 22 percent graduation rate when students are tracked for 150 percent of "normal" time. That rate goes up to 28.4 percent when they are tracked for 200 percent of normal time.[24] If students who graduate after transferring were included, then the graduation rate would be higher, although if part-time students (who account for a majority of community college students) were included, then the rate would be lower.

A recent release of the 2004/2009 Beginning Postsecondary Students Longitudinal Study (BPS), which tracked first-time college students beginning college in the 2003–4 academic year for six years through the 2009–10 academic year, shows six-year graduation rates incorporating completions for students who transferred (table 3.2). Among students who started in a two-year college, 34.5 percent completed some kind of degree or certificate within six years. At the end of the six-year period,

TABLE 3.2.   Outcomes for community college entrants: percentage of entering cohort that achieved certificates and degrees within time of study

| Study and dates[a] | Graduation time frame | Credential received | | | Total % completing a credential |
		Certificate	Associate's degree	Bachelor's degree	
BPS 2004/ 2010	6 years	8.5	14.4	11.6	34.5
BPS 1995/ 2001	6 years	9.7	15.7	10.3	38.5
NELS 1988/ 2000	8 years	6.5	15.4	17.5	39.4

SOURCES: BPS 2004/2010—Alexandria Walton Radford et al., *Persistence and Attainment of 2003-04 Beginning Postsecondary Students: After Six Years* (Washington, DC: National Center for Education Statistics, 2010), table 2; National Center for Education Statistics, *National Education Longitudinal Study: 1988-2000 Data Files and Electronic Codebook System, Base Year through Fourth Follow-up*, ECB/CD-ROM 2003-348 (Washington, DC: Institute of Education Sciences, U.S. Department of Education, 2003), NELS 1988/2000—National Center for Education Statistics, *National Education Longitudinal Study: 1988-2000 Data Files and Electronic Codebook System, Base Year through Fourth Follow-up* (Washington, DC: U.S. Department of Education, 2003). Calculation by the author.

NOTE: Percentages refer to all students who started their college education in a community college.

[a]Beginning Postsecondary Students (BPS) longitudinal studies tracked first-time college students entering a community college in the specified year up through the ending year specified. The National Education Longitudinal Study (NELS) followed eighth graders in 1988 until 2000.

almost 20 percent were still enrolled, and 46 percent were no longer enrolled, never having earned a degree or certificate. These completion rates have been quite stable over the last decade. These graduation rates are higher than the IPEDS 150 percent rates but nevertheless show that after at least six years, more than 60 percent of community college entrants have not completed any award.

An additional problem with graduation rates is that they are closely related to race and SES. Black, Hispanic, and low-income students complete at much lower rates than white middle-class students. For example, while 29.5 percent of white community college entrants complete a bachelor's or associate's degree, only 16.5 percent of black entrants do. The disparity is only slightly less for Hispanic students.[25]

These completion rates define the challenge facing reformers seeking to substantially increase community college graduation rates in order to meet the completion goals. How can these rates be increased?

Research on What Works to Raise
Persistence and Completion

While there has been a large quantity of research on persistence and retention in college, only a small share is focused on community colleges.[26]
One reason for optimism is that this general neglect has changed, and
there is a growing body of experimental and quasi-experimental research on community college practices and innovations. Some of these
studies do indicate that new policies and practices can improve student
outcomes. We will review some of these studies and draw some general
conclusions about the potential of these reforms.

Too many students arrive at community colleges academically unprepared for college-level work. Nearly 60 percent of recent high school
graduates who enter higher education through community colleges are
referred to at least one remedial course, and fewer than half of these students actually finish the remedial sequence to which they are referred.[27]
Many reforms are designed to address this problem. Programs in California and Texas that administer high school assessments to determine
the potential need for remediation and then provide academic services
when needed have been shown to reduce remedial enrollments in college by about 10 percent.[28]

Learning communities are a popular strategy to improve outcomes
for students needing remediation, but random assignment studies have
found that one-semester-long learning communities have no influence
on longer-term persistence.[29] In the Accelerated Learning Program
(ALP) at the Community College of Baltimore County, developmental
students are integrated into college-level courses and are also enrolled
in a supplemental course to provide extra support. A quasi-experimental
analysis found that among ALP students who place into the highest level
of developmental writing, participating in the program is associated
with a 13 percentage point difference in English completion.[30] Washington State's Integrated Basic Education and Skills Training Program
(I-BEST) provided remedial instruction linked to occupational areas and
increased the likelihood of certificate attainment by over 7 percentage
points and college credit attainment by almost 10 percentage points.[31]

Counseling, advising, and other types of student support services
are also considered important determinants of student outcomes. Most
community colleges have very high student-to-counselor ratios—often as
high as 1,000 to 1.[32] A random assignment study of an enhanced student

services program that significantly reduced the student-to-counselor ratio and provided a modest stipend had no effect on persistence one semester after the program ended.[33]

Student success courses are in effect strategies for providing group counseling. These courses vary widely, but they are all designed to help students learn how to be successful in college and to provide information and support. Students in Florida community colleges who enrolled in a student success course were 10 percent more likely than other students to earn a degree or transfer to a public university within six years.[34] A random assignment study of a program that included a mandatory college success course in California for students on probation found that participation in the success course almost doubled the percentage of program students who achieved good academic standing during the two semesters of the program.[35]

Performance-based financial aid programs have been found to increase persistence and graduation. A program for low-income students in New Orleans increased the number of students who registered for a class by 8 percent, and students in the program earned an average of 12.6 credits, compared with 9.2 credits for the control group.[36] Another program in Ohio increased the number of credits earned by 14 percent but did not influence persistence.[37] A state-wide merit aid program in West Virginia increased the overall number of graduates by about 10 percent, and merit aid programs in Georgia and Arkansas also raised the overall college attainment rate by about the same amount.[38]

What do these results tell us about the potential to increase significantly the number of community college graduates? Although weak outcomes for popular reforms such as learning communities and enhanced student services are disappointing, this research does suggest that strengthened practice and incentives can be used to increase some student outcomes. Innovations in developmental education and student services can increase success in college-level courses, persistence, and even completion. To what extent do positive impacts on intermediate outcomes translate into increased rates of graduation? The most positive of these outcomes suggest a 5–10 percent improvement over "business as usual." If these interventions could be extended to all students and maintained through to graduation, then even some of the ambitious completion targets might be attainable. But most of these outcomes are a long way from increasing institutional graduation rates. Many of the most reliable studies are targeted to particular groups—for example, students on probation or low-income parents who are facing multiple barriers—or are conducted on small samples of students. An increase in the number of credits earned in one or two semesters by a relatively small group of students will not influence completion rates unless the programs can be sustained and expanded to a much larger share of a college's students.

The potential for reforms of this type to lead to very large increases in the numbers of graduates depends on two factors. First, can the programs be scaled to a large enough group of students to influence overall graduation rates? And second, will intermediate outcomes, such as completing a developmental or first-level college course or one-semester retention, translate into completions?

The evidence on scaling up is discouraging. There are few examples of pilot programs that were institutionalized and "brought to scale." For example, in the Achieving the Dream Initiative, a program explicitly designed to bring about institution-wide change, relatively simple, low-intensity programs enroll 25 percent or fewer of students eligible for the service. More intensive programs generally enrolled fewer than 10 percent of the eligible students.[39]

How effectively are intermediate outcomes translated into completions? We do know that attainment of intermediate outcomes is associated with a greater probability of graduation.[40] But that does not necessarily mean that a program that induces completion of a given number of credits will also increase completion. Indeed, in some of the rigorous evaluations we have reviewed, such as the studies of learning communities and enhanced counseling, initial achievement during the program semester faded in the long run. This at least suggests that programs must be sustained. One-semester programs often show effects during that semester, but nonparticipants tend to catch up after the program ends. Of the reforms reviewed above, the merit aid programs in West Virginia, Georgia, and Arkansas did apply to all students in the state and were continued throughout the student's college career; these programs did increase the number of graduates by 10 percent.

Scaling and keeping programs going involves increased costs, costs that cannot be sustained by funding from special programs or by foundation support. So far I have focused on the effect of reforms on outcomes without considering cost, and indeed, most evaluations do not analyze costs. Results presented earlier suggest that even without considering the cost, the programmatic reforms typically introduced at community colleges do not have large enough effects to achieve the very ambitious goals currently being discussed. Introducing a consideration of costs, when data are available, reinforces that conclusion. For example, one of the most positive results came from the study of I-BEST in Washington State, but I-BEST students are funded at 1.75 times that for a regular full-time equivalent student.[41] The Accelerated Learning Program at the Community College of Baltimore County was also more costly, but the additional cost was offset by the increased course completion rates—so the cost per course completion was equivalent.[42]

Douglas Harris and Sara Goldrick-Rab have conducted a cost-effectiveness analysis of a wide range of reforms, many of which are being implemented in community colleges, including college access programs, financial aid initiatives, instructional reforms such as increased faculty-student ratios and increased reliance on full-time faculty (rather than adjuncts), and programs to enhance student services.[43] In essence, they compared the typical cost-per-degree at two- and four-year institutions with the cost incurred by the relevant reforms of yielding an additional degree. Using this methodology, they found that three practices were more cost-effective than the normal practices at community colleges: developmental education, a call center that contacted students who registered but failed to show up for classes, and a shift from part-time to full-time professors. Other programs that they studied were no more cost-effective than the regular operational practices of the colleges. The call centers had very small effects and were for a narrowly defined group but were cost-effective because they were cheap. The conclusions about the other two practices were only suggestive because of methodological issues with the underlying research.[44] With the possible exception of an increased use in full-time faculty, these results do not suggest that any of the current practices that Harris and Goldrick-Rab studied would be cost-effective approaches to significant, broad-based increases in graduation rates.[45]

Lessons from More Successful Institutions

Earlier I discussed the range of graduation rates, and it seems reasonable to ask whether we can learn anything from that variation. A significant increase in total completions would occur if colleges with single-digit graduation rates could increase their rates to the average (in the 20s). Other than an emphasis on certificates, which was discussed earlier, what differentiates the low-graduation-rate colleges from the apparently more successful institutions?

Analysis of the correlates of variation in community college graduation rates suggests that the following variables are associated with higher graduation rates: smaller size, a low share of minority students, a lower percentage of part-time students (note that the graduation rate was only for students who started as full-time students), and higher instructional expenditure for full-time-equivalent students.[46] These results may provide some guidance for colleges. Perhaps colleges should avoid getting too large (although the analysis did not take account of the cost side) or encourage their students to attend full time. Increasing instructional expenditures is not very useful in practice, since we are looking for ways to improve outcomes at equal or lower costs. Unfortunately, most of these characteristics are not useable policy or program practices. IPEDS, the source of the data used in the analysis, does not include information on institutional practices that colleges or policy makers might use to increase graduation.

Several studies have used qualitative analysis to identify the characteristics of colleges that have high completion rates (or other measures of student outcomes), although only one studied community colleges. In a comprehensive review of these studies, Davis Jenkins cites the following characteristics identified by at least one study as possible factors: leadership with a strong focus on student success; well-coordinated, proactive student support services; innovation in teaching and methods for improving student success; use of data analysis to monitor student progress and guide program improvements; targeted programs that provide advising and academic support specially designed for at-risk students; emphasis on engaging students, particularly in the first year; committees or work groups that monitor and promote student success efforts; collaboration across departments, with broadly shared responsibility for ensuring student success; small class sizes, even in freshman introductory courses; and a strong institutional culture, particularly a willingness to see changes through, even if results take time to become evident.[47]

The structure, organization, and processes of many for-profit institutions contrast to typical characteristics of public community colleges. Perhaps there are lessons for community colleges in the experience of the for-profits.[48] The fundamental argument is that for profits use more structured and simplified programs and guidance systems. Rather than offering students many choices and electives, the for-profit institutions more often provide highly structured programs with few choices. They also emphasize getting students through their programs quickly, encouraging students to attend full time and offering compressed schedules and many start dates. The for-profits also put relatively less emphasis on liberal arts programs and general education, instead focusing on specified occupational preparation. Many for-profits also have very strong ties to local employers.

Of course, many community colleges have programs with these characteristics, and indeed, these characteristics of the for-profits are similar to those of certificate programs in public institutions. Brian Bosworth, who has written another chapter in this book, argues that higher completion rates for certificate programs can also be explained by their more structured and simplified organization.[49]

As I argued earlier, so far there is little empirical evidence of the superior performance of the for-profits for similar students in similar programs. Nor have the benefits to community college students of more structured and simplified organization been definitively measured. On the other hand, there is growing support in general for the proposition that people faced with complex and multidimensional decisions make poor choices.[50] And, we do know that community college students are confronted by a complex and confusing set of processes and choices. Recent evidence also suggests that many students in community colleges never enter a coherent program of study, a requirement for completion of any degree or certificate. Students who do not get established in a program during their first year rarely catch up.[51] One-on-one counseling does not seem to be effective in helping students to navigate these complications and get well established. Some form of simplification or a better structuring of student pathways and choices seems like a logical response, in addition to a more explicit focus on helping students choose and enter coherent programs.[52]

This list of characteristics that emerges from an emphasis on organizational change contrasts with the more specific programmatic focus of much of the evaluation research. The organizational change perspective is based on the notion that changing overall performance of an institution requires a broader, comprehensive set of reforms, an argument that is consistent with the empirical results that conclude that the effects of individual reforms fade after students return to business as usual. This perspective may help explain the often-discouraging results of evaluations of individual programs. Anthony Bryk and his colleagues also find that institutional reforms in elementary and secondary schools that have little effect when implemented alone are effective only when combined with other measures.[53]

The Achieving the Dream community colleges count initiative was expressly designed to bring about broader organizational change, to move beyond specific individual programmatic innovations. The Achieving the Dream model called for colleges to strengthen their practices in five broad areas: leadership commitment; use of data to prioritize actions; stakeholder engagement; implementation, evaluation, and improvement of strategies; and establishment of a culture of continuous improvement. An evaluation of progress in the 26 colleges that joined the initiative in 2004 found that most colleges had made progress in these areas, but there were no statistically significant change in persistence or two-year completion rates, although the direction of the changes was positive.[54]

The outcome data from Achieving the Dream, therefore, do not, at least so far, provide strong evidence that the initiative has led to the types of improvements that would be necessary to realize the ambitious degree goals. The authors of the evaluation report suggest several reasons for the weak results. First, three years may not be enough time for ambitious organizational changes to be reflected in outcomes data, especially graduation rates. Second, despite widespread discussion of the need for broad organizational change, a majority of the colleges devoted most energy to more focused interventions that touched only small numbers of students. Third, most colleges did not emphasize instruction or faculty development and involvement with the initiative, especially for part-time faculty.

A recent report by McKinsey and Company assesses the cost and feasibility of a significant increase in the number of graduates per year based on broad organizational reform.[55] The authors conclude that by emulating some of the practices of what they refer to as "highly productive institutions," the U.S. higher education system could increase efficiency by 23 percent and therefore produce an additional one million graduates a year by 2020 without additional costs per full-time-equivalent student. They do not provide separate estimates for community and four-year colleges. The report concludes that practices that would be particularly effective for community colleges include "systematically enabling students to reach graduation" and "reducing unproductive credits." While the conclusions are encouraging and these are reasonable suggestions, the report does not provide much detail about the policies and practices, nor does it describe its methodology in enough detail to evaluate the validity of the conclusions.

In early 2011, the Community College Research Center completed a set of analyses of research on a variety of community college reforms. The series included reports on developmental education assessment and placement, the acceleration of remediation, pedagogy for math developmental education, contextualization of basic skills instruction, online learning, student support services, institutional and program structure, and organizational improvement.[56] While these reports came to conclusions about the specific topics, they all examined the broader organizational restructuring that would be needed to improve the chances that individual reforms would be effective. Broadly, the series concluded that colleges needed to simplify the structures and bureaucracies that students must navigate; that they should engage faculty much more intensively in the mission to support student success, including involving faculty actively in student support activities; and that they should be encouraged to align course curricula, define common learning outcomes and assessments, and set high standards for those outcomes.

Research on broad organizational change in community colleges is at a very early stage. Frustration with programmatic initiatives has led to efforts to bring about more ambitious reforms, but these organizational features are hard to measure. Cost-effectiveness analysis of broad institutional change in education is notoriously difficult.[57] These types of reforms have been shown to be effective in other sectors, but research is just beginning to test them in community colleges.

Conclusion and Discussion

This analysis has suggested that the goals set by the administration and by the Gates and Lumina Foundations are very ambitious. In the end, the goals represent a conviction that the country needs more college graduates. What would colleges have to do to reach those goals?

In the midst of the discussions about international competitiveness and the needs of the economy, it is easy to forget the continuing gaps between student achievement and student aspirations and between postsecondary achievement of lower- and higher-income students and among students of different racial and ethnic groups. Low-income students enter college at lower rates, are more likely to attend less selective colleges (controlling for relevant academic characteristics), and have less success when they do enroll in college. And the gap between their stated aspirations and their achievement is larger than it is for higher-income students. These gaps may be among the strongest reasons to set ambitious goals for college completion. Indeed, in their influential book, *The Race between Education and Technology*, Claudia Goldin and Lawrence Katz argue that technological development is outpacing educational achievement in the United States, and that one of the most important problems, if not the most important problem, with these trends is that they exacerbate inequality.[58]

The key question is, can community colleges increase degree production well beyond historical attainment rates? In general, the goals suggest that this increase above recent trends would have to be between 5 and 10 percent a year. Enrollment increases, while important, would require immense increases in capacity, without increases in graduation rates. Recently, educators have become enthusiastic about the potentially positive role that certificates can play in efforts to increase the number of higher education awards.

Increased graduation rates must be a substantial part of any increase in community college degree production. Recent evaluations of specific programs designed to improve student outcomes are not particularly encouraging. Some popular strategies have not been shown to be successful. Other interventions have shown positive effects in the 5 to 10 percent range, but in most cases these are small programs that lead to intermediate outcomes, such as completion of a first-level college course or additional credit accumulation. Translating these into similar percentage improvements in degree production would require taking the programs to "scale," a notoriously difficult process, and sustaining the positive outcomes through the whole college career to graduation. Positive program benefits tend to fall off after the enhanced services end, suggesting at least that those enhanced services need to be sustained.

Innovative programs will clearly need to be part of any ambitious strategy, but they will need to be accompanied by broader and more comprehensive organizational changes. So far, reform initiatives in community colleges based on institutional design and change have not shown strong effects, but this is a new field; discrete program innovations have dominated the community college reform agenda until only the last decade. Furthermore, institutional and state-level data on student outcomes at the institutional level have increased significantly in the last decade. These data allow a more detailed analysis of student problems and a better understanding of institutional performance.

Empirical evidence from research on K–12 and from the private sector suggest that coordinated programs that combine components have stronger positive effects on student (and other) outcomes than the application of those same components in isolation. Insights from those sectors and growing experience in comprehensive reform in community colleges suggest that a successful strategy will probably require significant progress in several areas.[59]

College systems need to be simplified to reduce confusion among students and to alleviate the need for complex counseling. Administrators and faculty need to focus on designing coherent programs and working to get students into those programs as soon as possible. Technology must be intelligently exploited to provide information and to track student progress (and lack of progress) in real time. Reformers need to turn their attention, much more than in past initiatives, to pedagogy, instruction, and professional development. Finally, faculty (including part-time faculty) need to be more broadly engaged in reform efforts. Employee engagement has been the foundation of organizational reform in the private sector, but reform efforts in community colleges have tended to rely on a small number of faculty activists.

There is no question that this set of ambitious goals will be difficult to achieve. Anything that looks like business as usual will certainly not succeed. Evidence suggests that reforms have succeeded in improving student outcomes, but in order to significantly increase degree outcomes, these improvements will have to be sustained and expanded and incorporated into organizations that support students and faculty in comprehensive ways that go beyond the current experience of most colleges.

ACKNOWLEDGMENTS

I would like to thank Sung Woo Cho for help with background research. Madeleine Weiss did the IPEDS calculations. Betsy Yoon and Gladys Perez-Mojica edited the manuscript.

NOTES

1. At the White House Community College Summit held in October 2010, both President Obama and the summit chair, Jill Biden, referred to the OECD

data in their arguments for a concerted effort to strengthen community colleges. The president also cited them again in the 2011 State of the Union Address and further emphasized the need to strengthen community colleges.

2. OECD, *Education at a Glance: 2010* (Paris: OECD, 2010), table A1.3a.

3. International comparisons are notoriously difficult. The comparisons made by OECD have been criticized for being misleading and for exaggerating the comparative deficiencies of U.S. degree production. See Arthur Hauptman's discussion in chapter 1, above, and Clifford Adelman, *The Spaces between Numbers: Getting International Data on Higher Education Straight* (Washington, DC: Institute for Higher Education Policy, 2009).

4. Patrick J. Kelly, *Closing the College Attainment Gap between the U.S. and Most Educated Countries, and the Contributions to Be Made by the States* (Boulder, CO: National Center for Higher Education Management Systems, 2010).

5. Lumina Foundation for Education, "The Big Goal," accessed Dec. 30, 2011, www.luminafoundation.org/goal_2025.html.

6. Bill and Melinda Gates Foundation, "Postsecondary Education," accessed Dec. 30, 2011, www.gatesfoundation.org/postsecondaryeducation/Pages/default .aspx.

7. Anthony Carnevale, Nicole Smith, and Jeff Strohl, *Help Wanted: Projections of Jobs and Education Requirements through 2018* (Washington, DC: Georgetown University, Center on Education and the Workforce, 2010), available at www9.georgetown.edu/grad/gppi/hpi/cew/pdfs/FullReport.pdf; Kelly, *Closing the College Attainment Gap*.

8. Comparing the community college and overall goals is further complicated by the inclusion in the 5 million goal of certificates of at least one year; these would not be included in the overall goal of 8 million, since the certificates are not counted in the OECD calculations.

9. See chap. 1, above.

10. Gates Foundation, "Postsecondary Education."

11. Brian Bosworth, *Certificates Count: An Analysis of Sub-Baccalaureate Certificates* (Washington, DC: Complete College America and Future Works, 2010).

12. Recent analyses of certificates have suggested that while certificates of one year or more in some fields have good labor market payoffs, less than one-year certificates have uncertain value. Ibid.

13. The projections generally imply compounded growth rates. This is reasonable if the increase in degrees is driven primarily by enrollment increases. However, if attaining completion targets depends significantly on increasing completion rates, then the compounding assumption is more difficult to defend.

14. Including all institutions would make attaining the 5 million degrees easier, since the baseline number of degrees (in 2009) is higher and therefore requires a lower percentage growth to achieve a fixed number (5 million). The complication, though, is that total associate's degrees and certificates have grown faster (3.5% per year) than those awards conferred by community colleges (2.5% per year); therefore, if one projects the 3.5% growth rate forward, there would

have to be additional total graduates to meet the goal of 5 million *additional* awards, since the projected number of graduates would be higher if we include all institutions rather than only community colleges.

15. These calculations are available from the author.

16. Calculations by the author from restricted public use data from the National Center for Education Statistics, *National Education Longitudinal Study: 1988–2000 Data Files and Electronic Codebook System, Base Year through Fourth Follow-up*, ECB/CD-ROM 2003-348 (Washington, DC: Institute of Education Sciences, U.S. Department of Education, 2003).

17. Shanna Smith Jaggars, *Online Learning: Does It Help Low-Income and Underprepared Students?* (CCRC Working Paper no. 24, Assessment of Evidence Series, Community College Research Center, Teachers College, Columbia University, New York, 2011). In addition to the use of online education, colleges could increase the efficiency of their capacity utilization by using buildings during weekends and at night, a step many colleges have already taken.

18. Indeed, Kelly and Schneider argue that overall completion rates could be increased by encouraging students to shift from colleges with low completion rates to those with higher rates. Andrew P. Kelly and Mark Schneider, *Filling in the Blanks: How Information Can Affect Choice in Higher Education* (Washington, DC: American Enterprise Institute for Public Policy Research, 2011).

19. Louis Jacobson and Christine Mokher, *The Effect of Career and Technical Education on Employment and Earnings: Evidence from Florida*, CNA Education working paper (Alexandria, VA: CNA Education, 2010); Bosworth, *Certificates Count*.

20. David Prince and Davis Jenkins, "Building Pathways to Success for Low-Skill Adult Students: Lessons for Community College Policy and Practice from a Statewide Longitudinal Tracking Study" (CCRC Brief no. 25, Community College Research Center, Teachers College, Columbia University, New York, 2005).

21. Bosworth, *Certificates Count*; Anthony Carnevale, "Valuing Certificates: Defining the Value of Certificates" (presentation, Georgetown University, Center on Education and the Workforce, Washington, DC, Mar. 20, 2009), www9 .georgetown.edu/grad/gppi/hpi/cew/pdfs/certificatesdone.pdf.

22. Certificate programs are much more specific than most associate's degree programs so may attract students with clearer goals than associate's programs. Shifting less-directed students to certificate programs may lower certificate program completion rates.

23. James Rosenbaum, Regina Deil-Amen, and Anne Person, *After Admission: From College Access to College Success* (New York: Russell Sage Foundation, 2006); Jennifer L. Stephan, James E. Rosenbaum, and Ann E. Person, "Stratification in College Entry and Completion," *Social Science Research* 38 (2009): 572–93; Guilbert C. Hentschke, "For-Profit Sector Innovations in Business Models and Organizational Cultures," in *Reinventing Higher Education: The Promise of Innovation*, ed. Ben Wildavsky, Andrew P. Kelly, and Kevin Carey (Cambridge: Harvard Education Press, 2011), 159–96; William G. Tierney and

Guilbert C. Hentschke, *New Players, Different Game: Understanding the Rise of For-Profit Colleges and Universities* (Baltimore: Johns Hopkins University Press, 2007).

24. Laura Horn, *Tracking Students to 200 Percent of Normal Time: Effect on Institutional Graduation Rates*, NCES 2011-221 (Washington, DC: National Center for Education Statistics, 2010).

25. Alexandria Walton Radford et al., *Persistence and Attainment of 2003–04 Beginning Postsecondary Students: After Six Years*, NCES 2011-151 (Washington, DC: National Center for Education Statistics, 2010).

26. For a review of research as of the middle of the decade 2000–2010, see Thomas Bailey and Mariana Alfonso, *Paths to Persistence: An Analysis of Research on Program Effectiveness at Community Colleges* (Indianapolis: Lumina Foundation for Education, 2005), available at www.luminafoundation.org/publica tions/PathstoPersistence.pdf.

27. Thomas Bailey, "Challenge and Opportunity: Rethinking the Role and Function of Developmental Education in Community College," *New Directions for Community Colleges* 145 (2009): 11–30; Thomas Bailey, Dong Wook Jeong, and Sung-Woo Cho, "Referral, Enrollment, and Completion in Developmental Education Sequences in Community Colleges," *Economics of Education Review* 29 (2010): 255–70.

28. Jessica Howell, Michal Kurlaender, and Eric Grodsky, "Postsecondary Preparation and Remediation: Examining the Effect of the Early Assessment Program at California State University," *Journal of Policy Analysis and Management* 29 (2010): 726–48; Thomas Bailey, Heather Wathington, and Thomas Brock, "Developmental Education: What Policies and Practices Work for Students?" (Presentation at National Center for Postsecondary Research Webinar, New York, Dec. 15, 2010), available at www.postsecondaryresearch.org/confer ence/pdf/webinar2010.pdf.

29. Susan Scrivener et al., *A Good Start: Two-Year Effects of a Freshmen Learning Community Program at Kingsborough Community College* (New York: MDRC, 2008), available at www.mdrc.org/publications/473/full.pdf; Mary Visher et al., "The Learning Communities Demonstration: Rationale, Sites, and Research Design" (NCPR Working Paper, National Center for Postsecondary Research, New York, 2008); Mary Visher et al., "Scaling Up Learning Communities: The Experience of Six Community Colleges" (NCPR Working Paper, National Center for Postsecondary Research, New York, 2010).

30. Davis Jenkins et al., "A Model for Accelerating Academic Success of Community College Remedial English Students: Is the Accelerated Learning Program (ALP) Effective and Affordable?" (CCRC Working Paper no. 21, Community College Research Center, Teachers College, Columbia University, New York, 2010).

31. Matthew Zeidenberg, Sung-Woo Cho, and Davis Jenkins, "Washington State's Integrated Basic Education and Skills Training Program (I-BEST): New

Evidence of Effectiveness" (CCRC Working Paper no. 20, Community College Research Center, Teachers College, Columbia University, New York, 2010).

32. W. Norton Grubb, "Like, What Do I Do Now? The Dilemmas of Guidance Counseling," in *Defending the Community College Equity Agenda*, ed. Thomas Bailey and Vanessa Smith Morest (Baltimore: Johns Hopkins University Press, 2006), 195–222.

33. Susan Scrivener and Michael J. Weiss, *More Guidance, Better Results? Three-Year Effects of an Enhanced Student Services Program at Two Community Colleges* (New York: MDRC, 2009), available at www.mdrc.org/publications/524/full.pdf.

34. Matthew Zeidenberg, Davis Jenkins, and Juan Carlos Calcagno, "Do Student Success Courses Actually Help Community College Students Succeed?" (CCRC Brief no. 36, Community College Research Center, Teachers College, Columbia University, New York, June 2007).

35. Susan Scrivener, Colleen Sommo, and Herbert Collado, *Getting Back on Track: Effects of a Community College Program for Probationary Students* (New York: MDRC, 2009), available at www.mdrc.org/publications/514/full.pdf.

36. Lashawn Richburg-Hayes et al., *Rewarding Persistence: Effects of a Performance-Based Scholarship Program for Low-Income Parents* (New York: MDRC, 2009).

37. Paulette Cha and Reshma Patel, *Rewarding Progress, Reducing Debt: Early Results from the Performance-Based Scholarship Demonstration in Ohio* (New York: MDRC, 2010).

38. Judith Scott-Clayton, "On Money and Motivation: A Quasi-Experimental Analysis of Financial Incentives for College Achievement," *Journal of Human Resources* 46, no. 3 (2011): 614–46; Susan Dynarski, "Building the Stock of College-Educated Labor," *Journal of Human Resources* 43, no. 3 (2008): 576–610.

39. Elizabeth Rutschow et al., *Turning the Tide: Five Years of Achieving the Dream in Community Colleges* (New York: MDRC, 2011).

40. Prince and Jenkins, "Building Pathways to Success for Low-Skill Adult Students."

41. Zeidenberg, Cho, and Jenkins, "Washington State's Integrated Basic Education and Skills Training Program (I-BEST)."

42. Jenkins et al., "A Model for Accelerating Academic Success of Community College Remedial English Students."

43. Douglas Harris and Sara Goldrick-Rab, *The (Un)productivity of American Higher Education: From "Cost Disease" to Cost-Effectiveness*, La Follette Working Paper no. 2010-023 (Madison: Robert M. La Follette School of Public Affairs, University of Wisconsin, 2010).

44. The analysis of remediation relied on one study with positive findings, but three other studies found no positive effects. The conclusion about the full-time faculty in community colleges was based on one study, and because of data limitations, there were alternative explanations for the results. The authors'

primary goal in writing the paper was to promote the use of cost-effectiveness analysis, and the difficulty they had in carrying out the analysis is itself an argument for paying more attention to these issues.

45. Research by Bettinger and Long found a mixed effect of the use of adjuncts. They found that adjunct-heavy schedules increased student dropout rates, but that the use of adjuncts had positive effects on student enrollment patterns in fields related to particular occupations. Eric P. Bettinger and Bridget Terry Long, "The Increasing Use of Adjunct Instructors at Public Institutions: Are We Hurting Students?" in *What's Happening to Public Higher Education?* ed. Ronald G. Ehrenberg (Baltimore: Johns Hopkins University Press, 2006), 51–69; Eric P. Bettinger and Bridget Terry Long, "Does Cheaper Mean Better? The Impact of Using Adjunct Instructors on Student Outcomes," *Review of Economics and Statistics* 92, no. 3 (2010): 598–613.

46. Thomas Bailey et al., "Is Student-Right-to-Know All You Should Know? An Analysis of Community College Gradution Rates," *Research in Higher Education* 47 (2006): 491–519.

47. Davis Jenkins, "Redesigning Community Colleges for Completion: Lessons from Research on High Performance Organizations"(CCRC Working Paper no. 24, Assessment of Evidence Series, Community College Research Center, Teachers College, Columbia University, New York, 2011).

48. Thomas Bailey, "Increasing Competition and Growth of the For-Profits," in *Defending the Community College Equity Agenda*, ed. Thomas Bailey and Vanessa Morest (Baltimore: Johns Hopkins University Press, 2006), 87–109; Rosenbaum, Deil-Amen, and Person, *After Admission*; Hentschke, "For-Profit Sector Innovations in Business Models and Organizational Cultures"; Tierney and Hentschke, *New Players, Different Game.*

49. Bosworth, *Certificates Count.*

50. Judith Scott-Clayton, "The Shapeless River" (CCRC Working Paper no. 25, Assessment of Evidence Series, Community College Research Center, Teachers College, Columbia University, New York, 2011).

51. Davis Jenkins, "Get with the Program: Accelerating Community College Students' Entry into and Completion of Programs of Study" (CCRC Working Paper no. 32, Community College Research Center, Teachers College, Columbia University, New York, 2011).

52. Scott-Clayton, "The Shapeless River."

53. Anthony S. Bryk et al., *Organizing Schools for Improvement: Lessons from Chicago* (Chicago: University of Chicago Press, 2010). These authors point out what they consider to be five essential supports for school improvement: school leadership, parent and community ties, professional capacity of the faculty and staff, a student-centered learning climate, and an instructional guidance system. Schools that combined all of these supports experienced significant improvements in student outcomes. Making significant improvements in one or two of these elements has very little effect.

54. Rutschow et al., *Turning the Tide.* The authors emphasized two impor-

tant factors. First, there is wide variation among outcomes for individual colleges, with some making large gains while others saw outcomes fall. Second, although these changes (or lack of changes) are suggestive, they cannot necessarily be attributed to the initiative because other important factors not accounted for in the analysis may also have driven the changes.

55. Byron G. Auguste et al., *Winning by Degrees: The Strategies of Highly Productive Higher-Education Institutions* (New York: McKinsey and Co., 2010).

56. For a summary of the series, see Thomas Bailey, Shanna Smith Jaggars, and Davis Jenkins, "Introduction to the CCRC Assessment of the Evidence Series" (Community College Research Center, Teachers College, Columbia University, New York, 2011).

57. Henry M. Levin, *The Cost Effectiveness of Whole School Reforms*, Urban Diversity Series no. 114 (New York: ERIC Clearinghouse on Urban Education, 2002).

58. Claudia Goldin and Lawrence Katz, *The Race between Education and Technology* (Cambridge: Harvard University Press, 2008).

59. Jenkins, "Redesigning Community Colleges for Completion"; Scott-Clayton, "The Shapeless River."

CHAPTER FOUR

Certificate Pathways to Postsecondary Success and Good Jobs

BRIAN BOSWORTH

In this chapter I argue that the United States faces a decline in the educational attainment of the labor force that will reduce economic growth and limit national prosperity. We will not be able to halt this decline or reach national postsecondary attainment goals established by the Obama administration unless significantly higher percentages of working adults and low-income and minority youth complete college credentials with labor market value. Further, and more to the central point here, these two groups are unlikely to reach ambitious attainment objectives without a rapid expansion of nondegree credentials—specifically, sub-baccalaureate certificates awarded for completion of carefully organized, occupationally focused programs of study of at least one academic year in duration.

This is a big challenge to postsecondary education, but there is good news here. First, careful review of labor market research indicates that most certificates of one year or more have significant value in the labor market. Second, it seems feasible to quickly ramp up certificate programs; some colleges in some states are showing the way, boosting enrollment in these programs and producing large numbers of quality certificates. Third, there is evidence that completion rates in some of the best, most rigorous certificate programs are significantly higher than in degree offerings. Fourth, there is evidence to suggest that certificate programming can be economically efficient both for students and for state and federal higher education investors. Finally, there are strong indications that low-income and minority youth and working adults can find in certificate programs the success that has been so elusive in degree programs.

I will consider the evidence and make recommendations about sub-baccalaureate certificates as a pathway to postsecondary attainment. The first section of the chapter examines the demographic factors that underlie the importance of boosting attainment of working adults and low-income and minority youth who are now without postsecondary credentials. In the second section I summarize the current status of and trends in certificate production, attainment, completion rates, and costs; and in the third section, I review findings from research about the labor market value of certificates. The fourth section considers the advantages of certificate programs in meeting the needs of working adults and low-income and minority youth. This section describes the certificate programs of the Tennessee Technology Centers as an example of how certificates can boost the attainment of populations not now served well by traditional degree offerings. The final section concludes with recommendations for action at the federal, state, and institutional level that could increase certificate awards.

This chapter is not an argument that low-income and minority youth and working adults should be "tracked" into certificate programs rather than into degree programs, where long-term economic and social returns may be greater (for the relatively few who manage to complete them). Good certificate programs are stepping-stones to further degreed education, not a dead-end alternative to it. However, they are also stepping-stones to good jobs.

In the contemporary economy, where some form of postsecondary credential is increasingly the ticket of entry to family-supporting jobs, America's inverted pyramid of sub-baccalaureate education, which produces half as many associate's degrees as bachelor's and half as many one-year-or-more certificates as associate's degrees, makes little sense. A national commitment to expand high-quality certificate programs of at least one year offers a strategy to reverse the probable decline in labor force educational attainment, meet postsecondary attainment objectives, serve hard-to-serve populations, and strengthen economic growth.

The Importance of Increased Education Attainment in the Labor Force

Over the past several decades, rising educational attainment in a rapidly growing labor force contributed very significantly to productivity, economic growth, and national competitiveness in an increasingly global economy. A Joint Economic Committee report in 2000 found several estimates of the effect of human capital gains on economic growth in the range of 15 to 25 percent.[1] That review and other studies also have underscored the indirect contribution of educational advances in fueling innovation and the adoption of new technology.[2]

From 1960 to 2000, the labor force more than doubled, from about 70 million to about 141 million workers. The number of workers in their prime productive years, ages 25 to 54, increased by over 130 percent in that 40-year period. This stunning growth in the labor force was accompanied by huge gains in educational attainment. In 1960, just 41 percent of the population over the age of 25 had completed high school, but by 2000, 80.4 percent had at least at high school diploma. College attainment of the labor force grew at an even faster pace. In 1960, only 7.7 percent of adults (ages 25 and older) had a bachelor's degree or higher, but by 2000 this had increased to 24.4 percent. Especially from 1970 to 2000, workers entering their prime working years of 25 to 54 had much higher levels of education than those aging out of the prime-age group and those leaving the workforce altogether.[3]

But these advantageous trends have fully played out. Over the years 2000–2040, the labor force will not grow at anywhere near the rate of growth of the years 1960–2000. The Bureau of Labor Statistics projects overall labor force growth of only 29 percent between 2000 and 2040 and growth of only 16 percent among prime-age workers.[4]

Slow labor force growth is only half the story. From 2000 to 2040, we can expect very little gain in the educational attainment of the work-force, at least as a consequence of young adults moving into and through the labor force. The older cohorts in the current labor force (from ages 35 to 54) are now as well educated as the younger cohorts (ages 25 to 34), especially in the percentage with at least a high school degree, but also in the percentage with some postsecondary attainment. That means over the next several decades, there will be no "automatic" attainment gain as current workers age and older workers leave the labor force. In fact, without some big changes in the pattern of attainment by age, race, and economic status, it is likely that the newer workers coming into the workforce will have lower levels of attainment than the older workers leaving. Workforce attainment levels will stagnate or decline, and future economic growth will slow as a consequence.

In the face of these trends, President Obama proposed to the February 2009 joint session of Congress that "by 2020, America will once again have the highest proportion of college graduates in the world." Efforts to clarify and quantify that goal, led by the National Center for Higher Education Management Systems (NCHEMS), have produced a general consensus that taking international leadership in postsecondary education would require U.S. college attainment rates to reach 60 percent in the cohort of young adults ages 25 to 40. In 2008, only 37.8 percent of this age group had degrees at the associate's level or higher; at present rates of growth, degree attainment would increase to only 41.9 percent by 2020. To close the gap, NCHEMS projects the need to increase degree production 4.2 percent every year between 2008 and 2020.[5]

The White House has added two complementary goals of increasing community college graduates to five million between now and 2020 and providing all Americans with a year of credentialed education or training beyond high school.

Meeting these goals will be a huge challenge. Even with the most optimistic assumptions about high school graduation, college continuation, and degree completion, there simply are not enough traditional students to meet ambitious goals within existing patterns of attainment. A realistic appraisal of demographic trends and historic attainment patterns can lead only to a conclusion that increasing workforce attainment—or even maintaining current levels of attainment—requires big changes in the postsecondary enrollment and completion of two groups in particular: minority youth and working adults.

Younger age cohorts are more racially and ethnically diverse than adults now in the labor force, with greater representation from groups that historically have not been well served in either K–12 or postsecondary education. By 2050, the proportion of the labor force made up by Hispanic and black Americans will grow rapidly, reaching 24 percent and 15 percent, respectively, while the share made up by whites will shrink to 53 percent.[6]

Unfortunately, blacks and Hispanics are far less likely than white students to complete high school, attend college, and complete a postsecondary credential. According to National Center for Education Statistics (NCES) data compiled by the College Board, enrollment rates for recent black high school graduates increased from just 40 percent in 1975 to 56 percent in 2008. The rates for Hispanics increased from 53 percent to 62 percent. But these gains failed to keep pace with gains for whites, whose direct-from-high-school enrollment rates increased from 49 percent to 70 percent over that same period.[7]

Beginning Postsecondary Students (BPS) data for 2004/2009 indicate that the college completion gap between whites and blacks and Hispanics is not getting any smaller. A study of students beginning their enrollment in 2004 found that 66.9 percent of white students had completed a credential or were still enrolled five years later, while for Hispanics this rate was 57.9 percent and for blacks it was 56.6 percent. The six-year bachelor's or associate's degree achievement rate for whites, Hispanics, and blacks was 46.6, 25.3, and 24.3 percent, respectively.

There are about 62 million adults (ages 25 and older) in the labor force who do not have postsecondary credentials of any kind. Many have been reading the signals of the labor market, and more and more of them have been enrolling in college. The percentage of credential-seeking undergraduates ages 24 and older in postsecondary institutions increased from only about 27 percent in 1970 to about 40 percent by 2000, even as overall undergraduate enrollment more than doubled over that same period.[8]

Unfortunately, working adult undergraduates have very high levels of attrition before college completion as compared with traditional students. An analysis of all students of all ages who began their postsecondary education in 2004 revealed that by 2009, 49.4 percent had completed a credential and an additional 15.0 percent were still working on one. The remaining 35.6 percent were no longer enrolled and had received no credential. However, of those who were between the ages of 24 and 29 when they enrolled, only 34.9 percent had completed any sort of credential, 14.2 percent were still working on one, and more than half had dropped out without receiving any credential. Students who were above the age of 30 when they enrolled had significantly lower rates of completion.[9]

Yet minority youth and working adults who have found limited success in traditional degree-focused educational pathways can find more success in high-quality certificate programs. The next two sections provide some basic information about certificates and their labor market value.

Sub-Baccalaureate Certificates

The Integrated Postsecondary Education Data System (IPEDS), a system of interrelated surveys gathering information annually from all postsecondary institutions that participate in federal student financial aid programs, asks institutions to report sub-baccalaureate certificates by field of study in one of three categories, as follows:

1. certificates acknowledging completion of an "organized program of study" at the postsecondary level of less than one academic

year—that is, programs that, with full-time enrollment, can be completed in less than one academic year, defined as 30 semester hours, 45 quarter hours, or 900 contact hours;

2. certificates for programs of at least one but less than two academic years, designed for completion in 30–60 semester credit hours, 45–90 quarter hours, or 900–1,800 contact hours; and

3. certificates for programs of two to four years, designed for completion in at least 60 but fewer than 120 credit hours, or in at least 1,800 but fewer than 3,600 contact hours.

Measuring Annual Certificate Production

There are some limitations with use of the IPEDS data for research into the production of certificate awards. First, there is no state or other secondary-level oversight of reporting, and institutions sometimes report incorrectly (e.g., reporting awards for noncredit programs when they are asked to report only awards for credit programs, or placing programs into the wrong reporting category). Anecdotally, there seem to be more reporting errors in IPEDS certificate data than in degree data.

Second, there is wide variation in the length of certificate programs within the IPEDS categories. Awards for very short programs of 3–6 semester hours and for longer programs of 25–29 semester hours are all reported as "less-than-one-year certificates." One- to two-year certificate awards can represent just 30 semester hours—or they can represent nearly twice as many credits, even within the same institution. This huge variation in the length of study is unique to certificate programs; credit hours required in degree programs rarely vary more than 5 to 10 percent from institution to institution, across all the states.

Third, many institutions acknowledge that there is much less oversight of certificate programs by state authorities and by regional accrediting bodies than of degree programs. As a result, programs of the same name that purport to be aimed at the same occupational entry can vary dramatically in length and content from one institution to another, even within the same state. This creates obvious difficulties in making comparisons among different programs and different institutions.[10]

As indicated in table 4.1, the number of certificates awarded in programs of all lengths reached just over 800,000 in 2009, nearly tripling over 15 years from almost 300,000 in 1994. While much of that increase came in awards for completion of short-term programs, awards for com-

TABLE 4.1.   Sub-baccalaureate certificate awards, all institutional sectors, in all states and District of Columbia, 1994–2009

	No. (%) of certificates awarded			
Program length	1994	1999	2004	2009
Less than 1 year	118,962	228,973	338,465	435,733
	(41.4)	(48.3)	(51.5)	(53.4)
More than 1 year	168,681	244,266	318,896	379,601
	(58.6)	(51.6)	(48.5)	(46.6)
Total	287,642	473,239	657,451	815,334
	(100.0)	(100.0)	(100.0)	(100.0)

SOURCE: Compiled by author from Integrated Postsecondary Education Data System (IPEDS).

pletion of programs of one year or more than doubled. (In this summary, certificates for one to two years of study and for two to four years of study are grouped as "more than one year" or as "long-term" certificates.) This is significantly faster than the pace in increase in postsecondary degree production. From 1994 to 2009, associate's degree awards from all post-secondary sectors grew 53.2 percent, while bachelor's degrees increased only 38.3 percent over those 15 years.

It appears that this 15-year pace of increase in certificate awards has slowed slightly over the past five or six years, especially in awards for programs of one year or more. The certificate production data shown in table 4.1 suggests this slowdown can be attributed in large part to relatively flat growth in production of long-term certificates among public two-year colleges.

From 1994 to 2009, public two-year colleges increased their production of certificate awards for long-term programs by just 33 percent while increasing their production of awards for short-term programs by 169 percent (table 4.2). In 1994, public two-year colleges produced 66.2 percent of all long-term certificates, but by 2009 their share had fallen to only 39.2 percent. Nationally, public two-year colleges have ceded almost all the growth in long-term certificates to for-profit institutions. Public two-years have increasingly concentrated their sub-associate awards in short-term programs.

In all institutional sectors, certificate awards are heavily skewed toward healthcare programs. In 2009, 44.1 percent of all certificates were awarded for completion of health care–related programs; 41.9 percent of

TABLE 4.2. Sub-baccalaureate certificate awards, public two-year colleges, in all states and District of Columbia, 1994–2009

Program length	No. (%) of certificates awarded				Increase over 15-year period
	1994	1999	2004	2009	
Less than 1 year	81,529 (42.2)	92,136 (45.2)	169,765 (56.3)	219,099 (59.5)	169%
More than 1 year	111,584 (57.8)	111,609 (54.8)	132,032 (43.7)	148,837 (40.4)	33%
Total	191,113 (100.0)	203,745 (100.0)	301,797 (100.0)	376,936 (100.0)	

SOURCE: Compiled by author from Integrated Postsecondary Education Data System (IPEDS).

the long-term awards were for health care. At the associate's and bachelor's degree level, only 11.9 percent of awards were related to health care occupations.

The number of certificate awards for programs of at least one year and the increase in such awards are very uneven among the states. On a per population basis, some states produce over twice the national average, while other states produce as little as one-third of the national average. Some of the states producing a lot of long-term certificates on a per population basis do not award significant numbers of associate's degrees. However, certificate production does not have to come at the expense of associate degree production. Arizona, Florida, Minnesota, Kansas, Iowa, and Wyoming are among the top per capita producers of both long-term certificates and associate's degrees. In fact, if every state produced as many long-term certificates per capita as does Arizona, the annual number of these long-term certificates would more than double, to almost 800,000.

Certificate Completion Rates

It is unfortunately not feasible to compare completion rates across certificate programs and degree programs within institutions. Colleges report their graduation rates to IPEDS by tracking a cohort of beginning students enrolling on a full-time basis without differentiating in that reporting whether the students are enrolled in a certificate program or a degree program. That information is often not available even in state student record systems, since many colleges do not maintain records separating the beginning cohort by credential objective.

However, several states have non-degree-granting, certificate-only institutions with one- and two-year programs, and it is feasible to compare their IPEDS-reported completion rates with those of institutions that both award certificates and grant degrees. According to IPEDS, in 2008 the combined graduation rate for 150 percent of normal completion time for all 1,010 public two-year degree-granting institutions in the 50 states was 20.4 percent. That rate is based on and includes the entire cohort of first-time, full-time students from 2005, as well as those in all certificate and degree programs. In 2008 these institutions produced 526,525 associate's degrees and 334,002 certificates; 38.6 percent of the certificates were for completion of long-term programs.

In 2008, the combined graduation rate for 150 percent of normal completion time for all 362 public one- and two-year non-degree-granting, certificate-only institutions in the 50 states was 60.6 percent. Of course, this includes students pursuing short-term certificates as well as long-term certificates (as it does in the degree-granting institutions). In that year, 54.6 percent of certificate awards from this sector were for completion of programs of at least one year. This indicates a much higher rate of program completion for programs in certificate-only institutions than in degree-granting institutions and suggests a higher rate of completion for certificates than for degrees.

The Cost of Certificate Programs

Again, the only way to compare certificate costs relative to degree costs at a national level is by examining the cost structure of public certificate-only institutions versus public degree-granting institutions. Use of this comparison must be attended by some careful caveats that acknowledge the big differences between these sectors in terms of mission, scale, and instructional content. Many certificate-only institutions have limited general education instruction, at least very little that is separate from the general education content embedded within the occupation and technical programs.

On a cost per FTE basis, public certificate-only institutions appear to be more costly than degree-granting institutions, according to analysis of data available through IPEDS. In 2007–8, the 362 public, non-degree-granting one- and two-year colleges and the 1,010 public degree-granting two-year institutions reported the following total core expenditures and total 12-month FTEs:

	Expenditures	No. of FTEs	Average cost/ FTE
Non-degree-granting	$ 1.64 billion	127,840	$12,800
Degree-granting	$41.35 billion	4,147,350	$ 9,970

In terms of "years of attainment" per FTE, however, there is a different story. By this measure, in 2007–8 the degree-granting institutions produced about 0.30 years of attainment per FTE, and the certificate-only institutions produced about 0.42 years of attainment per FTE.[11] That is a 40 percent difference. While this is an imperfect indicator of efficiency comparing institutions, not programs, it nonetheless offers hints that, even after accounting for the different program lengths, certificate-oriented programs are probably more economically efficient than associate's degree–oriented programs.

Estimating Current Certificate Attainment

Counting the annual production of certificates, even with the limitations of IPEDS, is less difficult than trying to estimate the stock of current certificate holders—the number of people in the population who actually have a certificate as their highest level of postsecondary credential. The American Community Survey (ACS) annually surveys a sample of the population to determine education attainment but does not ask if the respondent has attained a certificate. For someone with less than an associate's degree, any attainment beyond high school can be classified only as either "some college credit, but less than one year of college credit" or "one or more years of college credit, no degree."

Both of these categories include individuals who may have obtained a postsecondary credential below the degree level—including a certificate award for completion of a short-term program or an award for completion of a long-term program. Obviously, however, both categories also include many more individuals who may have enrolled in college with certificate or degree objectives but dropped out before obtaining any credential.

The Census Bureau calculates that in 2009 there were about 33.8 million individuals aged 25 and over with some college but no degree.[12] Taking into account enrollment, persistence, and attainment patterns revealed by NCES studies, as well as IPEDS-reported annual production data for the last 25 years, it seems likely that at least two-thirds of these 33.8 million have no postsecondary credential. It might be generously calculated that 8 to 10 million have a sub-baccalaureate certificate as their highest level of postsecondary attainment, and of those, it might be reasonably estimated that about 4 to 6 million have a certificate representing completion of an organized program of study of at least one year.

Labor Market Returns for Certificates

National level research on the labor market returns for certificates is quite limited. As noted above, decennial census and annual ACS data do not specifically identify certificate holders. Individuals who might have completed a discrete program of occupational preparation are indistinguishable from those who might have taken only a few scattered general education or technical courses. Although there are widely available estimates for median earnings by level of education that include the attainment category of "some college, no degree," these are of no help in estimating returns for certificates.

Without decennial census or ACS data to compare with wage data for certificate holders, most national-level research relies on longitudinal surveys of education and employment carried out by the U.S. Department of Education and supplemented by wage and occupational surveys of the Census Bureau and the Bureau of Labor Statistics. The National Education Longitudinal Study (NELS) program analyzes the educational, vocational, and personal development of a sample of individuals beginning with their elementary or high school years and following them over time as they move into the workforce. The NELS program now consists of five studies, three of which are useful for tracking labor market outcomes of postsecondary education: the National Longitudinal Study of the High School Class of 1972 (NLS-72), High School and Beyond (HS&B), and the National Education Longitudinal Study of 1988 (NELS:88).

The big limitation of these longitudinal surveys is that while they can track certificate awards and earnings for certificate holders relative to individuals with degrees or those with no awards, they do not differentiate among certificates based on the length of the program of study. Thus, certificate awards for programs of just a few credit hours cannot be distinguished from programs of one to two years or more.

On the other hand, research that draws on these surveys is generally consistent in reporting that one year of study after high school results in earnings significantly above of the level of those with no postsecondary participation. Estimates of the improvement in earnings from one year of study range from 5 to 10 percent and generally find that earnings and wages rise further with credits completed above one year. This research also indicates that postsecondary participation of less than one year seems to have very little earnings return. Further, research drawing on these national longitudinal surveys generally finds no evidence that certificate attainment, without regard to length of study, consistently results in higher earnings.

Taken together, these findings from national-level survey-based research suggest that certificates for short-term programs of less than one year do not demonstrate significant labor market returns. However, these same findings suggest that certificates for programs of study of a year or more have strong labor market returns. Some of the research specifically identifies an advantage to completing a long-term certificate versus merely accumulating postsecondary credit, but not all findings are conclusive in this regard.[13]

Research at the state level on returns for certificates is less ambiguous and more consistently finds significant earnings advantages to certificates for programs of one year and more. Most of this state-level research rests on matching student records against wage data available through the state-maintained unemployment insurance records. This approach has some advantages over NCES surveys. It is not self-reported data, as is the case with the national longitudinal surveys. It can examine the returns for education for individual students by comparing earnings before the start of the education program with earnings after completion of the program. It also permits comparisons of wage records between students who have completed programs of various lengths and wage records of students who started but did not complete these same programs.

It is unfortunate that all states do not routinely make these earnings comparisons or, if they do, choose not to make this information publicly accessible. However, enough do to conclude from the research that certificates for programs of at least one year almost always offer good labor market returns for recipients and that they provide a platform for career entry and advancement in occupations paying family-supporting wages. Taken as a whole, this state-level research suggests that individuals who complete long-term programs of study make significantly more money that those who enroll but do not finish. Individuals who complete short-term programs of study do not make significantly more money that those who enroll in these programs but do not complete them. That is generally true across all fields of study.

Field of study is an important predictor of earnings outcomes. In some fields, the average earnings of those who complete long-term certificates are comparable to the average earnings of those who complete associate's degree programs. That seems to be because certificate completers pursue and earn awards in fields with relatively high labor market returns and then take jobs where they can realize those returns. Many who gain associate's degrees do not go on to higher attainment, and a significant number of them hold majors in areas that offer limited labor market prospects for job seekers with less than bachelor's degree.[14]

There is significant and immediate labor demand for individuals who have completed long-term certificate programs. The Center on Education and the Workforce at Georgetown University forecasts that the U.S. economy will create 47 million job openings over the 10-year period from 2008 to 2018. Nearly two-thirds of these jobs will require at least some postsecondary education. Further, half of the jobs that must be filled by workers with postsecondary education—14 million jobs—will be accessible to individuals with a sub-baccalaureate credential, that is, an associate's degree or a long-term certificate.[15] In fact, Bureau of Labor Statistics occupational employment projections suggest that jobs requiring only an associate's degree or a postsecondary vocational award (a certificate) will grow slightly faster than occupations requiring a bachelor's degree or more. This demand represents an opportunity for very rapid growth in the annual production of occupationally oriented associate's degrees and long-term certificates.

With this foundation of information about certificate programs and their labor market value, we now return to the argument that more aggressive certificate programming can offer an important strategy for boosting postsecondary attainment.

Certificates: Pathways to Success for Working Adults and Low-Income Youth

Given the accumulating evidence about demand, earnings, and relative efficiency, it seems both feasible and desirable to ramp up certificate offerings and aim them directly at low-income and minority youth and working adults who are not having much success in traditional pathways to degrees. These two groups are already finding some success in certificate programs, and with a more intentional approach to the design and expansion of long-term certificate awards, they could find still more success.

BPS survey data indicate that older students are much more likely to earn certificates than degrees when they do enroll in either four-year or two-year institutions. Of students who enrolled in 2004 at ages 24 to 29, 19.5 percent received a certificate by 2009, and only 15.4 percent received a degree. Of those 30 years of age and older, 17.8 percent received a certificate, while only 14.4 percent gained a degree.[16]

In 2007, the black and Hispanic share of all associate's degrees was 22.7 percent versus 63.6 percent for whites. The black and Hispanic share of one- or two-year certificates was significantly larger—32.7 percent versus 55.2 percent for whites.

A study of educational and employment outcomes for low-income students in Florida suggested that certificate programs, in addition to leading generally to good economic outcomes for completers, may have some particular advantages for students from low-income families.[17] That study drew from a longitudinal student record system in Florida that integrates data from students' high school, college, and employment experience. It followed two cohorts of Florida public school students who entered the ninth grade in 1995 and in 1996.

The Florida research suggested that strong earnings effects of degree attainment (associate's, bachelor's, and advanced) were confined largely to students who had performed well in high school. In postsecondary study such students were continuing a trajectory of success apparent in high school. However, the research found that even for students who did not necessarily perform well in high school, obtaining a certificate from a two-year college significantly increased their earnings relative to students who attended college but did not obtain a credential. These students were finding new success in certificate programs, changing the trajectory of their high school years. Moreover, the Florida study confirmed other research that found strong returns for completion of good certificate programs, even relative to associate's degree completers.

The Tennessee Example

A close examination of Tennessee's large state system of certificate-granting institutions offers some insight into what might make certificate programs a particularly good investment for working adults and recent high school graduates who struggle for success in more traditional community college degree programs.

Tennessee has 27 postsecondary institutions that offer only certificate-level programs and serve nontraditional students almost exclusively. The Tennessee Technology Centers began as secondary-level, multidistrict vocational and technical schools in the 1960s under the supervision of the State Board of Education and began to serve adults in the 1970s. In most states, analogous institutions were merged into community or technical college systems, but in Tennessee (as in a few other states), they continue to operate as a discrete set of non-degree-granting postsecondary institutions.[18]

The Technology Centers uses the term "certificate" to denote short-term programs of about 500 to 900 clock hours and the term "diploma" for programs that exceed 900 clock hours. Diploma programs average about 1,400 clock hours, and some exceed 2,000 clock hours. They are all designed to lead to immediate employment in a specific occupation. In 2008–9, the centers awarded 2,066 certificates and 4,696 diplomas, serving 12,112 students on an FTE basis. Collectively, the Technology Centers offer about 60 programs, some just at the shorter-term certificate level but most at the longer-term diploma level. Some of the more popular diploma programs are practical nursing, business systems technology, computer operations, electronics technology, automotive service and repair, CAD technology, and industrial maintenance.

Most students in the Technology Centers are low income. Nearly 70 percent come from households with an annual income of less than $24,000 per year, and 45 percent report a household income of less than $12,000 annually.[19] Thus, most students enrolling in full-time and part-time programs qualify for Federal Pell Grants; many receive Workforce Investment Act support for costs of attendance. The percentage of black and Hispanic students is greater than the percentage of minorities in the state population. The average age of students is 32 years, and all the Technology Centers report a mix of new high school graduates, young adults getting serious about career development, and older adult workers seeking the postsecondary credentials they decided not to pursue when they were younger.

The 2007 IPEDS-reported "150 percent of time" graduation rate for full-time first-time students in the Tennessee Technology Centers was 70 percent. The 2007 IPEDS national average among all public one-

and two-year non-degree-granting institutions was about 66 percent, but that includes many institutions whose average program length is almost certainly much shorter than the average length of programs of the Tennessee Technology Centers.[20] In comparison with more comparable institutions in Ohio, Oklahoma, Florida, and a few other states, most of Tennessee's Technology Centers clearly are national leaders in graduation rates. Every year for the past several years, at least 80 percent and sometimes as many as 90 percent of the Technology Centers' graduates who are available for job placement are employed in jobs related to their program 12 months after completion of training. The Council on Occupational Education accredits the Technology Centers, and one of its requirements is that institutions maintain annual job placement rates of at least 75 percent. While Tennessee does not use unemployment insurance data to track the labor market returns for its Technology Center graduates, internal surveys indicate consistently high earnings compared with industry and occupational averages.[21]

A growing consensus in Tennessee holds that the key explanation for the high completion rates in the Technology Centers can be found in the program structure. Tennessee's Technology Centers operate on a fixed schedule, consistent from term to term (usually from 8:00 a.m. to 2:30 p.m., Monday through Friday), with a clearly defined time-to-degree based on clock hours of instruction. The full set of competencies for each program is prescribed up front; students enroll as a cohort in a single coherent, block-scheduled program instead of individual courses. The programs are advertised, priced, and delivered to the students not as separate courses but as integral programs of instruction. Progression though the program is based not on seat time, but rather, on the self-paced mastery of specific occupational competencies.

Clearly, this approach discourages part-time attendance. It asks students to commit to an intensive program of full-time instruction. But it consolidates the classroom time into a fixed period each day, and it offers a clear and predictable timetable. The Technology Centers have found that this certainty allows students to work part-time and to meet family responsibilities. Transparency about tuition, duration, success rates, and job placement outcomes (published clearly in college brochures and on websites) apparently enables students to assess costs and benefits, see the reasons for continued attendance, and make the sacrifices necessary to achieve program goals.

The Technology Centers also build necessary remedial education into the programs, enabling students to start right away in the occupational program they came to college to pursue, building their basic math and language skills as they go and using the program itself as context for basic skill improvement.[22] Getting immediately into the program skills that attracted these students to the college in the first place seems to strengthen their motivation and encourage persistence and completion. While the students are held to a common and rigorous basic skill and workforce readiness standard, connecting basic skills development to technical skills demonstrates relevancy and seems to promote success.

Certificate Program Structure in Most States

Most community colleges and many non-degree-granting institutions do not offer certificate programs with Tennessee's completion-focused structure. At most community colleges students seeking an occupationally oriented certificate pursue a traditional "collegiate" pathway to the credential that is very similar to degree pathways. Generally, they must complete 10 to 12 separate courses, each typically counting for three credit hours. Courses usually meet for 60 to 90 minutes twice a week for 16 weeks over the semester. Many courses have prerequisites, so taking the right courses in the proper sequence is critical (and some courses are not offered every semester).

Just as in degree programs, newly enrolled students in many certificate programs are sometimes required to take "developmental education" courses (over one, two, or even three semesters) to build their math and language skills before they can even enroll in the program-level math and English courses that often represent a gateway into their fields of study. These "dev-ed" courses are credit bearing but do not count toward the certificate requirements. Piecing together a coherent academic pathway to a credential from an array of individual courses that sometimes are awkwardly and inconsistently scheduled in small chunks over 16-week semesters is hard for students who are often not well-prepared, typically face severe and immediate financial pressures, frequently have family responsibilities, and do not have supports or academic advisors to help guide them through the multiple choices required by complex conventional academic systems. Most students respond to these scheduling challenges by attending only part-time, trying to squeeze in one or at most two courses each semester and occasionally dropping out for a full semester. The pathway to a certificate, especially one that represents completion of a program of at least one year, is long and choppy; things go wrong; students simply quit.

Recommendations for Action

Increasing the number of certificate awards for completion of organized programs of study of at least one year is a desirable and feasible strategy for increasing overall postsecondary attainment pursuant to White House goals. More concretely, it is a good strategy for heading off the loss of skilled workers in the national labor force that would otherwise occur as older, more educated workers age out of their working years and are replaced by less educated younger workers. However, boosting certificate programs for working adults and low-income and minority youth will not happen without purposeful action by national, state, and college leaders. The trajectory of increase in long-term certificate awards is positive but gradual, and it has slowed over the past several years even as certificate growth has outstripped gains in degree awards on a long-term basis.

Concerted action at the national, state, and institutional levels is necessary if certificate programs are to achieve their promise in increasing postsecondary attainment for working adults and low-income and minority youth who are not now succeeding in traditional degree pathways to credentials.

At the National Level

Federal government authorities in the administration and at the Departments of Education and Labor can play an important policy leadership role by promoting sub-baccalaureate certificate attainment—above the threshold of one-year programs—as a viable component of national postsecondary attainment planning and as a valuable outcome of postsecondary participation. Important needs include better tools for the Census Bureau for tracking changes in attainment, more rigorous reporting requirements for IPEDS, more critical research about certificates by the National Center for Education Statistics, and more careful work by the Department of Labor to relate certificate pathways to occupational outcomes.

National and regional accrediting bodies should step up to greater responsibility in their oversight of long-term certificate programs. That means, among other things, acknowledging the importance of whole-program, competency-based programming rather than relying exclusively on course-by-course seat time requirements; supporting, not discouraging, the compression of classroom time through hybrid course design; and promoting the effective use of applied math, English, and general education content.

National employer groups should encourage their affiliates to pay sharper attention to certificates as a measure of postsecondary attainment. Of special importance is the need to help employers see the advantages of long-term versus short-term certificates for current and prospective employees. There is inevitable tension between the logical desire of most employers to squeeze postsecondary education and training of current employees into work-related short chunks that can be incorporated into employee development plans, and their longer-term shared interest in a more highly skilled workforce with the higher competencies and platform skills typically associated with longer-term credentials. National employer groups can help promote the importance and legitimacy of long-term certificates as a strategy to pull underprepared youth and adults to postsecondary attainment.

At the State Level

State higher education authorities should ensure that the financial and regulatory framework for public postsecondary education encourages enrollment and success in long-term certificate programs, especially in state community colleges. They should encourage community colleges to build certificate programs with labor market payoff. They should also work with statewide and regional employer groups, general business and sector-specific, to promote the advantages to both employers and working adults of high-value certificate programs.

State workforce development and higher education agencies have a special responsibility—which few are now meeting—to measure the labor market returns for certificates as well as for all occupationally oriented programs at the associate's degree level. State agencies should routinely match postsecondary student records against administrative records of state-maintained unemployment insurance programs. Ideally, states would assess earnings outcomes for completers versus noncompleters in every program area and also compare earnings of those having postsecondary credentials with a sample of those without in all occupational categories.

Importantly, this information should be made widely available to students, prospective students, and their employers.

In some states, public postsecondary institutions have left the certificate marketplace to the for-profit sector. This is not a sound strategy for the long haul. It works for the for-profits as long as federal tuition subsidies are generously available, but it drives them toward high-margin programs and toward students willing to incur high levels of debt. Some proprietary institutions have better success in getting students to completion than do most community colleges, but many have poor graduation rates.

At the Institutional Level

Most of the hard work in developing the promise of high-value certificate programs needs to be done at the college level by staff and faculty, who have a shared interest in promoting better success at their institutions. In a few states, non-degree-granting one-year and two-year institutions can be a major player in this work, but in most states, it is the community colleges that must lead.

The first step is to examine the scale and scope of existing certificate programs with a view toward expanding the range of programs in high-value occupational fields and boosting enrollment in those programs, especially by working adults and low-income and minority youth. If there is a single state model to hold up for comparison, it is probably Arizona, where the community colleges have built an impressive array of certificate programs with some apparent consistency statewide but also demonstrating responsiveness to regional labor markets. Arizona's community colleges also offer a strong example of aggressive outreach to increase the participation of working adults and low-income and minority youth.

But for colleges, the issue is not just scale and scope and expanding access. The Tennessee Technology Center model demonstrates the importance of program structures that promote success and completion. Many community colleges see the completion advantage of certificate programs exclusively in their relatively short duration, but that is not an adequate foundation for success for strong certificate programs with high labor market relevance and good earnings returns. Time to credential is important and is usually one of the reasons that students enter certificate pathways: they see them as shorter and therefore less daunting than degree offerings. But good programs are often nearly as long as degree programs. Merely limiting credit or clock hours is not always feasible and by itself does not necessarily build success.

Several interrelated educational strategies and practices are frequently associated with high completion rates in both certificate and degree programs. These strategies and practices should not be seen as a *menu* from which colleges might pick and choose. Rather, they should be viewed as a flexible *recipe* for building new programs and rebuilding existing ones in ways that directly promote student success and credential completion.

- *Integrated program design.* The full set of competencies for each program would be prescribed up front, and students would enroll in a single, coherent program—not individual, unconnected courses. Students would not be required to navigate through complex choices or worry about unnecessary detours. Instructors would share accountability for helping the students successfully complete the whole program.
- *Compressed classroom instruction.* Non-classroom-based, asynchronous instruction methods using contemporary technology would supplement traditional classroom instruction to compress seat-time requirements and strengthen the curriculum.
- *Block schedules.* Programs would operate on a fixed classroom-meeting schedule, consistent from term to term. The students would know their full schedule before they begin, and they would know when they would be done.
- *Cohort enrollment.* Students would be grouped as cohorts in the same prescribed sequence of classroom and non-classroom instruction. This would promote the emergence of in-person and online learning communities widely acknowledged as an effective strategy for improving student outcomes.
- *Embedded remediation.* Most remediation would be embedded into the program curriculum, supplemented as necessary through instruction that is parallel and simultaneous to the program, rather preceding it. Students would develop stronger math and English skills as they build program competencies, using the program as context. There would be clear expectations about learning basic skills, with rigorous assessment.
- *Transparency, accountability, and labor market relevance.* The programs would be advertised, priced, and delivered as high-value

programs tightly connected to regional employers and leading to clearly defined credentials and jobs. Clear and consistent information about tuition, duration, success rates, and job placement outcomes would enable students to assess costs and benefits, see the reasons for continued attendance, and make the sacrifices necessary to achieve program goals. Programs would be held accountable to rigorous and consistent national accreditation standards.

- *Program-based student support services.* Even as these changes in the fundamental structure of certificate programs accelerate persistence to completion, schools should also anticipate that many students will require support services to overcome problems of transportation, child care, and other personal, family, and economic pressures. Ideally, these supports would be embedded into the programs themselves, with faculty helping to identify student needs and supporting resources and using technology and partnerships with employers and community-based organizations to supplement traditional support services.

If community colleges expanded their certificate offerings to all high-demand, good-wage jobs in their regional economy, and if they applied in those certificate offerings the strategies and practices associated with high rates of completion, certificate awards and attainment levels could increase much more rapidly than degrees. If we do them right, certificate programs can be a vitally important national strategy in boosting postsecondary attainment and maintaining the advances in labor force skills that have helped drive national economic growth.

ACKNOWLEDGMENT

An earlier version of this chapter appeared as "Expanding Certificate Programs" in *Issues in Science and Technology,* Fall 2011, pp. 51–57. Used with permission of the University of Texas at Dallas, Richardson, Texas.

NOTES

1. *Investment in Education: Private and Public Returns,* Joint Economic Committee, U.S. Congress, Jan. 2000.

2. See in particular J. Bradford DeLong, Claudia Goldin, and Lawrence F. Katz, "Sustaining U.S. Economic Growth," in *Agenda for the Nation,* ed. Henry J.

Aaron, James M. Lindsay, and Pietro S. Nivola (Washington, DC: Brookings Institution Press, 2003).

3. U.S. Census Bureau, *A Half-Century of Learning: Historical Statistics on Educational Attainment in the United States, 1940–2000* (Washington, DC: U.S. Census Bureau, 2006).

4. Mirta Toossi, "A Century of Change: The U.S. Labor Force, 1950–2050," *Monthly Labor Review*, May 2002.

5. Patrick J. Kelly, *Closing the College Attainment Gap between the U.S. and Most Educated Countries, and the Contributions To Be Made by the States* (Washington, DC: National Center for Higher Education Management Systems, April 2010). These calculations do not include undergraduate certificates because attainment data collected by the U.S. Census Bureau do not include certificates and because only certificates longer than two years in duration would count as "tertiary education" within international frameworks. Efforts are under way to include a new question on the Current Population Survey or the American Community Survey that will capture the percentage of adults in the population that have earned certificates.

6. Toossi, "A Century of Change."

7. Sandy Baum, Jennifer Ma, and Kathleen Payea, *Education Pays, 2010: The Benefits of Higher Education for Individuals and Society* (Washington, DC: The College Board, 2010).

8. Ali Berker and Laura J. Horn, *Work First, Study Second: Adult Undergraduates Who Combine Employment and Postsecondary Enrollment* (Washington, DC: National Center for Education Statistics, 2003).

9. Alexandria Walton Radford et al., *Persistence and Attainment of 2003–04 Beginning Postsecondary Students: After 6 Years*, NCES 2011-151 (Washington, DC: National Center for Education Statistics, 2010).

10. Some colleges also observe that regional accrediting bodies tend to be driven by traditional academic practices in their limited oversight of occupational programming and often are seen as obstacles to effective certificate programming—failing, for example, to acknowledge applied learning practices.

11. The years-of-attainment measure counts two years for each associate's degree and two- to four-year certificate, one year for each one- to two-year certificate, and half a year for each less-than-one-year certificate.

12. U.S. Census Bureau, *Current Population Survey, 2009: Annual Social and Economic Supplement* (Washington, DC: Government Printing Office, April 2010).

13. A more detailed review of national-level research on labor market returns for certificates is available in Brian Bosworth, *Certificates Count: An Analysis of Sub-Baccalaureate Certificates* (Washington, DC: Complete College America and Future Works, 2010), available at www.completecollege.org/resources_and _reports.

14. For a detailed review of state-level research on labor market returns for certificates, see ibid.

15. Anthony Carnevale, Nicole Smith, and Jeff Strohl, *Help Wanted: Projections of Jobs and Education Requirements through 2018* (Washington, DC: Georgetown University, Center on Education and the Workforce, 2010).

16. Alexandria Walton Radford et al., *Persistence and Attainment of 2003–04 Beginning Postsecondary Students: After 6 Years*, NCES 2011-151 (Washington, DC: National Center for Education Statistics, 2010).

17. Louis Jacobsen and Christine Mokher, *Pathways to Boosting the Earnings of Low-Income Students by Increasing Their Educational Attainment* (Washington, DC: Hudson Institute and CAN, November 2008).

18. There are thirteen community colleges in Tennessee. They are comprehensive institutions offering pre-baccalaureate-oriented associate's degrees that transfer directly to four-year colleges, as well as workforce-oriented associate's degrees and some certificates for programs designed to prepare students for more immediate employment. The enrollment in the community colleges was 92,226 in the fall term of 2009, with 59,993 FTEs. In 2008–9, the community colleges awarded 6,760 associate's degrees and 1,591 certificates. Nearly half of the associate's degrees were pre-baccalaureate and designed specifically for transfer to four-year institutions. Some of the other degrees might transfer to some four-year institutions, but they are designed primarily for occupational results.

19. Tennessee Higher Education Commission, *Wilder-Naifeh Technical Skills Grant Program Report* (Nashville, 2010).

20. The national average for public two-year degree-granting institutions was 20.8%.

21. John Hoops, *"A Working Model for Student Success: The Tennessee Technology Centers"* (unpublished report prepared for Complete College America, 2010).

22. An exception to this approach can be found in certain healthcare programs (mostly the LPN programs) where applicants are required to demonstrate baseline competencies in math and English. Statewide, the waiting list for LPN programs in the Technology Centers exceeds three years.

CHAPTER FIVE

Apprenticeships as an Alternative Route to Skills and Credentials

DIANE AUER JONES

Concern about the rising cost of a college education, the growing need for remedial and developmental education among first-time college students, and low persistence and graduation rates among the most at-risk college students has prompted education officials and policymakers alike to look for ways to *fix* college in order to reduce costs and improve student outcomes. But maybe college isn't broken.

Perhaps the real problem is that too many students enroll in college not because they want to be there, or because they are enthusiastic about learning, or even because they believe that the college environment provides the right kind of learning experience, but instead because they lack other career preparation alternatives. Students may have heard from parents, high school officials, policymakers, elected officials, and the media that only by going to college can they enjoy a financially secure future and social prestige. Sometimes even against their better judgment, students decide to give college a try (or even a second or third try) without fully understanding the personal commitment they must make to be successful in higher education.

It is highly likely that students who are genuinely committed to the hard work of traditional college learning and who have time to take advantage of academic and other support services can be successful, even if they come to college underprepared academically. However, not all students who enroll in college are willing to put forth the effort needed to be successful, and even among those who are, some find that the demands of work and family leave precious little time to devote to their studies. For other students, however, the classroom is never going to provide the optimal learning environment because they learn best by engaging in activities that yield tangible products. Kinesthetic learners learn best by doing, and some college programs provide very little "doing" time relative to the amount of listening or reading time. These learners may enjoy only limited success in a traditional lecture-based classroom.

Instead of trying to fix college or even fix students, a more effective approach might be to expand the postsecondary options available to students—and respected by employers, academics, and the public—so that each student can find the right pathway to success on the basis of personal and professional goals, life circumstances, learning style, and academic preparedness. Included among the expanded postsecondary options should be alternatives to traditional classroom education, including high-quality, centralized, and well-recognized apprenticeship programs.

What Is an Apprenticeship?

An apprenticeship is a formal, on-the-job training program through which a novice learns a marketable craft, trade, or vocation under the guidance of a master practitioner. Most apprenticeships include some theoretical classroom instruction in addition to hands-on, practical experience in the workplace. Classroom instruction can take place at the worksite, on a college campus, or through online instruction in partnership with public or private sector colleges.

The apprentice is paid a wage for the time he or she spends learning in the workplace, and while some apprenticeship sponsors cover the costs associated with the classroom-based portion of the program, other sponsors require apprentices to pay tuition out of their wages. Some sponsors pay apprentices for the time spent in class as well as their time on the job, while others pay wages only for time spent in the workplace. All of these details are part of the apprenticeship contract, which provides the apprentice with a clear understanding of the requirements of the program, the expectations of the apprentice, and the obligations of the sponsor, including wages and tuition support.

In many countries, such as Germany and Switzerland, apprenticeships are a critical part of the secondary education system, and the majority of students complete an apprenticeship even if they plan to pursue postsecondary education in the future. It is not uncommon for German or Swiss postsecondary institutions to require a student to complete an apprenticeship prior to enrolling in a tertiary education program. Alternatively, in the United States, apprenticeships are generally considered to be labor programs rather than education programs, so they are not a conventional part of most secondary or postsecondary systems or programs.

What Are the Benefits of Apprenticeship Programs?

Put simply, an apprenticeship program is an efficient and effective way to prepare students for jobs in a variety of fields. While we typically think of apprenticeships as an appropriate way to train students for positions in the skilled trades or crafts, apprenticeships are used in other countries to train engineers, nurses, teachers, finance workers, and myriad other professionals. Apprenticeships may be a particularly effective way for kinesthetic learners to excel, and to provide pathways to success for those who may not have been successful in a traditional classroom environment during their K–12 years or during prior postsecondary experiences.

Unlike in the traditional college setting, where a student may be forced to complete years of theoretical training before ever having the opportunity to apply that new knowledge to a practical challenge or problem, in an apprenticeship the student participates in real work from the first day of his or her program. Alignment between theoretical and practical learning is likely to improve student mastery, and the challenges that arise naturally in the workplace provide authentic opportunities to cultivate critical thinking skills in ways that the contrived classroom environment cannot. Additionally, master practitioners may be a more credible source of information and training for some students than are academics, who may not have direct experience working in the field for which they are preparing students.

Apprenticeships also provide advantages to learners by surrounding them with ready-made role models and mentors who help the novices develop and then refine their skills, while introducing them to the culture of the work environment and the mores of the field for which they are training. Apprentices have an opportunity to see firsthand what is required of those who seek career advancement and to observe the personal characteristics common among those who have been successful in the field. Apprenticeship programs make efficient use of skilled trainers and subject matter experts as well as facilities and equipment that already exist in the workplace. Perhaps most importantly, in the workplace apprentices are more likely to learn not just how to use a piece of equipment but also how to maintain and repair it. This rarely occurs in the traditional classroom setting.

On a practical level, the apprenticeship program provides those students who must earn income while in school with the opportunity to engage in work that supports and reinforces learning rather than distracting from it. Students who attend traditional colleges, but who must also work considerable hours outside of school, often feel torn between the demands of work and the demands of school, which are generally unrelated. For apprentices, on the other hand, school is work and work is school, so learning and working occupy the same space and time, rather than competing for the student's attention.

Are Apprenticeship Opportunities Available in the United States?

Apprenticeship opportunities do exist in the United States, but they lack standardization and are vastly underutilized, decentralized, and undervalued by students, educators, parents, and policymakers. The first successful federal legislative effort to promote and coordinate apprenticeships was the National Apprenticeship Act of 1937, commonly known as the Fitzgerald Act. This act treated apprentices not as students but as laborers, and it authorized the Department of Labor to establish minimum standards to protect the health, safety, and general welfare of apprentice workers.

Today the Office of Apprenticeships exists within the Education and Training Administration at the Department of Labor, where it receives an anemic annual appropriation of around $28 million.[1] The Office of Apprenticeships administers the Registered Apprenticeship Program as part of the National Apprenticeship Program, a highly decentralized state-administered effort to certify apprenticeship sponsors, issue certificates of completion to apprentices, protect the safety and welfare of apprentices, and monitor Equal Opportunity Plans of participating companies to ensure that women and minorities are not the victims of discriminatory practices. The state apprenticeship agencies that register programs and apprentices must be recognized by the Department of Labor as official registration agencies. Individuals who complete a registered apprenticeship program are awarded a certificate of completion by the registration agency upon the request of their sponsors.

The Department of Labor has been working over the last decade to modernize and improve registered apprenticeship programs and ensure greater accountability among them. From 2006 through 2008, the Department of Labor worked in partnership with the Apprenticeship Advisory Council and various stakeholders to develop and promulgate new regulations that, among other things, expand the ways in which program completion can be measured. In addition to the traditional, time-based approach that requires an apprentice to complete a minimum of 2,000 hours of on-the-job training and didactic instruction, the new regulations introduce a competency-based approach as well as a hybrid model for determining the parameters of successful program completion.[2] The competency-based approach requires the apprentice to successfully demonstrate acquired skills as well as complete related technical instruction, whereas the hybrid approach requires the apprentice to complete a minimum number of on-the-job learning hours (at least 2,000) and related technical instruction hours (generally 144) to demonstrate competency in the defined subject area.

In an effort to improve program quality, the revised regulations introduce new performance standards in addition to those already in place. New to the program is the requirement to track and report program completion rates, which must be at or above the national average for the field. In addition, program performance evaluations must include the use of sponsor-developed quality assurance assessments and Equal Opportunity Compliance Reviews.

Sponsors of registered apprenticeship programs are employers, or groups of employers, often in partnership with labor unions. Sponsors recruit and hire apprentices, determine the content for training, identify partners for classroom instruction, and develop formal agreements with apprentices regarding the skills to be taught and learned, wages to be paid, and the requirements of classroom instruction. State apprenticeship agencies make sure that the program complies with state standards, and they also register programs and students. In order to remain registered, apprenticeship programs must support at least one apprentice each year. Programs that yield completion rates below the national average must be provided with technical assistance by the state apprenticeship agencies to ensure improved program quality and outcomes.

Unfortunately, it is difficult to find information about the apprenticeship opportunities available in most states, to learn the wage level being paid by an individual sponsor, to understand the long-term outcomes enjoyed by program completers, or even to compare the components and requirements of similar programs offered by two different sponsors. While some states administer the registered apprentice program through their offices of labor, economic development, or workforce improvement, others rely on their Workforce Investment Act (WIA) OneStop centers to administer the apprenticeship program and disseminate information primarily to individuals actively seeking but unable to find work.

Current Statistics on Registered Apprentices in the United States

In 2007, there were about 28,000 registered apprenticeship sponsors who were training approximately 465,000 apprentices.[3] That year, the Education and Training Administration commissioned a survey to learn about what sponsors value, dislike, or would like to see changed about the program. In general, the sponsors' responses were quite positive. They indicated that they would "'strongly recommend' registered apprenticeships to others." In addition,

- employers reported a high rate of program completion on the part of the apprentices they sponsored;
- sponsors did not feel that the use of current employees to train new workers was too costly or burdensome;
- sponsors were somewhat concerned about trained apprentices being poached by other employers, but not enough to see this possibility as a deterrent to apprentice sponsorship;
- sponsors were likely to identify their industry as construction, utilities, or retail trade; and
- most sponsors conceded that they were dependent upon current employees to identify new apprentices for their programs.[4]

The appendix at the end of this chapter presents a more comprehensive summary of these survey results.

According to the Department of Labor, most U.S. apprenticeships are offered in the following fields and industries: construction and building trades; building maintenance; automobile mechanics; steamfitting; machinist, tool and die; and childcare. While some apprenticeship programs are offered through high schools and correctional facilities, most are offered by individual employers and labor unions.

Since 2003, the Department of Labor has worked with various federal agencies and external constituencies to explore the feasibility of expanding the use of registered apprenticeship programs to train workers for health care fields and green energy technologies. A recent Department of Labor report indicates that since the beginning of this effort, apprenticeship programs have been developed in 40 health care occupations, with the total number of health care apprenticeship programs increasing from around 200 to 350 during this time period.[5] The department is working with several large industry partners to develop apprenticeship programs in clinical care, nursing management, and health care IT.

While the Labor Department is encouraged by the development of new models for apprenticeship programs, the agency's leaders admit that a number of significant challenges must be addressed in order to fully implement these apprenticeship models. In particular, the Department of Labor has found that in the health care industry, few employers are aware that the Registered Apprenticeship Program exists or understand the benefits that are derived from this type of training. At this point, it is unclear how meaningful the apprentice certificate of completion in health care will be for individuals who seek to move from a sponsoring employer to another institution or company.

In its environmental scan of workforce opportunities and needs in the area of green jobs, the Labor Department reports numerous opportunities to utilize the Registered Apprenticeship Program to provide specialized training in green technologies and processes. However, stakeholders expressed concern about the growing need to provide pre-apprenticeship training in order to increase the number and diversity of qualified applicants to apprenticeship programs. In particular, stakeholders highlighted the need to provide additional pre-apprenticeship training in mathematics, science, writing, computer literacy, and customer service to many applicants, and in particular to women and to young people from impoverished communities, in order to help them qualify for apprenticeship programs.[6]

Why Expand Formal Apprenticeship Programs in the United States?

Given our need to prepare workers for the jobs that will exist in the future while also improving college completion rates, apprenticeship programs could fill an unfortunate gap in our postsecondary system. Filling this gap will be increasingly important given the current regulatory environment, which discourages institutions of higher education from serving high-risk students and those who formerly entered college as Ability to Benefit students (those who have earned neither a high school diploma nor a GED). Though not a replacement for college, apprenticeships are another avenue for career preparation which, if designed well, could also play an important role in helping adults complete a GED or otherwise prepare for more advanced college courses.

Apprenticeship sponsors report very high completion rates, with 44 percent of sponsors reporting apprenticeship completion rates of 90 to 100 percent, 21 percent reporting completion rates of between 70 and 89 percent, and 17 percent reporting completion rates in the range of 50 and 69 percent.[7] Without understanding more about which programs fall into each category and about the number of apprentices each program prepares, it is difficult to determine a national average for completion rates among all apprenticeship programs. However, it is noteworthy that 65 percent of sponsors reported completion rates at or above 70 percent.

Although these strong completion statistics are compelling, it would be inappropriate to compare them with completion rates of students enrolled in college-based certificate programs. While the participants in work-based apprenticeship programs may be demographically matched with students in college-based certificate programs, apprenticeship programs use a selective admissions model rather than the open-admissions policy of most certificate-program providers.[8]

In addition, the high completion rates among apprentices may very well be the result of the employee-employer relationship that exists between apprentice and sponsor. After all, a sponsor who is paying a wage to an apprentice may have a greater ability than a classroom instructor to capture the apprentice's attention and motivate a commitment to learning. The apprentice may be more inclined to perform well on the job versus in a classroom if he or she wishes to be hired or to remain employed by the sponsor following completion of the apprenticeship program. It is also possible that learning is simply easier and more meaningful when it occurs in the context of a real job, or that the careful alignment between what is being learned in the classroom with what is being done on the job yields a higher degree of mastery.

On the other hand, it is possible that high completion rates in apprenticeship programs are the result of minimal rigor and low standards as compared with school-based certificate programs. Without a careful examination of the assessment tools and methodologies employed by apprenticeship sponsors and school-based certificate programs to measure student learning and skill acquisition, it is impossible to draw conclusion about variations in completion rates, where they exist, between certificate programs and apprenticeship programs.

Some apprenticeships are offered as one-year programs, but most apprenticeship programs span a time period of three to six years, requiring 2,000 on-the-job hours per year. Reports of completion rates have not included information about each program's length, so it is unclear whether the length of the program has an impact on retention and completion rates. However, the Department of Labor recently introduced interim standards so that those who do not complete a full program can at least show evidence of certain skill competencies. There has not been a comprehensive effort to track apprentice outcomes beyond completion of the program, so we do not know if those who complete an apprenticeship, earning the title of journeyperson, enjoy improved job security, more rapid advancement, or higher earnings than those who enter their profession through some other means, including less formal on-the-job training, high school vocational training, or having earned a college-based certificate.

While the Registered Apprenticeship Program appears to provide good education and training options for a wide range of individuals, improvements in the program are needed before taking it to a larger scale. Critical issues to be addressed include developing mechanisms to improve the rigor, quality, and consistency of these programs; elevating the status of the credential; nationalizing elements of the curriculum and assessment systems to ensure better transferability of credentials; developing pathways that will allow registered apprentices to seamlessly apply their credential toward an undergraduate or advanced degree; and perhaps most important, improving public perception of apprenticeship programs by refuting the long-standing myths that apprenticeships serve individuals with low abilities who are destined for dead-end jobs.

The United States might look to the Swiss model, one of the most successful in the world, to identify ways to improve upon our own apprenticeship program.

The Swiss Apprenticeship Model

In other parts of the world, apprenticeships are considered a critical component of the national educational program. In Switzerland, for example, almost 70 percent of 16- to 19-year-olds participate in the dual-enrollment vocational education and training (VET) programs, which require students to go to school for one to two days per week, with the rest of their time spent in paid on-the-job training programs that last for three to four years.[9] Although the Swiss VET program is primarily a secondary school program, many of the principles upon which it operates could be incorporated into the U.S. postsecondary apprenticeship system.

There are numerous advantages for students enrolled in VET programs, including the ability to earn a wage while learning, to experience a career before making a lifetime commitment, and to learn under the guidance of a master practitioner. Beyond that, VET programs may have added social benefits in that 16-year-olds might be better influenced to make good decisions when surrounded by mature mentors and colleagues who serve as positive role models rather than when they are cloistered among their chronologically matched peers.

The Swiss VET model does not ignore the importance of developing core theoretical knowledge in addition to applied vocational knowledge. On the contrary, students are required to enroll in general education and vocational education classes taught in local vocational schools and industry learning centers, in addition to participating in the on-the-job training programs. Critical to the success of the VET system is the careful collaboration and coordination between the workplace trainers and the school-based educators, who work hard to ensure alignment between what the students are learning in school and at work.

Rigorous training and professional development are required of both institutional and workplace instructors. Vocational teachers are required to have a postsecondary credential (known in the Swiss system as a tertiary-level A or B degree), at least six months of professional experience, and 1,800 hours of preparation in VET pedagogy (300 hours if they teach part time). Teachers of general education subjects at vocational schools are required to have a university degree in their field but also must complete 1,800 hours of preparation in VET pedagogy so that they understand how to make general education relevant to vocational students. Teachers who already have a teaching diploma for general secondary education need 300 hours of preparation in VET specific pedagogy.[10]

Vocational trainers at host companies must complete 100 hours of training in pedagogy, VET law, and adolescent development. Instructors teaching industry-based courses are required to have 600 hours of pedagogical preparation. In addition, the third-party-certified examiners who administer the on-the-job assessments of vocational competencies for students enrolled in dual-track programs also receive training to make sure that their assessments are consistent across companies and cantons.

This administrative structure places equal value on pedagogical preparation and technical preparation, and fosters partnerships between educators with different experiences and strengths, in order to support the full intellectual development of the student. Unlike Americans, the Swiss place a higher value on vocational educators than on general educators since vocational educators are seen as having greater expertise and competency. These educators must have both educational and vocational knowledge and skills. Clearly, the Swiss educational authorities, unlike those who lead the American education system, do not believe that professional educators are the best people to teach technical skills, nor that technical competencies can be cultivated in traditionally educated teachers through a few hours or even a few weeks spent in professional development workshops.

Firms have a formal role in the development and oversight of VET programs. Their representatives, as well as those of professional organizations and trade unions, play a crucial role in working with representatives of the national government and various cantons to develop the national standards upon which apprenticeship programs are built, as well as the competency exams and assessments that should be utilized to evaluate student outcomes and success. This nationalized approach to standards and assessment may explain why apprenticeships are held in such high regard by Swiss citizens, employers, and academic institutions.

The roles of each partner in the collaboration are clearly defined. The national government (through its Federal Office for Professional Education and Technology) "ensures quality and strategic planning" and development of vocational education programs and ensures their consistent implementation across Switzerland. Cantonal vocational education agencies implement and supervise the vocational education programs, "provide career guidance, and inspect host companies and industry training centers. The professional organizations develop course content and develop qualifications and exams" and provide apprenticeship opportunities to students.[11]

Because VET programs are coordinated nationally, the student's credential is recognized anywhere in Switzerland, regardless of where the individual may have completed his or her apprenticeship. Small companies that have limited resources to contribute to apprenticeship training often form coalitions with other small companies to support apprentices who rotate through several companies. The national approach to standards development as well as third-party assessment of students ensures that the apprenticeship experience is focused primarily on common skills and standards rather than on company-specific training regimes.

Some who are critical of apprenticeship learning cite a lack of career mobility as the most significant disadvantage for those who complete these sorts of programs. However, researchers have found quite the opposite to be the case. Recent research sponsored by the Swiss Federal Office of Professional Education and Technology found that career placement and wages were higher for those who received workplace-based vocational training than for those (primarily in French-speaking cantons) who completed school-based vocational training programs; moreover, vocationally trained students did have the opportunity to transition to new careers, although most who did so made the decision earlier in their career and did experience initial wage reductions when moving to the new field.[12] This reduced wage is not a reflection of the lack of transferable skills but instead is the result of a premium that Swiss companies pay for those who have on-the-job experience in a given career area. Those who transfer to new companies but continue working in the same field do not experience wage depression and generally enjoy pay increases, since employers value the experience such an individual brings to the job.

The Swiss government currently recognizes 250 VET ordinances, which confer the legal basis for each program in Switzerland. VET programs, which are part of the upper-secondary education system, can last from two to four years. Students who successfully complete these programs are awarded either a VET certificate (for two-year programs) or a VET diploma (for three- or four-year programs).

The Swiss postsecondary education system is divided into two tracks: the tertiary B track, which provides vocational and professional degrees that can be earned in less than three years, and the tertiary A track, which provides traditional academic degrees that require at least three years of study (fig. 5.1). Individuals who have completed a VET at the secondary level can enter Swiss professional colleges (tertiary B institutions) to complete Professional Education and Training (PET) programs, although these are intended to serve individuals who, following completion of the

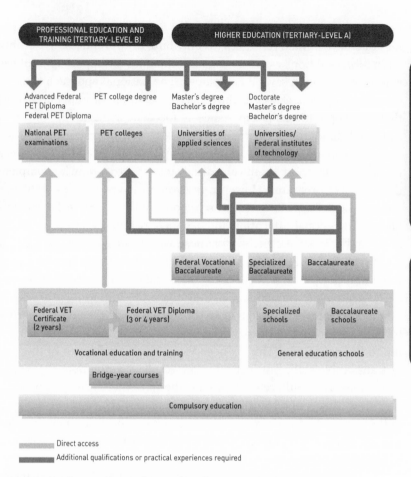

FIGURE 5.1. The structure of Switzerland's VET/PET system. *Source*: Federal Office for Professional Education and Technology OPET, Swiss Confederation

VET, have had several years of work experience. Individuals with work experience also have the opportunity to sit for the Federal Professional Education and Training (FPET) exam and the Advanced Federal PET (AFPET) exam to earn a well-recognized PET or APET diploma. There is no obligation to complete additional school-based education prior to taking the PET or APET exams; however, almost 94 percent of those interested in taking the exam do enroll in preparatory courses offered by private providers.

Professional education at the tertiary A level is provided by universities of applied sciences (UAS) that offer both bachelor's and master's degrees in occupational subjects. Those who earn a federal VET diploma and who pass the Federal Vocational Baccalaureate (FVB) Examination can enroll in a Swiss UAS at the tertiary A level. Or, with additional preparation, those who hold the FVB and pass the University Aptitude Test may enroll in a Swiss cantonal university, federal institute of technology, or university of teacher education. Those obtaining PET qualifications may also be eligible to attend a UAS.

By contrast, those who do not participate in a VET program and instead attend a secondary school, receiving a Swiss Academic Baccalaureate, may go directly to a cantonal university, federal institution of technology, or university of teacher education, or after at least one year of professional experience, may enroll in a Swiss UAS.

Disadvantages of the Swiss System

Of course, there are disadvantages associated with the Swiss VET program. The primary disadvantage is the cost to industry of providing such highly specialized and individualized training programs, although companies do have the ability to recover their investment through apprentice productivity and longevity during post-apprenticeship employment. Interestingly, while German firms pay less to support an apprentice (the equivalent of approximately $15,000 per apprentice per year) than do Swiss firms (which pay about $18,000 per apprentice per year), German firms claim a net loss during the apprenticeship period, while Swiss firms report a net gain as a result of apprentice productivity.[13] Swiss firms, as a result of paying higher wages and having a more flexible labor environment, focus on the productivity model in their apprenticeship programs (in which the apprentice must essentially earn his or her keep in real time). German firms pay a lower wage but have a heavy union presence and therefore tend to favor an investment model of sponsorship that assumes a longer-term payoff from the trained individual.

The greater union presence and power in Germany might explain why German apprentices tend to be given more menial tasks and less time on the job (thus yielding lower productivity but protecting low-wage union workers from displacement by apprenticeships) than their Swiss peers.[14] Swiss apprentices tend to have higher rates of mobility after completing the apprenticeship program, with 10 percent changing jobs within the first year after completion of the apprenticeship program.[15]

Since the private sector bears so much of the cost burden of training new apprentices, it is possible that a deep and extended recession could have a significant negative effect on the availability of placements for apprentices. The Swiss government and the cantons conduct regular surveys of apprenticeship opportunities and interested students in order to help match students with placement opportunities and to predict when shortages of apprenticeship slots may require government intervention. When students are not successful in finding apprenticeship placement, the government works with students to develop constructive gap-year programs and then helps such students locate apprenticeships the following year. Students also have the option to enroll in a school-based VET program, but these programs are more prevalent in the French-speaking cantons and the employment outcomes are inferior to those of dual-track VET programs.[16]

As international companies move to Switzerland, they may not embrace the VET program and may be unwilling to invest resources to prepare trainers, support apprentice wages, and introduce the culture of apprenticeship training to their organizations. If this were to become a widespread problem, it is possible that the government would impose an apprenticeship tax on all companies and then redistribute those monies to sponsoring companies so that a single company would not wind up investing resources to train individuals who might be poached by non-participating companies. This proposed system would be analogous to the French model, where companies pay a training tax unless they themselves are actively involved in the direct training of apprenticeships.

Finally, as student demographics shift and the number of young Swiss decline, there will be increased competition for students between VET programs and institution-based tertiary B and A programs, and the best students might be enticed away from VET programs. This would change the nature of the VET student population and could have a significant negative impact on the reputation and effectiveness of the entire dual-track system.[17] Encouraging individuals from all socioeconomic groups, ability levels, and educational backgrounds to participate in apprenticeship programs is key to maintaining an apprenticeship system that is well respected and leads to high-paying jobs.

Outcomes of the Swiss VET System

Apprentices in Switzerland are subjected to regular assessments in the classroom and on the job, culminating in final exams associated with certification. In 2008, the completion rate for Swiss apprentices was 79 percent, while the exam pass rate among program completers was 91 percent.[18] One of the main benefits of the Swiss apprenticeship system is that nearly 70 percent of all students participate in it, which means that students of all socioeconomic and ability levels are engaged in this form of learning. Such widespread involvement prevents the social stigmatization of apprenticeship programs, unlike in the United States, where social prestige is almost exclusively preserved for college-based education and training. Moreover, since students entering dual-track VET programs are frequently high performers, they are academically indistinguishable from the students who elect university education at the gymnasium rather than vocational training or dual education. The scores of Swiss dual-track VET students on OECD's Program for International Student Assessment (PISA) tests are generally higher than those of students engaged in apprenticeship programs in other countries, which means that Swiss students are likely to enter the workplace better prepared for work by possessing stronger academic skills.

Bridging the Gap between Labor and Education Programs: Expanding Apprenticeship Opportunities in the United States

While the Registered Apprenticeship Program could be an important component of a comprehensive postsecondary system, there are some barriers to wide-scale implementation.

Misinformation

Perhaps the greatest challenge to wide-scale implementation of high-quality apprenticeship programs in the United States is the public perception that only those with a college education will enjoy satisfying and financially rewarding employment. Public policy officials and education leaders are quick to tell students that a college degree practically guarantees higher lifetime earnings, when, in fact, there is no evidence that such is the case for a given individual.

Much of the rhetoric about lifetime earnings is based on the U.S. Census Bureau's 2002 report *The Big Payoff*, which projected future work-life earnings based on wage data collected during 1998, 1999, and 2000.[19] The results of this study—which suggested that those with a college degree could earn $1 million more over their work lifetime than those with just a high school diploma—have been misconstrued by many to constitute a guarantee that a college degree will increase an individual's earnings by $1 million.

Those who tout the results of this survey generally neglect to disclose what the authors included in the fine print, which is that there is a great deal of variability in earnings even among those who hold a bachelor's degree. The major the student selected, his or her personal ambition, the nature of the career path selected, the individual's work status (full-time versus part-time, continual versus intermittent employment), and individual effort all have a significant impact on actual wages. In other words, the average earning level of an individual with a bachelor's degree in business or engineering might be well above that of a similarly educated teacher, social worker, journalist, or dancer if the person remains in the field for which he or she trained. What the report actually shows is that the "big payoff" comes to those who earn a professional degree, such as a medical or law degree.

Unfortunately, the report aggregates all non-college-educated workers into a single category, failing to distinguish between the high earning potential of skilled trades and crafts people versus the low wage-earning potential of unskilled laborers. A more reasoned approach would have been to disaggregate non-college educated workers by occupation and skill level, similar to the way the study authors disaggregated college-educated workers by level of degree attainment.

Another report commonly cited as a justification for college completion is the Department of Commerce's *Occupational Outlook Handbook*.[20] Those who emphasize the importance of a college degree generally refer to this report's projections of the 20 fastest-growing careers, 12 of which require an associate's degree or higher, as the reason that everyone should earn a college credential. However, the percentage of growth is not the important number, since small occupations might experience a high growth rate while creating relatively few new jobs. Topping the list of fastest-growing occupations is biomedical engineering, where growth of 72 percent is anticipated. Unfortunately, the 72 percent growth equates to only 11,600 jobs over the next 10 years, or only 1,160 new jobs per year. This figure should not be used to encourage students to become biomedical engineers but, instead, should raise serious questions about why the United States is training so many biomedical engineers when so few are likely to get jobs in this field.

The important data table included in the *Occupational Outlook Handbook* is the one that lists the 20 occupations projected to have the largest numerical growth. One-third of all new jobs will be in the occupations listed in this table, so these are the jobs for which the large majority of workers should be prepared. Of the occupations listed in the table of occupations with the largest numerical growth, only three—home health aides, personal and health care aides, and computer software applications engineers—appear on the list of fastest-growing professions; and of those professions, only one requires a college credential. In fact, of the 20 occupations with the largest numerical growth, only 6 require an associate's degree or higher. Given these statistics, it is highly likely that certificate and apprenticeship programs will prove to be more efficient and effective than college degree programs in preparing workers for the majority of new jobs that will be created across the next 10 years.

In addition, the *Occupational Outlook Handbook* projects that earnings for workers in several of the skilled trades will exceed the national average for those with a college degree.[21] It is likely that a journeyman electrician, steamfitter, or plumber will significantly out-earn the average person with a bachelor's degree. And those skilled tradespeople who go on to own their own businesses may out-earn even those with professional degrees. It is overly simplistic and inaccurate to use average wage data to predict future earnings for any individual, but it is even worse to fail to distinguish between the earnings of skilled and unskilled workers when generalizing about worker wages.

Public Opinion

In order to eliminate the stigmatization of apprenticeship programs and those who work in skilled trades, we need to ensure that registered apprenticeship programs are inviting to all students and not just to low-income students or those who are poor performers in high school. Following the model of the Swiss, apprenticeship programs should be considered as a step along an educational continuum rather than a dead end. Moreover, apprenticeships should be developed for occupations traditionally associated with a liberal arts education, such as engineering, communications, banking, and teacher professional development. It is short-sighted to assume that only the economically disadvantaged or low-achieving students can benefit from apprenticeship training. However, without a concerted public awareness and information campaign, teachers and parents are unlikely to be supportive of the apprenticeship pathway, given U.S. policy focus on college completion.

Resources and Information

Another significant barrier to increasing apprenticeship enrollments is the failure to provide information to students, parents, and high school guidance counselors about the benefits of apprenticeship programs or even about how to identify and apply for admission to a high-quality program. The U.S. Department of Education, high schools, libraries, and community centers provide a number of resources to help students select a college, navigate the college admissions process, or apply for financial aid.

For example, College Navigator, a free tool provided by the Department of Education's National Center for Educational Statistics, helps students identify the right college based on location, program of study, cost, and a number of other variables. Similarly, College.gov is a website made available to middle and high school students to help them plot their course to college. It would be helpful if these resources also provided students with information about the career pathways available through apprenticeship training and about the apprenticeship opportunities across the country. The Office of Apprenticeship's own website is designed mostly to disseminate regulatory information to state agencies and provides little information that is of use to parents, students, educators, and potential applicants.

If apprenticeship programs were organized by field rather than by state, national advisory boards could set standards, develop assessments, and participate in third-party program evaluation and student testing, thereby blending the role that national advisory groups play in the Swiss system with the peer review system used in the U.S. higher education accreditation system. Some labor unions do provide *de facto* national standards for certain apprenticeship programs. It is unclear whether certain industries give preference to individuals trained through a union-supported apprenticeship program as opposed to those who earned school-based certificates or who trained through employer-based apprenticeship programs. States should continue to play an oversight role in inspecting local programs, monitoring apprentice complaints, and assisting programs that have fallen short on quality assessments and reviews.

Incentives

Public policymakers have created a number of incentives to encourage college participation, few of which are extended to individuals enrolled in dual-track apprenticeship programs (other than public subsidies made available to community colleges that provide the classroom-based portion of some apprenticeship programs).

High schools win awards for placing large numbers of students in AP courses rather than vocational education courses, regardless of whether students pass the AP exam upon completion of the course or whether the AP course is related to their personal or professional goals.

College enrollment may provide students with the opportunity to enroll in student health insurance at a group rate, whereas apprentices may not be given an opportunity to enroll in their sponsor's health insurance plan until they complete the apprenticeship program. There are also a number of tax advantages associated with saving for college (529 plans), paying college tuition, or paying interest on student loans. Meanwhile, there are no tax advantages to individuals or families whose children are learning as apprentices (although there may be tax advantages for businesses that hire apprentices who are displaced workers or who live in Empowerment Zones).

Even movie tickets are discounted for full-time students but not for full-time apprentices. The subtle and not-so-subtle messages are that college is valued above other forms of postsecondary training, regardless of whether college is the best way to prepare for the career an individual wants or is most likely to have.

A tremendous incentive for college participation comes in the form of federal grants and loans that allow individuals enrolled in accredited postsecondary programs to pay for college tuition, room, and board, and to purchase textbooks, sweatshirts, cars, designer coffee, vacations, or whatever else they wish to buy. There is no comparable loan program to help full-time apprentices purchase the tools they may need to successfully transition from apprentice to journeyperson, or to enable so-called lifestyle purchases that student loans enable among those enrolled in college.

While the government provides significant financial subsidies to nonprofit institutions of higher education to defray the cost of educating students, it does not provide the same level of direct subsidies to companies that are providing similar educational opportunities through apprenticeship programs. In addition, subsidies paid to institutions of higher education mask the true cost of education at public colleges and universities, which may make the cost of supporting an apprentice ($15,000–$18,000 per year) seem unreasonably high as compared to the sticker price at a public institution of higher education. Meanwhile, with taxpayer subsidies, capital investments, and tax abatements included, the cost of educating a student at a community college or public four-year college, especially in a technical field, is likely to be much greater than the amount paid by a company to support an apprentice.

A few states, such as South Carolina, provide tax incentives to companies that take on apprentices through the Registered Apprenticeship Program, but these sorts of programs have not yet been implemented on a national scale.

Awarding Academic Credit for Workplace Experience

A significant barrier to the integration of the Registered Apprenticeship Program into the postsecondary system is the absence of mechanisms for evaluating student achievement and assigning academic credit for the hands-on portion of an apprentice's training program. Following the model of the Swiss system, the use of outside third-party evaluators to assess student competencies may add credibility to student assessments and may allow for the development of standards for awarding academic credit for apprentice activities. The United States could also elect to adopt the Swiss system of exam-based certificates that individuals can earn to demonstrate their professional competencies as well as their readiness for advanced academic work.

The Role of Proprietary Colleges and Universities in an Expanded Apprenticeship Program

Proprietary institutions of higher education have become an important part of the American system of postsecondary education and would serve as ideal partners in an expanded apprenticeship program. Many of the larger proprietary institutions have a national presence, including campus locations or an online presence across the United States and abroad and, as a result, are not only knowledgeable about workforce trends across the country but could also be instrumental in setting standards and ensuring consistency among apprenticeship programs offered in different geographic regions. In addition, the investments that many proprietary institutions have made in sophisticated and effective educational technologies would allow apprentices to complete the didactic portion of their program at their worksite or at home, thereby reducing the additional transportation cost and burden associated with attending classes on a traditional campus.

Proprietary institutions have strong relationships with employers and are experienced in working with industry advisory boards to develop programs that are directly responsive to workforce development needs. In addition, these institutions have a highly flexible program development model that allows them to design and quickly implement courses that meet a particular industry's needs and standards. Similarly, their experience in recruiting, training, and evaluating an extensive pool of adjunct faculty, many of whom hold part-time or full-time jobs in the nonacademic workforce, makes them well prepared to hire new faculty who are knowledgeable about the field and willing to work closely with workplace-based vocational trainers to ensure strong coordination between the theoretical curriculum and experiential workplace learning.

At a time when state and local budget constraints are putting a strain on public institutions and forcing them to turn students away, proprietary institutions have the interest and the ability to provide new programs when and where they are needed. These institutions depend on market forces for revenue, as opposed to government largesse, which is subject to shifting political winds, and therefore have incentives to work in partnership with employers to meet the needs for trained workers.

Perhaps most importantly, proprietary institutions have considerable experience working with adult learners and understand the need to provide a flexible, respectful learning environment that accommodates each student's learning style and scheduling needs, facilitates accelerated credential completion, provides year-round learning opportunities, ensures access to supplemental support services at times convenient to the student, and welcomes transfer credits that students may bring from prior educational experiences. Moreover, proprietary institutions are likely to have protocols in place for assigning academic credit for knowledge and competencies that the adult learner may have gained from work experience, which is critical for apprentices who wish to continue their education in pursuit of a higher credential or degree following completion of the apprenticeship program.

Finally, since many proprietary institutions provide educational programs leading to a wide range of credentials—from certificate to advanced degree programs—a student who enrolls at a proprietary institution as part of an apprenticeship program is far more likely to have the opportunity to move seamlessly from one credentialing program to the next at that institution without losing time or money. In contrast, students who enroll in didactic programs at two-year institutions and then wish to pursue a bachelor's degree are likely to lose credits or be required to take additional credits when transferring from two-year to four-year schools.

Recommendations for the Future

In summary, it appears that a well-organized, well-publicized, and well-supported national system of dual-track apprenticeship programs would fill an important gap and address a number of growing concerns regarding shortcomings of the current U.S. system of higher education. Dual-enrollment apprenticeship programs that actively engage both traditional educators and master practitioners in a coordinated training and education effort have tremendous benefits for all involved. Traditional educators learn from master practitioners about real-world applications of the topics they teach. Master practitioners learn from experienced teachers how best to mentor and teach young workers.

Companies have a formal role in making curricular recommendations and developing assessments that will be used to evaluate student learning and skill development, which in turn also provides a formal mechanism to provide feedback to primary and secondary educators about the strengths and weaknesses of those programs. While there is a cost to companies of providing apprenticeship training, there are benefits associated with preparing workers with the skills they will need now and into the future. Companies also benefit from the ability to observe future employees in the workplace prior to making a long-term hiring decision. Firms making a financial contribution to the education of apprentices are far more likely to be engaged in the development of student curricula and assessments and to take responsibility for educating our youth, rather than constantly blaming teachers for all that ails American society.

Students benefit from the opportunity to earn a wage while learning a new trade or skill, and they often benefit from employer subsidies of the classroom instruction associated with their programs. They also appear to enjoy higher graduation and placement rates than their peers who do not participate in apprenticeship programs.

Taxpayers benefit from dual-track programs because the cost burden of educating future workers is shared by the employers who will benefit from having access to a well-trained workforce. In addition, the use of employer facilities and trained personnel reduces the capital investments taxpayers are expected to make to keep classroom facilities at public institutions up to date (which is an almost impossible goal) and to provide adequate professional development to classroom educators

In order to raise awareness, ensure consistent quality, and enable long-term career mobility among those who are interested in apprenticeship training, the following changes are required:

- The Office of Apprenticeships should develop a system similar to the higher education accreditation system to provide national oversight of apprenticeship programs based on the field for which apprentices are being trained. These accrediting bodies should be involved in the development of curricula, performance standards, and assessment of learning to ensure that apprenticeship experiences do not differ from one employer or one region to another. These bodies can also provide third-party validation of quality, which will improve the value and transportability of the completion credential.
- The Office of Apprenticeships should create a national database to improve the dissemination of information about registered apprenticeship programs, including the number of opportunities available in each geographic region, the requirements of each program, and the wages provided to each participant. Information about the application and selection process should also be publicly available, and students should be able to compare the various programs through a portal similar to College Navigator.
- Registered apprenticeships should be included as an important part of the postsecondary continuum and, in conjunction with this, the Department of Education should be required to include information about registered apprenticeships on all of its websites and to make available printed materials intended to help students prepare for and select a postsecondary path.
- Public policymakers should be careful to include apprenticeship training in any policies they develop or statements they make to encourage participation in postsecondary education and workforce preparation.

- National and regional accrediting bodies should work collaboratively to develop standards by which apprenticeship experiences can be evaluated for academic credit toward a degree in a related area.
- As in the Swiss system, workplace-based trainers and classroom-based instructors should be required to obtain certifications, based on significant professional development requirements, to address the unique aspects of vocational education. In addition, routine collaboration between classroom and workplace instructors should be required as a condition for participation in the Registered Accreditation Program.
- The federal government should engage in and support active marketing campaigns to promote the benefits of apprenticeship training, in the same way that they have invested heavily in marketing efforts to increase college access and completion.
- The federal government should explore the use of tax incentives to encourage greater participation by private sector firms in the sponsorship of dual-track apprenticeship programs, especially in light of the high completion rates achieved by apprentices as well as the cost savings these programs could achieve for taxpayers.

There is no doubt that today's adults need far more education than did adults who completed their compulsory education just two generations ago, but the signs are clear that traditional postsecondary education is not the only, or in some cases the best, way to prepare all individuals for the careers they are likely to pursue. The Swiss dual-track system, which requires collaboration between credentialed workplace trainers and experienced classroom instructors seems to be a good model for the United States to replicate, perhaps through the Registered Apprenticeship Program already being administered by the U.S. Department of Labor. Given the challenges we face in the current system of higher education, I would argue that it is indeed time to look back to the future in strengthening and revitalizing the age-old model of apprenticeship training in order to prepare workers for the highly skilled jobs many are likely to hold.

APPENDIX

The findings of the 2007 Department of Labor survey of registered apprenticeship sponsors can be summarized as follows:[22]

Sponsor characteristics. The majority of sponsors (36%) identified their industry as construction, with 11 percent indicating their organizations were in the utilities and 10 percent identifying their industry as retail trade. Approximately 26 percent of the sponsors indicated they were in programs jointly administered by employers and organized labor. Sixty percent of sponsors indicated that their program served only one employer, while 40 percent served multiple employers. Among programs with multiple employers, 38 percent had union involvement. Fifty-three percent of sponsors had small programs, with only one to four apprentices; 17 percent had no current apprentices, and 30 percent had five or more. Forty-eight percent of the sponsors had programs that were over 10 years old, and 31 percent had programs between 6 and 10 years old. About 3 percent of sponsors had programs that were less than one year old.

Program completion rates. Sponsors had high completion rates, with 44 percent saying that the completion rate for their program was between 90 and 100 percent, and 65 percent reporting completion rates at or above 70 percent. High completion rates were especially common in the aerospace, automotive manufacturing, energy, health services, retail, and transportation industries. Thirty-six percent of sponsors identified personal issues as the reason for noncompletion, making this the most frequently cited reason.

Sources for recruiting. About 60 percent of sponsors indentified current employees as an effective source for recruiting new apprentices, with 49 percent of sponsors indicating that educational institutions were an effective source. No more than 20 percent of the sponsors cited the Internet, community-based organizations, private vocational schools, and pre-apprenticeship programs as effective recruitment sources. Only 14 percent of sponsors indicated that the One-Stop Career Center system and unions were effective recruitment sources.

Related instruction. Fifty-eight percent of the respondents identified community colleges and public technical college as the providers of related instruction. Nearly one in four sponsors said that the related instruction was provided at a sponsor-owned or -operated facility, and about 17 percent reported that they used proprietary trade schools. Sponsors generally gave high marks to the quality of related classroom instruction. Seventy percent of sponsors said that employers provided the funds for related instruction, while 23 percent indicated that the apprentice covered such costs. A high quality of related instruction appeared to be correlated with higher percentages of individuals completing apprenticeship programs.

Value sponsors see in apprenticeships. Ninety-seven percent of sponsors of registered programs said that they would recommend the program to others, with 86 percent stating they would strongly recommend it and 11 percent indicating they would recommend it with reservations, primarily because of problems with accessing related instruction. The most frequently cited benefit of an apprenticeship program was that it helped sponsors meet their demand for skilled workers.

Drawbacks. The most commonly stated drawback was poaching by competitor firms, but while this was cited as a concern, it was not seen as a deterrent. Sponsors generally did not find cost to be a significant problem, and only 7 percent of respondents saw the costs of experienced workers' time to instruct apprentices as a significant problem, while 34 percent indicated it was a minor problem.

ACKNOWLEDGMENT

An earlier version of this chapter appeared as "Apprenticeships Back to the Future" in *Issues in Science and Technology*, Summer 2011, pp. 51–56. Used with permission of the University of Texas at Dallas, Richardson, Texas.

NOTES

1. Robert Lerman, "Expanding Apprenticeship: A Way to Enhance Skills and Careers" (Urban Institute, Washington, DC, Oct. 2010).

2. U.S. Department of Labor, *Apprentice Rule Fact Sheet*, www.doleta.gov/oa/pdf/Apprenticeship_Final_Fact_Sheet.pdf.

3. Robert Lerman, Lauren Eyster, and Kate Chambers, *The Benefits and Challenges of Registered Apprenticeship: The Sponsors' Perspective* (Washington, DC: Urban Institute, Mar. 2009).

4. Ibid.

5. U.S. Department of Labor, Employment and Training Administration, *Using Registered Apprenticeship to Build and Fill Healthcare Career Paths: A Response to Critical Healthcare Workforce Needs and Healthcare Reform*, www.doleta.gov/oa/pdf/Apprenticeship_Build_HealthCare_Paths.pdf.

6. U.S. Department of Labor, Employment and Training Administration, *The Greening of Registered Apprenticeship: An Environmental Scan of the Impact of Green Jobs on Registered Apprenticeship and Implications for Workforce Development*, June 2009, www.doleta.gov/oa/pdf/Greening_Apprenticeship.pdf.

7. Lerman, Eyster, and Chambers, *Benefits and Challenges of Registered Apprenticeship.*

8. Ibid.

9. Ibid.

10. Except as otherwise noted, information on the Swiss system in this section is from Kathrin Hoeckel, Simon Field, and W. Norton Grubb, *Learning for Jobs: Review of Switzerland, 2009,* OECD Reviews of Vocational Education and Training (Organisation for Economic Co-operation and Development, April 2009).

11. Ibid., p. 14.

12. Barbara Mueller and Juerg Schweri, "The Returns to Occupation-Specific Human Capital: Evidence from Mobility after Apprenticeship" (Swiss Federal Office for Professional Education and Technology, Jan. 2009).

13. Regina Dionisius et al., *Cost and Benefit of Apprenticeship Training: A Comparison of Germany and Switzerland,* IZA DP No. 3465 (Bonn, Germany: Institute for the Study of Labor, April 2008).

14. Ibid.

15. Mueller and Schweri, "Returns to Occupation-Specific Human Capital."

16. Hoeckel, Field, and Grubb, *Learning for Jobs: Switzerland.*

17. Ibid.

18. The information in this paragraph derives from Hilary Steedman, *The State of Apprenticeships in 2010* (London: London School of Economics and Political Science, Center for Economic Performance, 2010), http://cep.lse.ac.uk/pubs/download/special/cepsp22.pdf.

19. Jennifer Cheeseman-Day and Eric Newburger, "The Big Payoff: Educational Attainment and Synthetic Estimates of Work-Life Earnings" (U.S. Department of Commerce, Economics and Statistics Administration, U.S. Census Bureau, Special Studies, July 2002).

20. U.S. Department of Commerce, *Occupational Outlook Handbook: 2010–2011 Edition* (Washington, DC: Bureau of Labor Statistics, Office of Occupational Statistics and Employment Projections, 2010).

21. Ibid.

22. Lerman, Eyster, and Chambers, *Benefits and Challenges of Registered Apprenticeship.*

PART THREE

The Relationship between Policy and Completion

CHAPTER SIX

Financial Aid

A Blunt Instrument for Increasing Degree Attainment

ERIC BETTINGER

Higher education is a gateway to economic mobility, and as the returns on college degrees have increased over time, so too the demand for higher education has increased among every socioeconomic group. Yet, after years of emphasizing college access, policymakers have become increasingly concerned with college completion. The reason is simple. While attendance rates have risen dramatically for all socioeconomic groups in the United States over the last four decades, completion rates have not kept pace.

For example, between 1971 and 2001, total enrollment increased by 78 percent while degree receipt increased by only 48 percent. Additionally, while the percentage of 23-year-olds with some college experience increased by 31 percent between 1971 and 1999, degree completion by this age increased by only 4 percent.[1] Part of this decline is due to students' taking more time to complete degrees, yet whereas the United States previously led the world in the percentage of the population having bachelor's degrees, it has now lost that leadership.[2] Over the past three decades, cohort-based completion rates have increased by 2 to 3 percentage points across cohorts in the United States while other OECD countries such as the United Kingdom and France have seen 10 to 15 percentage point increases in completion rates.[3] While the change in leadership in completion rates may be as much about European policies and practices as any U.S.-related explanation, the change in leadership has brought renewed attention to completion rates in American higher education.

College affordability is one potential and often-cited reason that some students may start college but not complete it.[4] College affordability is frequently mentioned by policymakers, and college financial aid policies such as the Federal Student Loan Program and the Pell Grant program are the most visible federal policies aimed at changing college attendance and completion. Because of the increased concern with college retention, recent federal and state financial aid policies (e.g., Federal Academic Competiveness Grants) have specifically aimed at improving retention.

The efficacy of financial aid policies has been a subject of substantial interest to educators, policymakers, and academics. As is discussed below, most of the research in this area has focused on whether financial aid has increased college access and students' choices across colleges. Only recently have researchers begun studying the relationship between financial aid policies and college completion.

The focus of this chapter is on the relationship between financial aid and college retention and completion. After reviewing the literature in education, economics, and sociology that emphasizes how financial aid policies affect college outcomes, I discuss the cost-effectiveness of financial aid programs, specifically, the potential for state and federal financial aid programs to increase college attainment. I then look at innovative policies that can improve the efficacy of financial aid in increasing college retention and completion. The chapter concludes with remarks about the political economy of financial aid programs.

Federal and State Financial Aid Policies

There are several ways to partition financial aid programs. One can partition them by who provides the financial aid program. Federal and state programs are the largest and most visible programs; however, institutional aid and aid foundations are also prominent sources of financial aid. One could also categorize financial aid programs by the criteria used to award the financial aid. Need-based and merit-based aid are the most common forms of aid. Some special programs may use other special criteria for determining eligibility. For example, the GI Bill provides aid to military veterans regardless of need or merit. Another potential partition is the form of financial aid. The most visible types of aid are grants and loans, but aid also takes such forms as tax credits, employer tuition programs, work-study programs, and college savings programs. State subsidies to higher educational institutions may also be an indirect source of financial aid to students. Here, we narrow our focus to need-based and merit-based grant programs. These programs have received the most attention in the academic literature and have been highly visible in policy discussions.[5]

The College Board estimates that students in the 2009–10 school year received $154.5 billion in financial aid.[6] Of this, 18 percent, or about $28.2 billion, came through the Federal Pell Grant program. States provided an additional $8.6 billion in grants to students, and institutions provided an additional $26.0 billion. The largest component of aid is the Federal Student Loan Program, which makes up $65.8 billion, or about 43 percent, of all federal aid. Until recently, the federal government did not award merit-based financial aid. The Federal Academic Competitiveness Grant is the first federal award to include a merit component. Other federal grant programs, including the Academic Competitiveness Grant and SMART grants, made up an additional $12.0 billion in aid. The grants upon which I focus—the Pell Grants and state grants—make up about one-quarter of the overall financial aid awarded to students.

Prior Research on Financial Aid and College Outcomes
The Link between Financial Aid and College Access and Choice

Most of the existing literature on the effects of financial aid focuses on need- and merit-based grants and their impact on college attendance and college choice. Most of the work here is from need-based programs. Early reviews, such as the one by Larry Leslie and Paul Brinkman, suggest that college financial aid has a positive impact on the likelihood of attendance.[7] These two authors report that financial need significantly reduces the likelihood that low-income students would attend college. They argue that financial aid increases attendance by at least 20 percent in low-income families. The impacts were smaller for middle-class families. Thomas Kane as well as Ronald Ehrenberg and Daniel Sherman provide similar positive assessments of need-based aid.[8]

One of the weaknesses in the early financial aid literature was its limited capacity to identify statistically the causal impacts of need-based aid policies. The problem is that receipt and the size of students' federal need-based grants are correlated with several confounding variables. For example, poorer students are more likely to receive aid, and their aid awards are typically larger. By contrast, students who attend more selective and expensive colleges receive larger federal need-based grants than students who attend other institutions. Since academically prepared students are more likely to attend selective and expensive colleges, the size of aid awards may be larger for students with strong academic credentials than for others. In order to account for confounding factors, a number of researchers have turned to experimental and quasi-experimental methods to identify the impacts.

The first of these quasi-experimental studies focused on the introduction of the Pell Grant program. The results were largely disappointing: researchers failed to find any significant positive enrollment effect from the Pell Grant program.[9] Other studies have concluded that Pell Grants have not improved enrollment rates among low-income students and minorities but that they have affected which colleges students choose to attend.[10]

Starting in early 2000, a series of studies of need-based grants exploited other "natural experiments," such as discontinuities in aid awards, to identify the causal effects of financial aid programs. For example, Susan Dynarski used discontinuities arising from the removal of the Social Security Administration's Survivor Benefit Program.[11] By comparing students who were eligible in the last year of the program and students who would have been eligible had the program continued, Dynarski found sizable effects on both access and completion. The loss of financial aid led to a drop of almost 25 percentage points in the likelihood that students attended college.

Kane presented similar evidence.[12] He used discontinuities in the Cal Grant award program to estimate the impact of the program on college decisions. He found that the grant increased college attendance by 3 to 4 percentage points. He also concluded that the program affected college choice. Neil Seftor and Sarah Turner focused on how need-based aid affects older, nontraditional students.[13] After examining changes in the Pell Grant award which made some nontraditional students eligible, they found that Pell Grants cause increased enrollment by about 4 percentage points.

The most studied merit-based program is the Georgia HOPE Scholarship. The program awards free tuition to high school students who maintained a B average in high school. Susan Dynarski and Christopher Cornwell, David Mustard, and Deepa Sridhar examined the effects of the HOPE scholarship.[14] They found that enrollment increased by 3.7 to 4.2 percentage points in response to the program. There was also an increase of students who chose to attend Georgia colleges rather than an institution in another state. In summary, the evidence on the effectiveness of aid is mixed, with some more recent causal analyses suggesting that aid has a small positive effect on enrollment.

The Link between Financial Aid and College Retention and Completion

In terms of measuring the effects of aid on college outcomes, the literature is much less developed. In recent years, many studies have estimated the impact of need-based and merit-based awards on college graduation and retention rates.

Most of the studies focus on need-based programs. Dynarski found that the elimination of the Social Security death benefit reduced retention as well as attendance.[15] The results suggest that a $1,000 increase in aid improves retention by 3.6 percentage points. In an earlier study I used discontinuities in the Pell formulae caused by small differences in family size and the number of kids in college.[16] I found that Pell Grants increase students' persistence rates during their first year in college. This work implies that a $1,000 increase in Pell Grant awards leads to a 3 percent increase in persistence in a student's first year in college.

Recent work by Sara Goldrick-Rab, Douglas N. Harris, and Philip A. Trostel examined the effects of need-based awards on students' outcomes.[17] They evaluated a randomized experiment in Wisconsin which increased aid to some students after their initial enrollment in college. The first two years of the additional aid had no effect on persistence. After two years of the grant, individuals who received the extra grant were more likely to have completed at least 60 credits.

In a 2010 study I looked at the effects of a change in Ohio's need-based grant formula.[18] Ohio moved from using income and family size as the only determinants for aid to using students' estimated family contributions from the FAFSA form as the only criterion. Some students benefited from this change; some were not affected; and yet others were worse off as a result of the change. I found that students who benefited from the change were 2 percentage points more likely to persist after their first year in college as a result of the new program.

In terms of merit-based programs, Dynarski showed that large, state-run merit programs also increased persistence and completion rates.[19] She estimated that persistence rates increased by 5 to 11 percentage points and that degree completion increased by 3 to 4 percentage points.

The renewal of students' financial aid awards was contingent on academic success and progress in school. It is unclear whether the observed effects arose from the financial aid award, the conditionality of the awards, or some combination of both.

The most innovative work to date has come from MDRC. Over the last few years, MDRC has conducted a series of financial aid experiments aimed at testing new ways to improve retention and financial aid. Given that these policies shed light on possible effective innovations in financial aid policies, I review these studies in greater detail below.

The Potential of Grant Programs to Reduce the Gap

The evidence on the effects of need- and merit-based grants on college retention and completion suggests that grant aid can improve these outcomes. These results are certainly encouraging to individuals concerned about college completion. The real question is whether the effects are large enough and cheap enough to provide a cost-effective solution to improving college retention and completion. Or similarly, can grant aid be scaled up in a way that significantly reduces gaps in college completion and retention between socioeconomic groups?

If we want to understand whether grant aid can increase college retention and completion, we need to know to what extent the gaps in higher education completion are attributable to financial factors. If, for example, financial barriers are not the reason that students drop out, then we do not need more generous financial aid programs. The question is how much can and do we need financial aid to solve the completion problem.

Identifying the exact size of financial barriers is somewhat difficult. When we look at socioeconomic status, we see a persistent gap of about 30 percentage points between the poorest 40 percent of the population and the richest 20 percent in terms of college attendance. While this gap has narrowed slightly in recent years, it may suggest the magnitude of the gap. In their survey of the literature, Leslie and Brinkman found that 25 to 50 percent of students reported that they would not attend in the absence of aid.[20]

Students' responses on surveys also suggest that finances are a significant barrier. Edward P. St. John, Alberto F. Cabrera, Amaury Nora, and Eric H. Asker, for example, claim that half of the variation in student persistence can be explained by financial variables.[21] Other researchers have also reported that finances are a significant barrier.[22] In 2006, the Advisory Committee on Student Financial Assistance identified college costs as a major concern for academically prepared high school students. In the 2006–7 follow-up of the Beginning Postsecondary (BPS) Cohort, about 10 percent of students who dropped out claimed that finances were a significant reason for their decision.[23]

So where does that leave us? If we think that the gaps in college completion and attendance between rich and poor families are due to financial barriers, then the size of the gap is about 25 to 30 percentage points. This is a generous upper bound, since other factors such as culture, preparation, and information may contribute to the gap as well. On the other hand, if we believe the survey data from the BPS study, then the gap is about 10 percentage points.

Across the studies I reviewed, the estimated effect of $1,000 in need-based aid was a 2 to 4 percentage point increase in retention. The merit-based programs studied by Dynarski gave a $2,500 subsidy per student and had a slightly larger effect on persistence (5 to 11 percentage points) and degree completion (3 to 4 percentage points). As I noted above, funding in these programs was also tied to academic performance.

I will start by assuming that the effect on persistence is 3 percentage points per $1,000. I will further assume that this effect varies linearly with money, so that a $2,000 grant implies a 6 percent increase in retention. If we use the BPS statistic of 10 percent of students claiming that financial hardships were limiting enrollment, then there would need to be a $3,300 increase per student in order to convince the 10 percent of students who are making decisions based on money not to leave their first institution. If the number of students truly making enrollment decisions because of finances is greater than 10 percent, the estimated costs would be even larger.

There are a few problems with this simple extrapolation. First, this $3,300 increase is not just for the marginal students. Given our ability to identify students for whom financial aid would be most effective, the increase would have to be for all students who receive federal aid. To put this in perspective, this would require almost doubling the average 2009–10 Pell Grant award of $3,646. The increase that would be necessary is about 60 percent of the maximum 2009–10 Pell Grant award of $5,350. In 2009–10, about 7.7 million students received Pell awards. The added overall expenditure would be almost $30 billion dollars.

Second, the estimated effect may not be linear. The estimated impact of 3 percentage points per $1,000 may not be reasonable. As new policies affect students with greater financial need, the amount of resources needed could be greater and the responsiveness to resources could be even lower. Additionally, some of the studies show that the estimated effect for the marginal student is smaller than 3 percentage points.[24] In any of these cases, the overall expenditure would be even higher. Finally, we have assumed that colleges will not adjust their costs in response to an increase in Pell awards. I discuss this more below.

So could this increase be cost-effective? Most studies reviewed above have very little information about the cost-effectiveness of the programs reviewed. The researchers were primarily concerned with identifying the impacts of the program, and in many cases, they lacked information on the overall costs of the program. Moreover, the current studies identify the effects on the marginal student. We have to make assumptions on whether the effect is constant across other populations. In other words, in current studies, we might need $1,000 in aid to increase the likelihood that a "marginal" student stays. If we examine a student for whom financial aid barriers are even stronger, do we need more money? Do students become less responsive to aid? These questions are unanswerable with the current data, and so we have to make assumptions in any cost-benefit analysis.

There are two studies which have done extensive cost-benefit analysis. David Deming and Susan Dynarski have examined the cost-effectiveness of the HOPE scholarship programs that are scattered throughout the southern United States.[25] In their analysis of these merit-based grant programs, they include the annual cost of the scholarships, the forgone earnings of attending college (for those affected by the program), and the deadweight loss associated with additional taxation. They note that 80 percent of individuals receiving scholarships are completely unaffected by the program. These students would have made the same educational choices in the absence of the program. So the key is to compare the benefits of the program for the 20 percent affected by the program with the costs accrued by all. In this case, Deming and Dynarski find that the internal rate of return is about 7.9 percent.

I conducted a similar analysis of need-based aid policies in Ohio.[26] I computed effects on retention only for the first year and had to extrapolate how the effect of retention in the first year would translate into eventual effects on degree completion. In this study I outline a "best-case" scenario (the effect is constant across years to eventual degree completion) as well as a "worst-case" one (the effect attenuates over time). Like Deming and Dynarski, I incorporate costs of the subsidy and the opportunity costs. Deadweight losses from tax collection are not included. The costs are compared with the benefits accrued by the marginally affected students. The best-case scenario suggests that Ohio's change to Ohio's need-based grant program provides a 5 percentage point return while the worst-case scenario suggests a rate of return of -0.01 percentage points. The "best-case" scenario assumes that effects on first-year persistence are similar to effects on degree completion. In the need-based grant programs, the measured effect on persistence was much smaller (as much as half) than the measured effect on persistence in merit-based grant programs. If this is the case, then the rate of return and any cost-benefit analysis would be much lower and hence closer to the worst-case scenario.

In sum, we have two key concerns about the role of financial aid policies in increasing retention and completion rates. First, we do not know how much of the gap in college completion and retention between socioeconomic groups is attributable to financial factors. Given that the effects of need-based and merit-based aid are positive, it is clear that more generous financial policies can help, but we do not know the size of the gap that can be attributed to financial aid factors. At what point does increasing aid lose its effectiveness? The second and more severe problem is the magnitude and the potential cost-effectiveness of expanded grant aid policies. We have to make significant assumptions to get a positive rate of return on these programs. Given these concerns, we turn our attention to innovative programs which might represent more cost-effective ways to increase retention.

Examples of Innovative Policies

In recent years, a number of modifications to financial aid policies have been discussed or tested in the field. We can divide these policies into three categories: financial awards conditioned on student success, innovations that change financial aid framing and processes, and financial awards which improve targeting efforts.

Conditional Financial Aid Awards

Basing financial aid on attainment. One policy which has received attention links either additional or continued financial aid to a student's academic performance. For example, from 2008 to 2010, MDRC's Opening Doors Program tested a performance-based financial award in Louisiana.[27] In this program, the receipt of financial aid and additional support was conditional on the student's being enrolled at least part time and having at least a C average. Awards could be larger if individuals enrolled full-time.

According to MDRC's evaluation in Louisiana, students who were eligible for the $2,000 additional financial aid were 6.5 percent more likely to persist four semesters after the random assignment. These students had also completed more college credits and had spent more time attending college full time. On the basis of these results, MDRC is currently testing these scholarships across six states. The MDRC effect is larger than that found in the need-based aid programs we reviewed but similar to the effects found in Dynarski's evaluation of the HOPE scholarship programs, which also had a merit component.[28] In Georgia's HOPE scholarships, students' performance was evaluated at specific markers (e.g., 45, 90, and 135 quarter hours). Renewal of awards was conditional on academic progress and performance.

The Opening Doors intervention is probably much more cost-effective than HOPE or the need-based programs reviewed above because it is targeted at low-income, single-family households. The narrow targeting reduces the number of individuals to whom additional aid might be given inefficiently (i.e., individuals who do not require it for improved retention).

Changing Financial Aid Framing and Processes

Financial aid packaging. As in the United States, in Canada some students who are eligible for subsidized loans have not been using the Canadian subsidized loan program as a means for financing college. Boris Palameta and Jean-Pierre Voyer conducted a laboratory study attempting to determine why students fail to utilize the loan programs.[29] They gave students a hypothetical choice between receiving money today or an educational grant in the future. They observed which students selected an educational grant. They then made the same offer but included an optional student loan as part of the financial aid package. About 30 percent of students who had accepted the financial aid package the first time refused it when the package included an optional loan package.

Palameta and Voyer concluded that students' lack of familiarity with loan programs contributed to their reluctance to utilize the financial aid offered to them. They advocated attempting to decouple the award processes for grants and loans. They are currently conducting additional research on whether the decoupling process will lead to greater use rates.

Simplifying aid applications. One of the much-discussed difficulties in receiving financial aid is the complexity of the financial aid application process. Even the poorest families often have to submit more information to the U.S. Department of Education in the FAFSA form than they have to submit to the Internal Revenue Service in their annual tax filings. Bettinger, Bridget Terry Long, Philip Oreopoulos, and Lisa Sanbonmatsu offered a simplified process as well as assistance to individuals who were eligible for financial aid.[30] They found that the simplified process and assistance led to a 25 percent increase in college attendance. The preliminary results suggest that the increase in college attendance continued into at least students' second years in college. The simplified FAFSA process also helped students who already were attending college. Simplifying the application process increased the likelihood that students received financial aid.

"Paycheck" financial aid. Typically, financial aid is awarded in a lump sum at the start of a semester. MDRC is conducting a research project that changes the disbursement schedule. Instead of awarding financial aid as a lump sum, this project uses the paycheck model to disperse the aid funds at regular intervals. The premise is that students are not good at budgeting their funds, and they may spend their money early in the semester, with the result that they need additional funding at the end. Awarding financial aid in regular disbursements essentially takes care of the budgeting for students during the semester. Moreover, financial aid in the form of a paycheck may create the impression in students that the aid is conditional on effort and attendance during that period.

Improved Targeting

Targeting times of need. Many anecdotes suggest that students, especially nontraditional students, often experience sudden, unexpected financial hardships that make it difficult for them to continue in their schooling. The Lumina Foundation funded one such program—"The Dreamkeepers and Angel Fund"—to aid students in times of need. The fund provided students with "emergency" money for significant hardships. Transportation and housing were the most likely uses of the funds in practice. While there has not been a formal test of the program, reports from administrators suggest that the program's impact was positive.

Identifying Marginal Students

As mentioned above, one of the hurdles in financial aid policy is finding the truly marginal student. Policies which can identify these individuals are likely to be more cost-effective. However, the difficulty is trying to find characteristics that identify marginal students and then writing policies that can accurately track these students.

As an example, consider the change in financial aid in Ohio. That state switched its financial aid from a moderate program (the Ohio Instruction Grant, or OIG) to a very generous program (the Ohio College Opportunity Grant, or OCOG).[31] The new grant used the "expected family contribution" as defined from the FAFSA forms rather than just family income. About 25 percent of all students who filed the FAFSA in Ohio received additional awards. In the 2006–7 school year, 11,095 students received higher awards under OCOG than they would have received under its predecessor. On average, the state, under the new program, had to increase its expenditure by roughly $860 per student for 11,095 students. Of those 11,095 students, roughly 220 changed their plans and stayed in college for an additional year. The rest either dropped out as they had planned or stayed in college as they had planned. The entire stream of benefits was realized by these 220 students.

My point is not that families' expected family contribution (EFC) is a "bad" targeting measure. It may indeed target needy families, but as we think of incremental changes in financial aid policies, improving the targeting would make the programs much more cost-effective. For example, suppose that we could identify which students were most likely to benefit from additional aid in the case of the changes in Ohio. Improving the targeting would essentially reduce the total number (11,095) that receive additional aid. The problem, of course, is that it is difficult to change a policy to make it more directed. First we have to identify specific characteristics which are closely linked to students' likelihood of being "marginal" students. Then we have to convince policymakers to alter policies to track these characteristics. Such targeting could be either illegal (e.g., if race or ethnicity were a predictive characteristic) or politically improbable (e.g., if targeting limited financial aid opportunities for middle-income families). Improved targeting is a largely unexplored topic, and it likely sounds simpler than it truly is. Nonetheless, if future studies and interventions are sensitive to the role of targeting, our knowledge of and capacity to use better targeting measures will also increase.

Enacting Change

If we know that there are successful programs, are there ways for us to improve the likelihood that students will choose to participate in these successful programs? And if we identify policies that are not cost-effective, how do we shift away from these programs?

One of the primary barriers to change is a lack of knowledge about the cost-effectiveness and specific mechanisms surrounding new programs. Among the policies which are listed above, few have been tested on more than a few hundred individuals. We do not know what the effects of these programs would be if the programs were scaled up. Moreover, the interventions that have been evaluated generally do not include rigorous cost-effectiveness analysis. More information about costs would be useful for projecting the potential for these interventions to be scaled up.

I have written this last paragraph as if conducting financial aid studies is a simple endeavor. Unfortunately it is not. Altering financial aid packages requires substantial resources. MDRC's performance-based financial awards were $2,000 per individual. To estimate a 3 percentage point effect on retention (assuming a base retention rate of 20% and 80% power), we would need close to 1,000 people in the study. While not everyone will accept and use the awards, expenditures could quickly rise as more people took up the financial aid offer. Alternatively, if we wanted to have the capability to measure a smaller effect or to measure the effects for a specific subsample, that would require an even greater financial outlay—and all of these costs ignore the expenses associated with the evaluation. Unfortunately, no single foundation can support such an intervention by itself. Given the large outlay, they could be reluctant to have so much of their portfolio tied up in a single, unproven intervention.

To date, the federal government and most states have been reluctant to, or have not had the means to, test new financial aid schemes. Given that the federal government and state governments control most financial aid expenditures, they may be in a unique position to test new financial aid products on a larger scale.

While thus far I have focused on implementing and scaling up new interventions, I have made two naïve assumptions. First, I have assumed that existing financial aid policies are changeable. I have assumed that they could either be replaced with a set of more effective policies or that they could be modified in meaningful ways. Second, I have assumed that the political opposition to such change is largely nonexistent.

Unfortunately, financial aid policies have a unique place in educational policy. Higher education plays an important role in economic mobility and success, and the most visible issue in higher education is its cost. Parents (and potential voters) are greatly concerned about the cost of education and want policymakers to adopt policies that help them provide opportunities for higher education to their children. Moreover, the perception that affordability has led to significant, persistent gaps in educational attainment across socioeconomic lines only reinforces the perceived need for aggressive financial aid policies. If the infrastructure for these aggressive policies relies on existing programs, it may be that the expected overall effect mimics the small effects we currently see in financial aid programs.

Can the federal government and individual states find ways to eliminate ineffective programs? One could argue that the prolonged period during which policymakers allowed the spending power of Pell Grants to erode could be a response to that program's perceived ineffectiveness in promoting retention. Yet, given that "perceived ineffectiveness" is still hotly debated among researchers, it is not clear that policymakers had greater insights into the effectiveness of such policies. The lack of growth in the benefits probably had more to do with political pressures than with a conscious assessment of the costs and benefits of the Pell program. However, the strategy of not allowing a program to keep up with inflation is a way to eventually kill it.

Another way to eliminate an ineffective program is to shift ownership of its costs. For example, one of William Bennett's often-cited criticisms of financial aid policies was that they may have created incentives for individual schools to increase tuition. Higher tuition influenced decisions to increase need-based awards, and the Bennett hypothesis supposes that institutions respond to increases in financial aid by increasing their tuition. A similar set of incentives may exist when considering the interactions of state and federal financial aid policies.

For example, consider a state which has adopted a costly and largely ineffective financial aid policy. If the policy is politically popular, it is extremely difficult for the state to eliminate the program. Now suppose that the federal government dramatically increases the generosity of the Pell Grant program. Then the state does not need to increase the generosity of its program. In fact, it could either reduce the size of grants or retard the growth of its program. Such a maneuver would allow the state to keep a politically popular program while greatly reducing its generosity and overall cost. If individual states do engage in such efforts to cannibalize increases in Federal Pell Grants, then increases in the Pell Grant schedule may actually be simple ways for the federal government to offset states' budgetary woes. In ongoing work, I am focusing on measuring the responsiveness of state aid programs to increases in the Federal Pell Grants.

Most of the rhetoric in the news and elsewhere focuses on tuition growth. But there are other costs that can be manipulated. A state that engages in significant tuition subsidies as its financial aid policy of choice may find ways to increase the fees associated with attendance. For example, after the introduction of the Georgia HOPE scholarship, the Georgia legislature limited schools' abilities to raise revenue by limiting the tuition growth allowed. Limiting tuition growth reduced the overall expenditure in the state. How did the universities respond? Long shows that the universities increased the rate at which other fees were increasing to compensate for the lost revenue from capped tuition growth.[32]

The Role of Financial Aid Policies

In the discussion here, I have been purposefully and deliberately critical about the potential of grant programs to increase college retention and completion. I am not advocating removal or elimination of any program. Rather, I am recommending that the federal and state grant programs receive more scrutiny from policymakers and academics. Given that the effects of financial aid programs are only now being identified, we know little about their cost-effectiveness. Moreover, the Pell Grant program could be an anchor that impedes policymakers from introducing or testing new forms of financial aid. If these new forms of financial aid are more cost-effective than existing forms, then such innovation could improve overall welfare.

It could be that states and the federal government already have plans for innovation. In the most basic courses on the economics of state and local public finance, economists teach students that states can be laboratories for potential national policies. States might be experimenting with new forms of aid; then, if those programs turn out to be mistakes, states may find ways to step back from expensive programs by "gaming" changes in the federal financial aid policies.

Nonetheless, to date, there are few if any who claim that current federal financial aid policies have done much to encourage degree completion or to reduce the gaps in attendance between socioeconomic groups. Over the past 40 years, completion has been relatively stagnant, especially when compared with the increases in the number of individuals attending college at all. Additionally, the gaps in attendance between the richest and poorest 20 percent of the population have changed little over this time period.

One topic that I have not explored here is the contrast between what people say and how they act. A number of studies show that individuals tend to cite their financial state as their primary reason for discontinuing college. While many people may have to leave school because of finances, the proportion who blame their finances is much larger and potentially a different population than the proportion who actually accept more generous need-based financial aid. More study on this is warranted. Is it really students' finances, or is this a convenient scapegoat for other causes of dropout? Are the additional resources which have been the focus of the studies to date insufficiently generous to cover the financial need? If the financial need is much larger than what these programs provide, then more generous policies are needed. However, with the current targeting mechanisms available in federal financial aid policies, expanding the generosity of these programs may not be cost-effective. The marginal benefit might not be sufficiently large to offset the cost of a large-scale expansion in the programs' financial aid offerings. To expand the amount offered, we need either to identify more cost-effective forms of financial aid or to find ways to target aid programs more effectively toward the marginal students.

NOTES

1. Sarah Turner, "Going to College and Finishing College: Explaining Different Educational Outcomes," in *College Choices: The Economics of Where to Go, When to Go, and How to Pay for It*, ed. Caroline M. Hoxby, National Bureau of Economic Research Conference Report (Chicago: University of Chicago Press, 2004), pp. 13–62.

2. David Deming and Susan Dynarski, "The Lengthening of Childhood," *Journal of Economic Perspectives* 22, no. 3 (Summer 2008): 71–92.

3. Organisation for Economic Co-operation and Development, *Education at a Glance, 2007* (Paris: OECD, 2007).

4. Edward P. St. John et al., "Economic Influences on Persistence Reconsidered," in *Reworking the Student Departure Puzzle*, ed. John Braxton (Nashville, TN: Vanderbilt University Press, 2000), pp. 29–47. See also Larry Leslie and Paul Brinkman's "Student Price Response in Higher Education: The Student Demand Studies," *Journal of Higher Education* 58, no. 2 (March–April 1987): 181–204.

5. A comprehensive review of financial aid programs is provided in David Deming and Susan Dynarski, "Into College, Out of Poverty? Policies to Increase the Postsecondary Attainment of the Poor" (NBER Working Paper no. 15387, National Bureau of Economic Research, Cambridge, MA, Sept. 2009), www .nber.org/papers/w15387; and Bridget Long, "The Effectiveness of Financial Aid in Improving College Enrollment: Lessons for Policy" (unpublished manuscript, Harvard University).

6. College Board, *Trends in Student Aid, 2010* (Washington, DC: College Board, 2010).

7. Leslie and Brinkman, "Student Price Response in Higher Education."

8. Thomas J. Kane, *The Price of Admission: Rethinking How Americans Pay for College* (Washington, DC: Brookings Institution, 1999); Ronald G. Ehrenberg and Daniel R. Sherman, "Optimal Financial Aid Policies for a Selective University," *Journal of Human Resources* 19, no. 2 (1984): 202–30.

9. Charles Manski and David Wise, *College Choice in America* (Cambridge: Harvard University Press, 1983); Lee W. Hansen, "The Impact of Student Financial Aid on Access," in *The Crisis in Higher Education*, ed. Joseph Froomkin (New York: Academy of Political Science, 1983), pp. 84–96; Thomas, J. Kane, "Lessons from the Largest School Voucher Program: Two Decades of Experience with Pell Grants," in *Who Chooses? Who Loses? Culture, Institutions and the Unequal Effects of School Choice*, ed. Bruce Fuller and Richard Elmore (New York: Teachers College Press, 1996).

10. Kane, *Price of Admission*; Ehrenberg and Sherman, "Optimal Financial Aid Policies for a Selective University"; Leslie and Brinkman, "Student Price Response in Higher Education."

11. Susan Dynarski, "Does Aid Matter? Measuring the Effect of Student Aid on College Attendance and Completion," *American Economic Review* 93, no. 1 (2003): 279–88.

12. Thomas J. Kane, "A Quasi-Experimental Estimate of the Impact of Financial Aid on College-Going" (NBER Working Paper no. 9703, National Bureau of Economic Research, Cambridge, MA, 2003), www.nber.org/papers/w9703.

13. Neil Seftor and Sarah Turner, "Back to School: Federal Student Aid Policy and Adult College Age Enrollment," *Journal of Human Resources* 37, no. 2 (2002): 336–52.

14. Susan Dynarski, "Hope for Whom? Financial Aid for the Middle Class and Its Impact on College Attendance" (NBER Working Paper no. 7756, National Bureau of Economic Research, Cambridge, MA, 2000), www.nber.org/papers/

w7756; Christopher Cornwell, David Mustard, and Deepa Sridhar, "The Enrollment Effects of Merit-Based Financial Aid: Evidence from Georgia's HOPE Program," *Journal of Labor Economics* 24, no. 4 (2006): 761–86.

15. Dynarski, "Does Aid Matter?"

16. Eric Bettinger, "How Financial Aid Affects Persistence," in Hoxby, *College Choices*, pp. 207–37.

17. Sara Goldrick-Rab, Douglas N. Harris, and Philip A. Trostel, "Why Financial Aid Matters (or Does Not) for College Success: Toward a New Interdisciplinary Perspective," in *Higher Education: Handbook of Theory and Research* 24, ed. J. C. Smart (New York: Springer Science + Business Media B.V., 2009).

18. Eric Bettinger, "Need-Based Aid and Student Outcomes: The Effects of the Ohio College Opportunity Grant" (unpublished paper, Stanford University School of Education, May 2010).

19. Susan Dynarski, "Building the Stock of College-Educated Labor," *Journal of Human Resources*, Summer 2008, pp. 576–610.

20. Leslie and Brinkman, "Student Price Response in Higher Education."

21. St. John et al., "Economic Influences on Persistence Reconsidered."

22. Sharan Merriam and Rosemary Caffarella, *Learning in Adulthood: A Comprehensive Guide* (San Francisco: Jossey-Bass, 1999); Vincent Tinto, *Leaving College: Rethinking the Causes and Cures of Student Attrition*, 2nd ed. (Chicago: University of Chicago Press, 1993).

23. Author's calculations with Beginning Postsecondary Students Longitudinal Study.

24. Bettinger, "Need-Based Aid and Student Outcomes."

25. David Deming and Susan Dynarski, "Into College, Out of Poverty? Policies to Increase the Postsecondary Attainment of the Poor," in *Targeting Investments in Children: Fighting Poverty When Resources Are Limited*, ed. Phil Levine and David Zimmerman (Ann Arbor, MI: National Bureau of Economic Research, 2009).

26. Bettinger, "Need-Based Aid and Student Outcomes."

27. See Thomas Brock et al. *Rewarding Persistence: Effects of a Performance-Based Scholarship Program for Low-Income Parents* (New York: MDRC, 2009).

28. Susan Dynarski, "Hope for Whom?"

29. Boris Palameta and Jean-Pierre Voyer, *Willingness to Pay for Postsecondary Education among Underrepresented Groups* (Toronto: Higher Education Quality Council of Ontario, 2010).

30. Eric Bettinger et al., "The Role of Simplification and Information in College Decisions: Results from the H&R Block FAFSA Experiment" (NBER Working Paper no. 15361, National Bureau of Economic Research, Cambridge, MA, 2009), www.nber.org/papers/w15361.

31. Bettinger, "Need-Based Aid and Student Outcomes."

32. Bridget T. Long, "How Have College Decisions Changed over Time? An Application of the Conditional Logistic Choice Model," *Journal of Econometrics* 121, nos. 1–2 (2004): 271–96.

CHAPTER SEVEN

Remediation

The Challenges of Helping Underprepared Students

BRIDGET TERRY LONG

Although nearly three-quarters of high school graduates eventually go on to higher education, many are not prepared for the college curriculum. Research suggests that only 32 percent of all students leave high school ready to study college-level material, and the proportion academically prepared for higher education is even smaller among black and Hispanic students (20% and 16%, respectively).[1] Given that academic preparation is an important predictor of success in college, these students are often placed into remedial or developmental courses.[2] The classes are designed to address academic deficiencies and prepare students for subsequent college success. Estimates suggest that one-third or more of first-year students are required to take remedial courses in reading, writing, or mathematics.[3]

While remediation plays an increasingly important role in higher education, surprisingly little is understood about the effects of remediation on student outcomes and how to make the courses effective. There are also growing debates about how to best offer and regulate the courses. Perhaps due to a lack of best practices, states vary widely in where they offer and how they handle remedial and developmental programs. As many states and institutions look for cost-effective ways to deal with the increasing numbers of underprepared students who enter higher education each year, many are considering ways to limit remediation, shift its location, or pass on its costs to students or high school districts. For example, at least eight states, including Florida and Illinois, restrict remediation to two-year institutions; and several other states are currently considering such policies. States such as Texas, Tennessee, and Utah have imposed or are considering limits on the government funding of remedial coursework.[4] States are also implementing various policies in the effort to help students avoid college remediation.

This chapter examines how reforming remediation might facilitate the national goal to increase degree attainment. We will look at the basic facts about remediation—the students who need it, how it is organized, and how much it costs—as well as the major debates surrounding remediation. I review the research on what is known about the effects of remediation on student outcomes and then consider how to make remediation work, given current research on reforming and improving remediation programs.

Basic Facts about Remediation

The Students

During the twentieth century, the increased demand for higher education by students from all backgrounds accelerated the need for remediation in higher education. According to a 1996 study by the National Center for Education Statistics (NCES), 81 percent of public four-year colleges and all two-year colleges were offering remediation by 1995. The increasing numbers of students entering colleges unprepared for college-level material is reflected in the growing numbers required to take remedial courses. In that study, 39 percent of colleges surveyed reported that remedial enrollments had increased during the previous five years. Other colleges chose to expel rather than educate students with severe academic deficiencies. For instance, during the fall of 2001, the California State University system "kicked out more than 2,200 students—nearly 7 percent of the freshman class—for failing to master basic English and math skills."[5]

The students in remedial education come from two major groups. One group is composed of underprepared recent high school graduates, many of whom exit secondary school without grade-level competency or the proper preparation for college-level material. The need for remediation in college is closely tied to a student's high school curriculum. A 2002 study by the Ohio Board of Regents found that students who had completed an academic core curriculum in high school were half as likely to need remediation in college as students lacking this core training.[6] Similarly, studies by Cliff Adelman emphasize the importance of academic preparation in high school for success in college.[7]

However, completion of a high school core curriculum does not ensure that a student will avoid remediation in college. Many students who complete upper-level math courses in high school still require math remediation courses or need to repeat subjects in college.[8] The need for students who are supposedly academically prepared to take remediation suggests that the problem is larger than just poor high school course selection or the lack of a college-prep curriculum at some schools. High school rigor is certainly a concern. In addition, misalignment between the material defined as necessary by high schools and the competencies colleges require has been well documented.[9]

In addition to recent high school graduates, a substantial number of adult students enroll in developmental courses. Many of these are workers who have been displaced by structural shifts in the labor market and are seeking developmental courses to acquire the skills necessary for re-employment. Others in this group of adults are recent immigrants or welfare recipients. Nationally, about 27 percent of remedial students in 1998 were over the age of 30.[10]

The Colleges: The Organization and Delivery of Remedial Education

In most college systems, the purpose of remedial education is to provide underprepared students the skills necessary to complete and succeed in higher education. In addition, remediation may serve several institutional needs. First, it allows colleges to offer access to growing numbers of students. It also provides individual departments, especially English and math departments, the ability to generate enrollment. Moreover, by separating weaker students into remedial courses, remediation allows colleges to protect institutional selectivity, regulate entry to upper-level courses, and maintain the research functions of the college. Finally, remediation may serve as a tool to integrate students into the school population.[11]

The bulk of remediation is provided by nonselective public institutions, the point of entry for 80 percent of four-year students and virtually all two-year students. At some colleges, remedial courses are offered institution-wide; in others, the courses are within individual departments. Another option for institutions and states is to outsource remediation. At one point, Maryland and New York experimented with outsourcing remediation courses to private vendors—companies like Kaplan and Sylvan—but now such private contractors offer software and other teaching aids for remedial education rather than teaching classes.[12]

Because the average college student attends a nonselective institution to which he or she is almost ensured admission, the remediation placement exam that the student takes when first arriving on campus has become the key academic gatekeeper to postsecondary study. As Michael Kirst notes, since admission is virtually certain, the student's first hurdle is the placement test.[13] Nationally, the most widely-used placement exams are the Computerized Adaptive Placement Assessment and Support Systems (COMPASS) and the Assessment of Skills for Successful Entry and Transfer (ASSET), each published by ACT, and the ACCUPLACER, developed by the College Board. The tests consist of a variety of items that measure students' skill level. For example, the ASSET exam is a written test with as many as 12 subsections, including in-depth assessment of students' writing, numerical, and reading skills. While most students who need remediation are identified using these placement exams in reading, writing, and mathematics, some schools also use standardized test scores and high school transcripts to make assignments. After students have taken the placement exam, colleges assign them to specific math courses, often remedial courses, on the basis of their scores. Typically, administrators use "hard" cutoffs to make these designations: students scoring below a given threshold are assigned to a remedial course.

Placement into math remediation is more common than placement into English remediation (reading and/or writing), but participation in English remediation may be more important, as some evidence suggests that reading and writing deficiencies have more negative effects on a student's success. Remedial courses are often the gateway for students to enroll in college-level courses. Nationally, about two-thirds of campuses restrict enrollment in some classes until remediation is complete, and most schools prohibit students from taking college-level courses in the remedial subject area until remediation is complete.[14] Some go even further by barring students from taking any college-level work while enrolled in remediation.[15] Campuses do vary, however, in the extent to which they *require* versus *suggest* that underprepared students enroll in remedial or developmental work.

To the extent that remediation restricts students' class schedules and affects the classes they can take, it may also discourage them from focusing on certain majors and have major effects on the length of time a degree takes. For example, some majors are extremely demanding in terms of required credit hours and have little leeway for students to enroll in nonrequired classes. A student in remediation may have to take one or two semesters of preparatory classes before starting the courses for a major. While most colleges and universities offer academic credit for remedial courses, most do not allow remedial credits to count toward degree completion.

The Costs of Remediation

The true total cost of remediation is unknown, but some national estimates suggest an annual cost of over $2 billion.[16] In 2006, the Alliance for Excellent Education concluded that the cost of remediation was $2.8 billion, half of this in the form of direct costs and half in the form of what the nation loses in earning potential because remedial students are more likely to drop out of college without a degree. We do not have an accurate number because most states have few data on which to base assessments. A few states have studied this issue, however.

Ohio funded a detailed case study of the costs of providing remediation in that state. In 2000, Ohio public colleges spent approximately $15 million teaching 260,000 credit hours of high school–level courses to freshmen; another $8.4 million was spent on older students.[17] These figures only take into account state subsidies—the instructional subsidies that Ohio offers for courses granting academic credit. The additional costs associated with items such as tuition expenditures, financial aid resources, and lost wages are not included in this estimate. The cost of remediation for the 20,000 freshmen in the state amounted to an additional $15 million in tuition.

Texas also provides estimates of the cost of remediation at its public higher education institutions. In 2007 the Texas legislature appropriated $206 million in general revenue funds for the instructional costs of developmental education in state schools. (Private colleges and universities were not included.) The cost per semester credit hour varied by institution type. The Legislative Budget Board found that the average cost per credit hour was $256 at Texas public universities, $152 at public community colleges, and $189 at state technical colleges.[18] Along with the direct costs of remediation, a 2005 study by Hammons estimates that Texas loses over $13.6 billion annually in lower earnings potential, poor worker productivity, and increased spending on social programs.[19]

While remediation is expensive, it may be relatively less expensive to provide than other college courses. According to a 1998 study by the Arkansas Department of Higher Education, remedial education is less costly than or approximately the same as core academic programs. An analysis of expenditure data in 1996–97 found that the direct and indirect costs per full-time equivalent (FTE) student were $7,381 for remediation at four-year colleges and $6,709 at two-year colleges.[20] In comparison, the cost of core programs ranged from $7,919 to $12, 369 at the four-year colleges and $6,163 to $8,235 at the two-year colleges. The two primary reasons for the cost differences were larger class sizes and the higher prevalence of adjunct, lower-paid instructors in remedial courses.[21] Price Waterhouse found similar results examining the City University of New York (CUNY) system during 1996–97, which spent $124 million on re-mediation that year. The cost of remediation courses was approximately one-third less than the cost of other academic courses. Two-thirds of the costs for remediation were covered by tuition and student aid, with city and state funding providing for the rest.[22]

While the expense associated with remediation is quite high, the so-cial costs of not offering remediation are likely to be much larger than the institutional costs of the programs. Unskilled individuals generate expenses such as those associated with unemployment costs, government dependency, crime, and incarceration. Moreover, the increasing demands of the economy for more skilled workers encourages the nation to find an effective way to train its workers.

The Policy Debates

Given the significant costs of remediation, and the fact that many view remedial courses as double payment for skills that should have been ob-tained in high school, states and higher education institutions continually question whether they should cover any or all of the costs of remedial education.[23] In their consideration of reform, however, many policymak-ers have focused on reducing costs rather than searching for ways to improve remedial programs. Some states have decided to limit where remediation can happen or how much students can take. This section outlines some of the major policy debates and decisions.

Where Should Remediation Happen?

One major question is who should offer remedial courses. Nearly every state has taken the responsibility to offer some kind of remediation. How-ever, the states differ in which public institutions offer the courses. While many offer remedial courses at either their two- and four-year institu-tions, an increasing number limit the classes to only their two-year institutions. Even among former group, three states have some limitation imposed concerning remediation at the four-year institutions. These decisions are partly justified by the lower cost of offering courses at community colleges.

Florida was the first state to limit remediation at public colleges and universities to the two-year schools (with the exception of historically black colleges) in 1985. This type of policy shift has been much more visible in other states in recent years. In particular, New York's decision to phase out most remedial education within the CUNY four-year system in 1999 generated a great deal of debate and press. Starting in 1999, students have had to go through a two-step admissions process. First, they may be granted provisional admission based on high school grades and other nontest measures. Then, students must demonstrate "skills proficiency" with SAT scores or Regents test scores. Students who are unable to pass this second hurdle and require remediation are not accepted until they complete the remedial work at a community college and pass the CUNY/ACT Basic Skills Tests.[24]

More recently, a number of states—including Arizona, Florida, Montana, South Carolina, and Virginia—have decided to prohibit their in-state public universities from offering remediation education. For example, Virginia law mandates that community colleges should handle remedial education. Four-year public institutions therefore are expected to make arrangements with community colleges to handle the remediation of students accepted for admission. Virginia's private colleges are not affected by this requirement.[25] In North Carolina, the state legislature passed a law in 2001 (which was amended in 2003) that banned schools within the University of North Carolina (UNC) system from offering remedial education.[26] Instead, institutions were instructed to refer students to other schools to complete their remedial coursework. Since 1992, schools within the UNC system had been allowed to enter into contracts with community colleges; others have been encouraged to do so "when it improves the cost effectiveness or educational value of remedial coursework."[27]

California is another state that has moved towards concentrating remediation in the community college system. The University of California system does not officially offer remedial instruction, although some UC campuses have contracted with community colleges or folded their remedial classes into regular courses.[28] However, the California State University system did offer remediation without limitations until 1996, when the legislature passed laws whose intent was to reduce the number of incoming students in need of remediation to less than 10 percent.[29] Although the original goal was to begin denying admission to a CSU campus to students who needed remedial courses in 2001, the plan was quickly revised with a 2007 target instead. Since initiating the plan, CSU has done several things to reduce the need for remedial education. For example, the system offers more summer remedial education programs, has tried to strengthen teacher preparation, and is attempting to set clearer standards and communicate them to students, parents, and schools to ensure that graduates meet university admission requirements. The goal is to require recent high school graduates to demonstrate college-level skills in English and mathematics as a condition of admission.[30] This is part of a larger effort in California to encourage students to complete their remediation at two-year colleges before entering the four-year system.[31]

Other states continue to debate the possible benefits of limiting remediation at public institutions to the two-year colleges. With this movement away offering remediation at four-year institutions, an important question is what effects restricting remedial services to community colleges will have on student outcomes. By shifting the locus of remediation, states could change enrollment patterns, and eventual degree completion could fall as a result: research suggests community college students, perhaps because of a lack of resources, do not perform as well as similar students who initially enter four-year institutions.[32]

Should States Limit or Shift the Costs of Remediation?

There are other kinds of limitations that states and institutions could impose on the provision of remediation. Some states put a ceiling on the percentage of remedial students that an institution can accept. Other states and institutions impose limits on the amount of time students have to complete remedial courses or on the number of times a student can repeat a remedial course. These types of restrictions can also have important implications for students.

One state that has chosen to limit the number of students with remedial needs who can be admitted to a public university is Massachusetts. In a 1998 report, the Massachusetts Board of Higher Education voiced the opinion that developmental education should be a primary function of the two-year public college and not four-year institutions.

Therefore, it imposed a 5 percent cap on the enrollment of freshmen in remedial courses in four-year institutions.[33] The cap has been increased to 10 percent; students above that percentage are referred to community colleges.[34] Similarly, in Georgia, there has been some movement towards reducing the number of students in remediation, particularly within the University of Georgia system.[35]

Some institutions and states impose time limits. For example, Texas limits both the number of developmental credits that students can take and the number of levels of remediation can be offered by an institution. The Texas Success Initiative states that legislative appropriations may not be used for developmental coursework taken by a student in excess of "18 semester credit hours, for a general academic teaching institution," and "27 semester credit hours, for a public junior college, public technical institute, or public state college."[36] Other states limit the number of remedial courses that can be taken. California community colleges limit "precollegiate basic skills" courses to 30 semester or 45 quarter credits, except for ESL students or those with "verified learning disabilities."[37] In Georgia, students who do not meet the minimum standards for college-level work within the University of Georgia system are placed into Learning Support classes. However, only a maximum of 12 semester hours, or three semesters (whichever occurs first), may be taken in any area. If students do not meet this requirement, they are suspended for three years, pending an appeal.[38]

Another way states and university systems limit remediation is to not allow students to repeat remedial courses if they do not pass the first time. In Florida, for instance, in 1997 the state legislature imposed a penalty on students who enroll more than once in a remedial course. According to analysis by the Division of Community Colleges, this policy significantly reduced the percentage of students who retook courses. Senate Bill 1974, passed in 1999, amended the law to increase the number of times state funding would support students repeating a course to two. The current policy is that students pay the regular tuition price for the first two attempts of a remedial course. If they need to take the class a third time, they must pay the full costs of instruction, which are four times the regular tuition amount.[39]

Efforts to limit remediation, either in where is it offered or in how much is allowed, could have the effect of pressuring high school students to prepare better for college while pushing programs and college students to be more efficient with their time. However, such effects are unlikely because of poor information among students about these efforts and, importantly, because there is no clear evidence on how to build a successful remediation program. Therefore, while policymakers lament the problems of remediation, many of the efforts described above do little to reduce remediation rates or improve programs. Instead of moving forward the conversation on how to "fix" remediation, the policies being debated are orthogonal to the research and practice focused on identifying strategies to make remediation more effective.

Does Remediation Work?
Remedial versus Nonremedial Students

Remedial classes are designed to address academic deficiencies and prepare students for subsequent college success. They may improve student persistence by teaching material that students have not yet mastered. Students with similar deficiencies who are not in remediation may never gain a sufficient academic foundation and may be more likely to drop out. Remedial courses may also provide a safe environment in which students receive other kinds of support that could increase their chances of degree completion. Yet, there are several reasons that remedial courses may in fact have the opposite effect. By increasing the number of requirements and extending the time to a credential, remediation may lower the likelihood of degree completion. The literature also suggests that the stigma associated with remediation may also negatively impact students. Remedial courses may also lead to negative peer effects; similar students who are not placed into remediation might benefit from positive peer interactions with higher-ability students in nonremedial classes.[40]

While the use of remedial courses by postsecondary institutions is widespread, states and colleges know little about whether their remediation programs are successful along any dimension. Few states have exit standards for remedial courses, and only a small percentage have performed any systematic evaluation of their programs. One major problem has been a lack of good data; studies that have been able to overcome the information barrier often focus on one particular institution. Moreover, most of the research on remediation simply compares students in remediation with those not in the courses. Not surprisingly, these studies find that remedial students, who have less preparation, are less likely to succeed than their peers. Because students who are placed in remedial courses differ from those who are not placed into remediation, one would expect these students to be less likely to persist and complete a degree, even in the absence of remediation. Therefore, one must develop a way to separate the effects of lower preparation from the effects of being placed in a remedial course. Moreover, placement in remediation might differ as a result of college choice: a student wishing to avoid remediation might choose a college with a very low placement cutoff. Placement also differs by socioeconomic status, as wealthier students are more likely to repeat remediation exams in order to have additional chances of passing out of the courses.[41]

Does Remediation Work for Marginally Ready Students?

The recent availability of new data sources has prompted several large-scale studies that attempt to address these selection problems to get to an apples-to-apples comparison of students placed in remediation with *similar* students not in the courses. In 2005 and 2009 studies, Eric Bettinger and I used an instrumental variable strategy that combines between-college variation in remediation placement policies and the importance of distance in college choice to estimate the causal effect of remedial courses on higher education outcomes in Ohio.[42] This sort of comparison is possible in that state because institutional policies regarding remediation differ across the public colleges and universities. Therefore, two students with the same characteristics face dissimilar probabilities of remediation if they attend different schools. The 2009 analysis focused on degree-seeking, traditional-age, full-time undergraduates who initially entered a public college in fall 1998.[43] Our results suggest that remedial students at Ohio colleges are more likely to persist in college and complete a bachelor's degree than are students with similar test scores and backgrounds who are not required to take the courses.[44] These results support the assertion that remediation is a way to improve the chances of degree completion.

Another way to research the effects of remediation is to use a regression discontinuity methodology. Assuming that students who score just above and below the placement cutoff have nearly similar ability, especially because of the noise inherent in such tests, one can obtain a causal estimate of the effects of remedial placement on subsequent outcomes for those students at the margins of passing.[45] Juan Carlos Calcagno and I used this strategy in a 2008 study to examine the effects of remediation in Florida.[46] The results suggest that remediation might promote early persistence in college, but it does not necessarily help community college students make long-term progress towards a degree.[47] The impacts for math and reading remediation were positive in terms of total credits earned but no statistically significant difference was found in terms of total college-level (nonremedial) credits earned. Paco Martorell and Isaac McFarlin, in a 2011 study, used a similar method to examine the impact of remediation in Texas.[48] They also found that remediation had little effect on persistence and degree completion, along with a range of other educational outcomes. In addition, they found no effect on labor market earnings. Generally, their estimates were small and statistically insignificant.

The conflicting results from these studies suggest that the causal effects of remedial courses on student outcomes are mixed at best for students at the margin of passing out of remediation. However, it is puzzling that the estimated effects differ so much. One reason for the differences across studies could be variation in where states locate the cutoff for placement into remediation. Another possible explanation is that each study focused on different student populations. Calcagno and I included nearly the entire universe of first-time degree-seeking students in Florida. Meanwhile, Bettinger and I focused on traditional-age college students at two- and four-year public institutions, and Martorell and McFarlin limited their analysis to students who took all three placement exams (math, reading, and writing) and passed the writing section. Many educational interventions have had varying effects on students of different genders, races, and other demographic characteristics; and so it is plausible, as discussed below, that remedial courses could also have varying effects on different kinds of students.

Do the Effects Differ by Type of Student?

In additional work focusing on Florida, Juan Carlos Calcagno and I indeed find that the effects of remediation differ by student background and demographics.[49] Women experienced more positive effects from placement into remediation than men. This finding could relate to other differences documented by gender, such as learning styles, levels of engagement, or amount of study time—and this may give clues as to why remediation works for some but not others. However, the gender difference is also consistent with many other studies that have found women and girls to be more positively influenced by interventions.[50] Women also have higher degree completion rates, but it is unclear whether remediation plays any role in this difference. It is also curious that women assigned to developmental courses earned fewer nonremedial college-level credits than their female counterparts not assigned, thereby suggesting again that remediation does not have an overall positive effect.

Another interesting pattern is that older students placed into remediation realized more positive effects in a host of outcomes than younger students in remediation. This result could suggest that the outlook of the student is important to the potential impact of being assigned to developmental courses. Older students may be more focused, or ready to take advantage of "refresher" courses or the opportunity to "catch up." It could also be that older students have a greater need for developmental courses because they have been out of high school for a longer period. Therefore, older students who score high enough to just barely pass out of remediation might benefit from taking the courses regardless of placement status.

Income level also appears to be related to the effectiveness of remediation. Pell Grant recipients in remediation experienced more negative outcomes in terms of persistence, completion of associate's degrees, transfer rates, and credits earned. Because income is often highly correlated with high school quality, the underlying cause of these differences may be preparation. However, it may also be that affordability interacts with performance in remediation and afterwards. While these low-income students receive the Pell Grant, usually it does not cover the full costs of their educations. The patterns suggest that there should be further investigation of the interaction of financial need and experiences within and after remediation.

Do the Effects Differ by Level of Prior Preparation?

The studies mentioned above focused on students just on the margin of needing remediation courses. Little is known about the effects of remediation on students with much lower levels of preparation. Research that Angela Boatman and I have conducted expands the literature by examining the impact of remedial and developmental courses on the academic outcomes of students with varying preparation levels.[51] We focused on students who began at a public college or university in Tennessee in fall 2000. Because of the state's multitiered system, in which students could be assigned into one of four levels of math and one of three levels of reading or writing (remedial, developmental, or college-level courses), we were able to examine the effects of multiple levels of remediation, from students who need only one course to those who need several courses.

The results suggest that the impact of remedial and developmental courses on academic persistence is tied to the level of student preparation. As we saw with some of the studies discussed above, the largest negative effects were found for students on the margin of needing remediation: by comparison with their peers in college-level courses, students assigned to remedial courses were less likely to complete a college degree in six years. However, at the lower end of the academic ability spectrum, the negative effects of remediation were much smaller and sometimes positive. In the writing courses, Boatman and I found positive effects for those placed in lower-level courses. For example, students in the lowest levels of remedial writing persisted through college and attained degrees at higher rates than their peers in the next highest level course. These results suggest that the effects of remediation do differ by preparation level and that more, rather than less, remediation could be beneficial for students with weaker preparation. This study and others suggest that writing (or English) remediation has more positive effects than math remediation.[52]

What Else Do We Need to Know?

The existing research suggests that the effects of remediation are far more nuanced than a single effect experienced by all students. In essence, remedial and developmental courses appear to help or hinder students differently by state, institution, background, and level of academic preparedness. Therefore, states and schools need not treat remediation as a singular policy but instead should consider it as an intervention that might vary in its impact according to student needs. The results also present an interesting puzzle about why remedial and developmental courses have such different effects.

Understanding the reasons for the differences could spur some insight into how to make *all* developmental and remedial courses effective. The often negative effects found for students at the margin of needing remediation may also suggest that remediation is not needed for as many students as are currently placed in such courses. On the other hand, given the low levels of persistence and degree completion at many colleges, institutions need to find better ways to support the academic needs of their students. It may also be that some colleges and universities are more successful than others in helping underprepared students owing to differences in how they offer and teach their remedial and developmental courses. Future research needs to take a more critical look to identify which institutions do the best job.

Making Remediation Work

The research on remediation and how to improve it is still in its infancy. Still, there are many hypotheses about how to make remediation work. There are also some promising interventions currently being implemented that could provide direction. Some focus on figuring out ways to improve instruction, give students additional support, or accelerate the remediation process so that students are not delayed from accumulating college credits. This section considers these strategies and programs.

What Are the Best Practices for Colleges and Universities?

While the above results give a general sense of the impact of remediation, it may be that certain types of instruction and support are more beneficial than others. Research is needed to identify which practices are the most effective in remediation programs. The literature highlights factors that *might* matter in the success of a remediation program. According to a 1995 review of studies, these factors include clearly specified goals and objects, a high degree of structure, the provision of counseling and tutoring components, and the use of a variety of approaches and methods in instruction.[53] A more recent review of the literature confirms that little rigorous research exists to document best practices in remedial or developmental education. The authors conclude that the most promising strategies are to help students build their skills in high school, integrate remedial students into college-level courses, and provide opportunities for the development of skills for the workforce.[54] However, far more work is needed to compare the relative effectiveness of different models of delivery.

One factor on which current reformers have focused is the placement process itself. There is a lack of consensus on what it means to be prepared for college-level work, and consequently, there are differing views of what would necessitate placing a student in a remedial or developmental course. Even when there seems to be agreement about what skills are needed for higher education, translating those benchmarks into assessments has resulted in a variety of tools. As noted above, states vary a great deal in the types of instruments used and cutoffs imposed to determine placement into remediation. Remedial courses may be more or less effective for certain parts of the testing distribution, and so the placement of the cutoff could be an important determinant of the impact of the courses.

In a 2005 report, Heath Prince summarizes arguments for more standardized and consistent testing instruments and cutoff scores. He asserts that introducing policies that are "more consistent and predictable" would help to "establish a common definition of academic proficiency . . . which could accelerate the alignment of secondary and postsecondary academic requirements and expectations and enable colleges to send clear signals to high schools about the preparation students need to be college-ready."[55] In addition, he argues that more consistent policies would improve states' ability to track and evaluate their programs. Having a mandatory policy might also facilitate transfer, as students would be able to avoid duplication and arbitrary placement if they transferred to another institution in the state. However, even if standardization is preferred, it is not clear which assessment or assessments should be used and where the threshold for remediation should be drawn.

Other avenues for reform include examining how instructors (including adjunct faculty) are used and professional development for instructors.[56] One reason remedial courses tend to be less costly than college-level classes is that the inputs are cheaper: adjunct instructors are more likely to be used than full-time faculty, and class sizes have been larger. Yet, some research suggests that students who have adjuncts as instructors do worse in terms of educational outcomes. Moreover, larger class sizes, especially for students with academic needs who have already had past trouble engaging with material, could be detrimental to progress. Some institutions are thinking much more deliberately about how remedial courses are offered and conducted, in terms of instruction, pedagogy, format, and size.

Using Learning Communities in Remedial Courses

One model that may be beneficial in a remediation program is that of learning communities. In learning communities, students are organized into cohorts that take paired remedial and academic courses, such as a remedial writing course linked with an entry-level psychology course. In 2002, a report by the National Survey of First-Year Academic Practices found that 62 percent of responding colleges enrolled at least some cohorts of students into a learning community, although most of these programs involved only a small portion of students.[57] The use of learning communities is currently one of the fastest growing and most prominent approaches to remediation.

Proponents of learning communities suggest several reasons that this approach may be more effective than traditional models of teaching in helping students with low basic skill levels. Linking a course like remedial English with a course in a student's major may make the material more engaging and motivate the student to work harder. Students in learning communities are challenged to view course material from different perspectives, thereby building critical thinking skills and deepening their understanding of it. Finally, students in learning communities have the opportunity to form deeper ties with their peers and with faculty, thereby strengthening their support networks and their attachment to the institution.

Despite widespread enthusiasm for the learning community model, research analyzing its effectiveness as an instruction model is remarkably thin, as indeed is research on remediation in general. Vincent Tinto, in 1997 and 1998 studies, found positive results at LaGuardia Community College and Seattle Central Community College by comparing students who voluntarily enrolled in learning communities with students who did not.[58] More recently, MDRC conducted a random assignment evaluation of a learning communities program at Kingsborough Community College in Brooklyn as part of its Opening Doors Demonstration. The authors in this evaluation found that "relative to a control group of students in regular classes, students in the learning community moved more quickly through developmental English requirements, took and passed more courses, and earned more credits in their first semester." The evidence was much more mixed on whether the program increased college persistence. According to the MDRC report, "Initially the program did not change the rate at which students reenrolled. In the last semester of the report's two-year follow-up period, however, slightly more program group members than control group members attended college."[59] Further evaluation is needed to determine the effects of learning communities on academic achievement and persistence, particularly for students entering college with low basic skills.

Redesigning Remediation Courses: The Tennessee Example

Other institutions have tried much more drastic changes to their remedial offerings. In the fall of 2007, the Tennessee Board of Regents initiated a redesign of remediation using grants from the National Center for Academic Transformation (NCAT).[60] During the 2008–9 academic year, the state began piloting redesigns of the instructional approaches at four community colleges, with the goal of allowing students to spend less time in remedial courses. At these institutions, remedial courses are taught using technology to enable students to work at their own pace and focus on the particular skills in which they are deficient. These courses are tailored much more to students' specific needs and academic deficiencies.

Administrators and policymakers are optimistic that these types of changes can greatly improve student learning and long-term outcomes. Current evaluations simply report the remedial pass rates and test scores of students before course redesign and after, not accounting for the selection of students for these courses and the differences that may have occurred over time. Therefore, much more research is needed to determine whether this is a promising, cost-effective way to improve remediation. Moreover, previous research has looked only at a very limited list of outcomes. However, the pilots were found to improve course completion rates (as measured by a final grade of C or better), as well as reduce the instructional costs on average by 36 percent. The Tennessee Board of Regents plans to expand its redesigns for developmental courses, and by 2013 all its community colleges must have in place programs that have technology as an integral part and must focus on helping students master remedial subjects at their own pace.

Avoiding the Need for Remediation

Some states and institutions are trying to avoid the need for remediation altogether through the use of early placement testing. Such programs administer remediation placement exams to high school students in order to provide students with early signals that they may lack competencies critical to success in a postsecondary institution. These exams are usually administered during the 10th or 11th grade. The tests are designed to improve the information high school students have regarding their preparation for college and to encourage those who fall short to take additional coursework in their senior year. With their teachers, counselors, and parents, students can then determine what courses to take while still in high school in order to avoid college remediation. With costs considerably less than college remediation, early placement testing programs may be a much more affordable way to address the problem of preparation for some students; Ohio estimates the cost of the early testing program to improve a student's college math skills is $17.[61]

The earliest use of early placement testing was in Ohio in 1978. It began as an experimental program between one high school in Columbus and an Ohio State University math professor. Today, the Early Mathematics Placement Testing (EMPT) program is supported by the Ohio Board of Regents, with funding from the Ohio legislature. It remains closely tied to the Ohio State University math department, although all of Ohio's state-supported four-year universities, and some two-year and private colleges, have been incorporated into the program. On the other hand, the program has little connection with K–12 systems; and participation by high schools is voluntary, limited, and variable from year to year. For example, between the 2003–4 and 2004–5 school years, participation fell from 261 to 231 high schools.[62] Still, an evaluation found that participation in the EMPT program had a significant effect on mathematics placement at the college level; the evaluation further concluded that the program effectively reduced remediation. Students who participated in EMPT were more likely to place higher in math upon entering Ohio State University and less likely to require remediation.[63] Since 1978, at least 12 states have followed Ohio's example and implemented similar programs.

In California, the Early Assessment Program (EAP) provides high school juniors with information about their academic readiness for coursework at California State University campuses. One study by Jessica Howell, Michal Kurlaender, and Eric Grodsky examined the effects of the program as offered in spring 2004. Fifteen optional multiple-choice questions were added to each of the mandatory California Standards Tests in 11th-grade English and mathematics. Students who opted to complete those questions then received a letter the summer before their senior year denoting their performance level and providing advice about what courses to take in their senior year. They were also directed to additional resources to improve their readiness for college coursework. In an evaluation of the program, Howell, Kurlaender, and Grodsky found that "participation in the Early Assessment Program reduces the average student's probability of needing remediation at California State University by 6.1

percentage points in English and 4.1 percentage points in mathematics." They concluded that EAP increased students' academic preparation in high school and did not discourage poorly prepared students from applying.[64] This suggests that such programs have promise in reducing the need for remediation but that the framing of the information given to students is important.

Conclusion

For the past several decades, the United States has focused on increasing access to higher education, with the promise of substantial private benefits for the individual and public benefits for society. The reality is that many students seeking the benefits of a college degree are not academically prepared for college-level coursework. Remediation has grown to address this gap, allowing for the continued expansion of college access with the hope of giving students the foundational skills necessary to persist to degree completion.

It is questionable, however, whether remediation is currently living up to that hope; the little research available gives mixed estimates on whether remediation is working at all. There are also many unanswered questions about how and, more importantly, why the effects of remediation differ across students and institutions. For the 30 to 40 percent of first-year students who are placed in the courses, remediation can serve to delay the accumulation of college credits and prolong the pathway to completion. Many never complete their remedial coursework, thereby ending their pursuit of a postsecondary credential. "Fixing" remediation by identifying and developing better ways to conduct the courses is therefore essential to increasing educational attainment.

Of course, as the main gateway to college-level courses, especially given that most students attend nonselective institutions, remediation is a significant cost to taxpayers, institutions, and students. Debates about limiting or restricting remediation are therefore understandable, but they can be counterproductive to the goal of increasing degree attainment. As noted in a *Time* magazine article, eliminating remediation in higher education could "effectively end the American experiment with mass postsecondary education."[65] The low levels of academic preparation inherited by higher education are certainly a challenge, but solutions need to be found to address the problem if the country is serious about raising graduation rates. With only half of students completing their college degrees, to increase in degree completion we must figure out ways to address the needs and concerns of students in the bottom half of the distribution, most of whom are placed into remediation. By helping students gain the skills they need to succeed in college-level courses through the most cost- and time-effective methods, improved models of remediation could contribute significantly to the nation's goals of increasing educational attainment.

NOTES

1. Jay Greene and Greg Foster, *Public High School Graduation and College Readiness Rates in the United States* (Manhattan Institute, Center for Civic Information, Education Working Paper no. 3, Sept. 2003), define being minimally college-ready as (1) graduating from high school; (2) having taken four years of English, three years of math, and two years of science, social science, and foreign language; and (3) demonstrating basic literacy skills by scoring at least 265 on the reading portion of the National Assessment of Educational Progress (NAEP).

2. In this chapter, I refer to all types of below-college-level courses as remedial or developmental. This includes "basic-skills training" and "nontraditional coursework" as well as developmental or remedial courses with other names. I acknowledge that different areas of the country and stakeholders may have other preferred names.

3. National Center for Education Statistics, *Remedial Education at Degree-Granting Postsecondary Institutions in Fall 2000* (Washington DC: Department of Education, 2003); Eric Bettinger and Bridget Terry Long, "Addressing the Needs of Underprepared College Students: Does College Remediation Work?" *Journal of Human Resources* 44, no. 3 (Summer 2009): 736–71.

4. Education Commission of the States, "Recent State Policies/Activities: Postsecondary Success—Developmental/Remediation," Sept. 2003, www.ecs.org/ecs/ecscat.nsf/WebTopicPS?OpenView&count=1&RestrictToCategory=Postseco ndary+Success--Developmental/Remediation.

5. National Center for Education Statistics, *Remedial Education at Higher Education Institutions in Fall 1995* (Washington, DC: NCES, 1996); Rebecca Trounson, "Cal State Ouster Rate Rises Slightly," *Los Angeles Times*, Jan. 31, 2002.

6. Ohio Board of Regents, "The Preparedness of Recent High School Graduates Entering Ohio's State-Supported Colleges and Universities," *Ohio's High School Students Go to College, 2002: Profile of Student Outcomes and Experiences* (Columbus: Ohio Board of Regents, 2002).

7. Clifford Adelman, *Answers in the Toolbox: Academic Intensity, Attendance Patterns, and Bachelor's Degree Attainment* (Washington, DC: U.S. Department of Education, Office of Educational Research and Improvement, 1999); Clifford

Adelman, *The Toolbox Revisited: Paths to Degree Completion from High School through College* (Washington, DC: U.S. Department of Education, 2006).

8. For example, 25% of Ohio high school graduates who completed the academic core curriculum still required remediation in math or English. Ohio Board of Regents, *Making the Transition from High School to College in Ohio 2002* (Columbus: Ohio Board of Regents, 2002).

9. See Robert H. McCabe, "Developmental Education: A Policy Primer," *League for Innovation in the Community College* 14, no. 1 (Feb. 2001). Andrea Venezia, Michael Kirst, and Anthony Antonio, *Betraying the College Dream: How Disconnected K–12 and Postsecondary Education Systems Undermine Student Aspirations* (Stanford, CA: Stanford Institute for Higher Education Research, 2003), also detail how the standards for high school courses are entirely different from those for college classes.

10. Ronald A. Phipps, *College Remediation: What It Is, What It Costs, What's at Stake* (Washington, DC: Institute for Higher Education Policy, 1998).

11. Mary Soliday, *The Politics of Remediation* (Pittsburgh, PA: University of Pittsburgh Press, 2002).

12. By 2006, these companies had stopped providing most of their remedial teaching services. A former Sylvan executive cited some of the problems that led to the company to eliminate that part of its business, including the long period of time it took for colleges to decide whether to hire the company and opposition from faculty members who disliked the idea of outsourcing teaching duties. Goldie Blumenstyk, "For-Profit Education: Facing the Challenges of Slower Growth," *Chronicle of Higher Education* 52, no. 18 (2006): A13.

13. Michael Kirst, "Secondary and Postsecondary Linkages," in Stacy Dickert-Conlin and Ross Rubenstein, eds., *Economic Inequality and Higher Education: Access, Persistence, and Success* (New York: Russell Sage Foundation, 2007).

14. National Center for Education Statistics, *Remedial Education at Higher Education Institutions in Fall 1995* (Washington, DC: Office of Educational Research and Improvement, 1996).

15. Legislative Office of Education Oversight, *Remedial and Developmental Programs in Ohio's Public Colleges and Universities* (Columbus: Ohio General Assembly, 1995). Over four-fifths of campuses nationally restrict enrollment in some college-level classes until remediation is complete, and most require those in need of remediation to participate in the courses. National Center for Education Statistics, *Remedial Education at Degree-Granting Postsecondary Institutions in Fall 2000* (Washington DC: U.S. Department of Education, 2003).

16. Juan Carlos Calcagno and Bridget Terry Long, "The Impact of Postsecondary Remediation Using a Regression Discontinuity Design: Addressing Endogenous Sorting and Noncompliance" (NBER Working Paper no. 14194, National Bureau of Economic Research, Cambridge, MA, July 2008).

17. Ohio Board of Regents, *Ohio Colleges and Universities, 2001: Profile of Student Outcomes, Experiences and Campus Measures* (Columbus: Ohio Board of Regents, 2001).

18. Texas Legislative Budget Board, "The Cost of Developmental Education in Texas," in *Higher Education Performance Review* (Austin: Charles A. Dana Center, University of Texas at Austin, 2007).

19. Christopher Hammons, "The Education Deficit in the Lone Star State: The Financial Impact on Texas When Students Fail to Learn Basic Skills," Texas Public Policy Foundation, Austin, March 2005, www.texaspolicy.com/pdf/2005-03-remedial-ed.pdf.

20. Because these figures include indirect costs such as libraries, registration, and facility maintenance, they should not be used to determine the savings associated with eliminating remediation.

21. Phipps, *College Remediation*.

22. PricewaterhouseCoopers, *Report I: Financial Analysis of Remedial Education at the City University of New York* (New York: City of New York, Mayor's Advisory Task Force on the City University of New York, 1999).

23. It is important to distinguish between the remedial costs for recent high school graduates versus those for nontraditional college students, including adult learners and immigrants. While critics blame the K–12 system for the need to offer remediation to its recent graduates and suggest that high schools should contribute to the costs associated with these unprepared students, most treat older students who are returning to higher education to upgrade their skills as a separate category.

24. Tara L. Parker and Richard C. Richardson, "Ending Remediation at CUNY: Implications for Access and Excellence," *Journal of Educational Research and Policy Studies* 5, no. 2 (Fall 2005).

25. State Council of Higher Education for Virginia, *Remediation in Virginia Higher Education*, SCHEV Issue Brief (State Council of Higher Education for Virginia, Dec. 9, 2002).

26. North Carolina House Bill 1211, enacted in 2001.

27. Guidelines on Contracting with Community Colleges to Offer Remedial Instruction, University of North Carolina Policy Manual, Guideline 400.1.11[G], adopted July 9, 1992, available at www.northcarolina.edu/policy/index.php.

28. David W. Breneman, Robert Costrell, and William Haarlow, *Remediation in Higher Education: A Symposium*, Thomas B. Fordham Foundation, July 1, 1998, available at www.edexcellence.net.

29. David Ardenale, *Survey of Education Policies Concerning Developmental Education at the State and Federal Level in the U.S.* (National Association for Developmental Education, 1998).

30. Colleen Moore et al., *Beyond the Open Door: Increasing Student Success in the California Community Colleges* (Sacramento: Institute for Higher Education Leadership and Policy, California State University, 2007), available at www.csus.edu/ihelp/PDFs/R_Beyond_Open_Door_08-07.pdf.

31. California State University Office of Public Affairs, "Percentage of CSU Freshmen Needing Remedial Education Drops for First Time," March 14, 2000, available at www.calstate.edu/pa/news/2000/RemedialReport.shtml.

32. Bridget Terry Long and Michal Kurlaender. "Do Community Colleges Provide a Viable Pathway to a Baccalaureate Degree?" *Educational Evaluation and Policy Analysis* 31, no. 1 (March 2009): 30–53.

33. Massachusetts Board of Higher Education, Academic and Campus Affairs Meeting, no. ACA 99-02, Sept. 16, 1998.

34. Education Commission of the States, "Recent State Policies/Activities."

35. Associated Press, "Thousands of University Students Still Need Extra Help," Dec. 9, 2001.

36. Texas Success Initiative, Education Code sec. 51.3062, effective Sept. 1, 2003.

37. Judith James, Victoria Morrow, and Patrick Perry, "Study Session on Basic Skills" (presentation to the Board of Governors, California Community Colleges, July 2002), www.cccco.edu/Portals/4/Executive/Board/2002_agendas/july/13 -Basic_Skills.pdf.

38. Administrative Procedures for Learning Support Programs, University of Georgia Academic and Student Affairs Handbook, sec. 2.9.1, available at www .usg.edu/academic_affairs_handbook.

39. Katherine Boswell and Davis Jenkins, *State Policies on Community College Remedial Education: Findings from a National Survey*, Education Commission of the States, Sept. 2002, available at www.ecs.org/clearinghouse/40/81/4081 .pdf.

40. Research suggests that students who interact with peers who are higher achievers than themselves tend to improve. See, e.g., Bruce Sacerdote, "Peer Effects with Random Assignment: Results for Dartmouth Roommates," *Quarterly Journal of Economics* 116, May 2, 2001; David J. Zimmerman, "Peer Effects in Academic Outcomes: Evidence from a Natural Experiment," *Review of Economics and Statistics* 85, no. 1 (Winter 2003); Caroline Hoxby, "Peer Effects in the Classroom: Learning from Gender and Race Variation" (NBER Working Paper no. 7867, National Bureau of Economic Research, Cambridge, MA, 2000).

41. Calcagno and Long, "The Impact of Postsecondary Remediation Using a Regression Discontinuity Design."

42. Eric Bettinger and Bridget Terry Long, "Remediation at the Community College: Student Participation and Outcomes," *New Directions for Community Colleges*, no. 129 (Spring 2005): 17–26; Bettinger and Long, "Addressing the Needs of Underprepared College Students."

43. In the 2009 study we focused on students who were 18 to 20 years old when they initially began college. Also, to get data on past student preparation and performance, we limited the sample to students who took the ACT. This is not a strong restriction, given testing patterns among the group indicating they wanted to complete a degree.

44. Additionally, Bettinger and Long, "Remediation at the Community College," found that community college students placed in math remediation were 15% more likely to transfer to a four-year college and to take 10 more credit hours than students with similar test scores and high school preparation.

45. William R. Shadish, Thomas D. Cook, and David T. Campbell, *Experimental and Quasi-Experimental Designs for Generalized Causal Inference* (Boston: Houghton Mifflin, 2002); Guido Imbens and Thomas Lemieux, "Regression Discontinuity Designs: A Guide to Practice," *Journal of Econometrics* 142, no. 2 (Jan. 2008).

46. Calcagno and Long, "The Impact of Postsecondary Remediation Using a Regression Discontinuity Design." We also addressed concerns about noncompliance—i.e., the fact that some students choose not to follow the placement rules by taking the recommended level of course (remedial or college-level)—as well as concerns about endogenous sorting around the policy cutoff caused by some students' repeating the placement exam multiple times until they pass the cutoff.

47. More specifically, students on the margin of requiring math remediation were slightly more likely to persist to their second year than their nonremedial peers, but the likelihood of passing subsequent college-level English composition was slightly lower for remedial students.

48. Paco Martorell and Isaac McFarlin, "Help or Hindrance? The Effects of College Remediation on Academic and Labor Market Outcomes," *Review of Economics and Statistics* 93, no. 2 (2011): 436–54. During the focal time period of this study, Texas had a single placement exam and cutoff score.

49. Bridget Terry Long and Juan Carlos Calcagno, "Does Remediation Help All Students? The Heterogeneous Effects of Postsecondary Developmental Courses" (unpublished working paper, June 2010).

50. Clive R. Belfield et al., "The High/Scope Perry Preschool Program: Cost–Benefit Analysis Using Data from the Age-40 Followup," *Journal of Human Resources* 41, no. 1 (2006).

51. Angela Boatman and Bridget Terry Long, "Does Remediation Work for All Students? How the Effects of Postsecondary Remedial and Developmental Courses Vary by Level of Academic Preparation" (Working Paper, National Center for Postsecondary Research, 2010).

52. This was also found by Bettinger and Long, "Addressing the Needs of Underprepared College Students."

53. Michael F. O'Hear and Ross B. MacDonald, "A Critical Review of Research in Developmental Education, Part I," *Journal of Developmental Education* 19, no. 2 (1995).

54. Elizabeth M. Zachry and Emily Schneider, "Building Foundations for Student Readiness: A Review of Rigorous Research and Promising Trends in Developmental Education" (Working Paper, National Center for Postsecondary Research, 2010).

55. Heath Prince, *Standardization vs. Flexibility: State Policy Options on Placement Testing for Developmental Education in Community Colleges*, Policy Brief (Boston, MA: Jobs for the Future, 2005), p. 2.

56. Zachry and Schneider, "Building Foundations for Student Readiness."

57. Betsy O. Barefoot, Second National Survey of First-Year Academic Practices 2002, Administered by the Policy Center on the First Year of College (now

Gardner Institute), 2002, available at www.jngi.org/wordpress/wp-content/uploads/2011/12/2002_2nd_Nat_Survey_Responses_ALL.pdf.

58. Vincent Tinto, "Classrooms as Communities: Exploring the Educational Character of Student Persistence," *Journal of Higher Education* 68, no. 6 (1997); Tinto, "Learning Communities and the Reconstruction of Remedial Education in Higher Learning" (paper presented at the Conference on Replacing Remediation in Higher Education, Jan. 26–27, 1998, Stanford University, Stanford, CA).

59. Susan Scrivener et al., *A Good Start: Two-Year Effects of a Freshmen Learning Community Program at Kingsborough Community College* (New York: MDRC, 2008)

60. Initially, redesign efforts were planned at six colleges in Tennessee, but two colleges did not successfully implement the redesign efforts.

61. "Ohio Early Mathematics Placement Testing Program at the Ohio State University" (report issued by Ohio State University, 2003).

62. Data requested from Ohio Early Mathematics Placement Testing by the author on historical participation by high schools; received Jan. 23, 2006.

63. M. A. Zuiker, "The Ohio Early College Mathematics Placement Testing Program: Program Evaluation" (doctoral diss., Ohio State University, 1996).

64. Jessica S. Howell, Michal Kurlaender, and Eric Grodsky, "Postsecondary Preparation and Remediation: Examining the Effect of the Early Assessment Program at California State University," *Journal of Policy Analysis and Management* 29, no. 4 (Fall 2010).

65. John Cloud, "Who's Ready for College?" *Time*, Oct. 14, 2002.

CHAPTER EIGHT

Equalizing Credits and Rewarding Skills

Credit Portability and Bachelor's Degree Attainment

JOSIPA ROKSA

"College for all" has become a mantra of policymakers and foundations alike. In his first speech to a joint session of Congress in February 2009, President Barack Obama pledged: "We will provide the support necessary for you to complete college and meet a new goal: by 2020, America will once again have the highest proportion of college graduates in the world."[1] Many foundations have expressed similar goals, including the Lumina Foundation for Education, whose Goal 2025 aims to increase the percentage of Americans with high-quality degrees and credentials to 60 percent by 2025.[2] These commitments represent a recent shift in the national agenda, from focusing primarily on access to highlighting the issue of degree completion.

American higher education has historically been much more successful at facilitating access than degree completion. Between the high school cohorts of 1972 and 1992, the rate of entry into higher education increased from 48 percent to 71 percent while the bachelor's degree completion rate decreased: 51 percent of the class of 1972 and 46 percent of the class of 1992 graduated with a bachelor's degree within eight years.[3] A different way of examining the issue is to consider the educational attainment of different birth cohorts, which reveals that over the course of the twentieth century, the proportion of young adults with some college has increased, but the proportion with a bachelor's degree has at best remained stable.[4]

Amid the growing focus on degree completion, students' trajectories through higher education are gaining increasing attention. Even a cursory examination reveals that institutions operate under a premise of institutional autonomy, which gives them independence in crafting curricula and determining whether and how specific courses count toward their degrees. Students, on the other hand, operate under what could be referred to as a premise of credit portability, which assumes that one earns a degree by accumulating credits at multiple institutions. Students act on their premise: many of them attend more than one institution and are disappointed when credits they have earned at one institution do not count toward a degree at another.

An example provided recently in the *Chronicle of Higher Education* sounds much too familiar:

> Take a student who completes Technical Mathematics I for four credits at Bronx Community College, and consider the system's wacky credit-transfer rules. If that student transferred to CUNY's College of Staten Island, John Jay College of Criminal Justice, or New York City College of Technology, those credits would be accepted as if for a similar course offered there (although for only three credits at John Jay). At three other senior colleges in the system, the Bronx course would transfer only as elective credit, which tends not to count toward a major. Only Staten Island would apply the transfer credit toward general-education requirements. And five other colleges in the system wouldn't accept transfer credit at all—unless, in two cases, the student had completed an associate degree.[5]

The lack of consistency and transparency, even within a specific educational system, is remarkable. These types of observations have helped to generate an impression that credit portability (transfer of credits across postsecondary institutions, particularly from two-year to four-year schools) is a key hindrance to bachelor's degree attainment. A related expectation is that removing barriers to credit transfer, particularly for students transferring from two-year to four-year institutions, would substantially increase bachelor's degree attainment. This expectation is not supported by currently available research. While the research is not definitive and there are still unanswered questions, there is no convincing empirical evidence to suggest that streamlining credit transfer would increase degree attainment. This does not mean that the transfer process should not be more transparent and consistent. But it does mean that focusing on credit transfer as a primary strategy for increasing bachelor's degree attainment is not advisable.

Patterns of Multi-Institutional Attendance

Students' pathways through higher education have grown increasingly complex, with multi-institutional attendance becoming the modal pattern. In the sample examined in this chapter, just over 50 percent of students attended multiple institutions and approximately 20 percent attended more than two. Multi-institutional attendance is prevalent among students who begin in both two-year and four-year institutions.[6] Analyses presented in this chapter are based on a nationally representative sample of the 1992 high school seniors who entered higher education within approximately two years of high school graduation and were followed through 2000.[7] I do not consider all of the possible pathways through higher education but focus on a few that are analytically relevant to the concerns regarding credit transfer and have an adequate number of cases for examination.[8]

Bachelor's Degree Attainment

Are students who attend multiple institutions less likely to complete bachelor's degrees? Following students who matriculate in four-year institutions, descriptive results in table 8.1 suggest that those who attend multiple institutions have a lower rate of degree attainment than those who remain at one institution (64% vs. 74%). Students who begin at two-year institutions have a particularly low rate of bachelor's degree completion. This is largely because they do not transfer to a four-year institution, which is typically a necessary step on the path toward a bachelor's degree.[9] Only about one-third (36%) of traditional-age students who begin their postsecondary journeys in a two-year institution transfer to a four-year institution.[10] Among students who do transfer to a four-year institution, the completion rate is 53 percent.

Students who follow different pathways through higher education vary along multiple dimensions. Consequently, the lower bachelor's degree completion rates of students who change institutions and especially of those who start at two-year institutions may reflect these individual differences. Figure 8.1 shows results from a logistic regression model controlling for demographic characteristics, academic preparation, and enrollment patterns (delayed entry and part-time and continuous enrollment). All of the control variables are held at the mean when predicting bachelor's degree attainment. Even this basic set of control variables eliminates the gaps between the three groups of students and renders them not statistically significant. Whether students start at a four-year institution and attend only one college or university, start at a four-year institution and attend multiple colleges and universities, or transfer from a two-

TABLE 8.1. Bachelor's degree completion, by attendance patterns

	Bachelor's completion (%)
Starting at a 4-year institution	69.15
Only one 4-year institution	74.32
Multiple institutions	64.39
Multiple 4-year institutions	82.31
Multiple institutional types	50.34
Starting at a 2-year institution	19.53
Transferring to a 4-year institution	53.02

SOURCE: Author's calculations based on the National Educational Longitudinal Study (NELS), 1988–2000.

year to a four-year institution, they have similar likelihoods of bachelor's degree completion. Other recent studies focusing on community college transfers have similarly reported no differences in bachelor's degree attainment between community college transfers and rising juniors who started at four-year institutions.[11]

Figure 8.1 combines all students who start at four-year institutions and attend multiple colleges and universities into a single category. However, this category includes two distinct groups: students who attend multiple four-year institutions and students who attend multiple institutional types. Table 8.1 reports bachelor's degree completion rates for each of these subgroups. If the multiple institutions attended are all four-year institutions, students' completion rate is actually higher than for those who attend only one four-year institution (82% vs. 74%). Since students who engage in lateral transfer are more socioeconomically advantaged, their higher likelihood of degree attainment may reflect advantages in knowing how to navigate the higher education system.[12] Those who attend multiple institutions that are not all four-year schools have a much lower completion rate, as would be expected. Many of these students are "reverse transfers" (i.e., students who enroll in four-year institutions and subsequently transfer to two-year institutions), who tend to come from less advantaged family backgrounds and be less academically prepared.[13]

A regression model controlling for a range of individual differences based on the data used in this chapter reduces but does not eliminate the gap in degree completion between those two groups of students. Similarly, another recent study that used extensive controls and selection adjustments indicates that lateral transfers (students transferring among

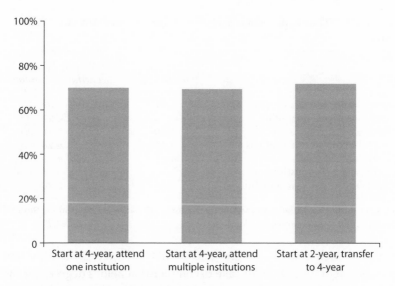

FIGURE 8.1. Predicted bachelor's degree completion, by attendance patterns. *Note*: Predictions based on a logistic regression model controlling for demographic characteristics, academic preparation, and enrollment patterns.

four-year institutions) have the same degree completion rate as students who attend only one four-year institution. Reverse transfers, however, continue to lag slightly behind their peers attending only one four-year institution, even net of controls and selection adjustments.[14]

Since students who move across four-year institutions have graduation rates similar to those of students who attend only one four-year institution, credit transfer does not appear to be a major issue for this group, or at least not enough to deter them from degree completion. Similarly, finding that there is no gap between students who transfer from two-year to four-year institutions and students who attend only one four-year institution, net of controls, implies that credit portability does not pose a challenge to their degree completion. These findings do not imply that students are not losing credits as they move across institutions, but they suggest that if students are losing credits, that is not deterring them from completing their degrees.

Time to Degree and Credits Earned

Even if students who follow different pathways through higher education have similar degree completion rates, there may be differences in other

TABLE 8.2. Time to degree for bachelor's degree recipients, by attendance patterns

	Years to bachelor's	Years to bachelor's, continuous enrollment
Starting at a 4-year institution	4.42	4.31
Only one 4-year institution	4.25	4.21
Multiple institutions	4.60	4.41
Multiple 4-year institutions	4.44	4.28
Multiple institutional types	4.81	4.59
Starting at a 2-year institution		
Transferring to a 4-year institution	5.43	5.20

SOURCE: Author's calculations based on the National Educational Longitudinal Study (NELS), 1988–2000 (descriptive results).

outcomes such as time to degree and credits to degree. Table 8.2 reports the amount of time students take to complete bachelor's degrees for each of the attendance patterns examined in this chapter. Descriptive results suggest that students who attend multiple institutions take longer to finish their bachelor's degrees; this is especially the case for students who begin in two-year institutions and subsequently transfer to four-year colleges and universities. However, students who attend multiple institutions, and particularly those who begin in two-year institutions, also tend to interrupt their enrollment, delaying degree completion.

The second column of table 8.2 thus provides data only for students who were enrolled continuously.[15] Students who start at four-year institutions have similar time to degree completion regardless of the pathway travelled. Students who begin in two-year institutions and subsequently transfer to four-year institutions take almost an additional year to complete their degrees, even if they do not interrupt their enrollment. This extra time could lead to higher debt loads and lower probability of graduate school attendance, as students may feel the need to immediately enter the labor market. However, it is difficult to discern whether these differences emerge from matriculating in two-year institutions or other factors. Students who begin in two-year institutions are not only more likely to interrupt their enrollment; they also differ from four-year entrants in many other respects, some of which, such as having to take remedial courses, can substantially lengthen time to degree.

Instead of relying on proxies such as time to degree, a more accurate representation of the role of credit transfer can be obtained by ex-

TABLE 8.3. Credits earned by bachelor's degree recipients, by attendance patterns

	Total credits	Total enrolled credits
Starting at a 4-year institution	137.37	134.33
Only one 4-year institution	134.41	131.86
Multiple institutions	140.51	136.94
Multiple 4-year institutions	139.10	135.58
Multiple institutional types	142.31	138.74
Starting at a 2-year institution		
Transferring to a 4-year institution	143.63	142.14

SOURCE: Author's calculations based on the National Educational Longitudinal Study (NELS), 1988–2000 (descriptive results).

amining the number of credits earned. If students are losing credits in the transfer process, those who follow more complex pathways through higher education should accumulate more credits. Table 8.3 shows the total number of credits earned by students who completed bachelor's degrees following different pathways through higher education. The table includes two measures of credits: the total number of credits earned and the total number of credits earned through enrollment (which excludes dual enrollment credits and credits earned through examination). Considering the total number of credits earned, students who attend multiple four-year institutions complete approximately five credits more than those who attend only one four-year institution on their path toward a bachelor's degree. When students move across institutional types, the gaps are slightly larger. Students who start at four-year institutions and attend multiple institutional types earn eight credits more toward their bachelor's degrees than those who attend only one four-year institution. Similarly, students who begin in two-year institutions earn over nine credits more than students who attend only one four-year institution.

The credit gap between students who start at two-year institutions and those who attend only one four-year institution has been frequently noted in policy discussions, serving as a critique of the current system and a call for transforming the approach to credit transfer.[16] However, one of the most notable findings shown in table 8.3 is that all groups of students are earning more than the 120 credits typically thought to be required for a bachelor's degree. Even students who attend only one four-year institution earn 134 credits, 14 credits more than would typically be expected; this is more than the gap between students starting at two-year institutions and those attending only one four-year institution. Since students who attend only one four-year institution are not changing schools, these "excess" credits are not related to issues of credit transfer. Future research is needed to examine why students are earning additional credits and to explore the extent to which individual and institutional factors contribute to the observed patterns.

National datasets, such as the one used in this chapter, are rarely adequate to examine variation across state systems as well as across institutions and fields of study. Fortunately, a number of states have begun collecting data on credit transfers within their systems, such as the recent audit study of Minnesota state colleges and universities and a survey of community college students in Maryland.[17] The findings of these state endeavors generally replicate the patterns reported in the national datasets. For example, a recent policy report focusing on California included a section titled "Many Transfer Students Graduate from a University with 'Excess' Units."[18] This report cited a finding from a recent study of the California State University (CSU) system which found that students who transferred from community colleges to four-year institutions graduated with an average of 141 semester units, which is remarkably similar to the national estimates presented here and, indeed, much in excess of the 120 credits typically considered to constitute a bachelor's degree.

The policy report then proceeded to consider different reasons for these "excess" units. However, at least in the CSU system, there appears to be no gap between credits earned toward a bachelor's degree between community college transfer students and students who begin in the CSU system. The same CSU report that noted that community college transfers graduated with 141 credits also noted that "native" CSU students graduated with an average of 142 credits.[19] Similarly, a recent report from Florida indicated that associate of arts transfer students completed 137 credits before graduation, while "native" four-year students averaged approximately 133 credits.[20] This 4-credit difference between four-year entrants and transfer students is small compared with the 13 "excess" credits completed by four-year entrants in pursuit of a bachelor's degree. Hence, although the system does appear to be inefficient, transfer is not the primary culprit for this inefficiency.

Even when there is a difference in the number of credits completed by students who transfer from two-year institutions and those who start at four-year institutions, the implications of this difference are not self-evident. On the one hand, this difference could reflect an issue with credit transfer. On the other hand, students who transfer and those who do not are different on many dimensions. It could be that transfer students would have completed more credits even if they had started at a four-year institution. Isolating the causal effect of transfer on credit accumulation is challenging, not only because of individual differences and self-selection, but also because of the issue of appropriate comparison groups. (For example, should transfer students be compared with all four-year students or only with rising juniors? Should all transfer students be considered or only those who reach a status of a junior?) At least one recent study, which used propensity score methods to compare community college transfers with rising juniors who started at four-year institutions, suggests that after adjustments for individual characteristics, there is no difference between the two groups in the number of credits earned.[21] These findings imply that credit transfer is not a major hindrance on the path toward a bachelor's degree.

Some readers may take issue with this interpretation, which suggests that the lack of difference in credits earned between transfer and non-transfer students *after* controls (or other statistical adjustments) implies that credit transfer is not an issue. Some of the characteristics included in the models, such as family background and academic preparation, may be related to credit transfer issues. If, for example, students from less advantaged family backgrounds and with lower levels of academic preparation are not completing degrees because they are losing credits, then those individual characteristics could in part capture issues related to credit portability. However, those groups of students tend to face challenges navigating the higher education system, even when attending only one institution.

A recent study found that 23 percent of students in private two-year institutions and 46 percent of students in community colleges reported taking a course that did not apply toward their degree.[22] These students probably would have accumulated more than the minimum number of credits required for a degree even if they had remained at the same institution. If these students attempted to transfer, they probably would have encountered even more challenges and, lacking "know-how" about higher education, possibly have accumulated excess credits in their new institutions as well. Students in two-year institutions, particularly those from less advantaged family backgrounds, face numerous challenges in streamlining their educational careers even when they attend only one school. Accumulating excess credits is thus not simply, or perhaps even primarily, a consequence of credit portability issues.

Articulation Policies and Transfer

Because of the recent concerns among academics and policymakers regarding the loss of credits in the transfer process, many states have adopted statewide articulation policies in an effort to manage the flow of students and credits across institutions.[23] Although the primary purpose of articulation policies is to preserve credits for students who have decided to transfer, the general expectation has been that these policies will increase transfer rates as well. The underlying assumption is that if the transfer process is easy and transparent, and if students know that they will be able to keep most if not all of their credits, they will be more likely to make the transition, particularly from community colleges to four-year institutions.

Studies relying on nationally representative datasets, however, find no relationship between the presence of statewide articulation policies and transfer rates from community colleges to four-year institutions.[24] This null finding holds whether all community college students are considered or only those aspiring to earn bachelor's degrees. It also holds when policies are disaggregated to consider their overall strength or specific components (e.g., common course numbering or common general education requirements). These findings indicate that articulation policies do not ease the transfer process, at least not in ways that would increase the number of students transitioning from community colleges to four-year institutions. Moreover, at least one study found that the presence of articulation policies does not reduce time to degree or credits needed to complete a bachelor's degree among transfer students.[25]

It is possible, however, that national-level studies are not able to identify the effects of articulation policies due to the great variation across states. A better place to look may be within the policies and experiences of specific states. I thus briefly review patterns in three states—California, Florida, and Arizona—which have adopted different articulation strategies. Even across these different contexts, a consistent pattern emerges: community college students who transfer to four-year institutions fare reasonably well in terms of degree completion and credits to degree; the main issue is that only a small proportion of community college students actually make a transition to the four-year system.

California

One of the key components of California's Master Plan for Higher Education is transfer from community colleges to the University of California (UC) or California State University (CSU) systems. California's legislature has long experimented with different strategies for facilitating transfer, while affording institutions a substantial degree of autonomy. A recent attempt at standardization included development of ASSIST (Articulation System Stimulating Interinstitutional Student Transfer)— an online repository of information which allows students to see whether and how their courses at community colleges will transfer to any of the four-year California institutions. More recently, California has introduced the Intersegmental General Education Transfer Curriculum (IGETC). Generally referred to as the "core transfer curriculum," IGETC is a standardized general education program that students can use to fulfill lower-division general education requirements, although it is neither required for transfer nor a guarantee of admission for potential transfer students; moreover, a number of science, nursing, and engineering schools within the UC system do not accept it.[26] In yet another attempt to streamline the transfer process, in the fall of 2010, California passed the Student Transfer Achievement Reform Act, which guarantees that community college students who earn specific associate's degrees aligned with California State University baccalaureate programs can enter the CSU system with junior status.

If California is tracking transfer data (transfer rates, degree completion, time to degree, and credits earned), researchers will be able, in a few years, to evaluate the impact of this latest intervention. But if the past, or other states, are any indication, this new initiative is not likely to lead to a notable increase in transfer rates or, by extension, overall bachelor's degree attainment in the state. The focus of this policy, as well as of earlier endeavors, is on preserving credits for students who make the transition to four-year institutions. That is an essential goal, and one that could be pursued as a matter of fairness and equity. However, its relationship to degree completion is less clear. California community college students who transfer to four-year institutions have relatively high bachelor's degree completion rates—80 percent of community college transfers to the UC system graduate within four years of transfer, and approximately two-thirds of transfers to the CSU system graduate within six years.[27] Rates for cohorts beginning in UC and CSU institutions are not provided in the same report, so a direct comparison is not possible, but those completion rates are quite high compared with average rates for public four-year institutions. At the same time, the transfer rate in California is very low: only about 20 percent of community college degree-seeking students transfer to four-year institutions.[28] Moreover, transfer rates appear to have remained largely stable over time.[29] Persistent efforts to address articulation in California have thus been accompanied with relatively low and stagnating transfer rates.

Florida

Florida has long had a state statute that guarantees junior status to community college transfers who complete an associate of arts (AA) degree. Earning an AA is a well-established pathway to four-year institutions, and approximately three-quarters of transfers complete an AA before moving to a four-year institution.[30] Moreover, AA transfers have comparable educational outcomes to four-year students.[31] Recent data available for the University of Florida, for example, indicate that the six-year graduation rate for the first-time-in-college four-year students is virtually identical to the four-year graduation rate of AA transfers.[32] There is also very little difference between transfer students and four-year entrants in credits earned to degree: AA transfers earn only about four credits more than students who begin in four-year institutions.[33] Thus, degree attainment and credits to degree do not appear to be major issues, even if slight adjustments to eliminate the existing credit-to-degree difference could be considered.

Although AA transfers have remarkable success rates, a relatively small percentage of community college students earn AA degrees. Among first-time degree-seeking students in community colleges, only approximately one-quarter complete an AA degree. If a sample is restricted to students who complete at least twelve nonremedial credits, the AA completion rates would increase to approximately one-third.[34] Students who complete AA degrees have very high transfer rates: three-quarters of them transfer to four-year institutions. However, since they constitute a very small portion of the total degree-seeking student body in community colleges, and since a relatively small proportion of students transfer in Florida without earning an AA degree, the overall transfer rate is not high—it is at best average.[35] Florida's 2+2 system thus produces very good outcomes for students who earn AA degrees and transfer to four-year institutions. However, this category includes a small proportion of degree-seeking students who begin their postsecondary journeys in community colleges. Consequently, this strategy is not a likely candidate for increasing the overall bachelor's degree production.

Arizona

Another state that has invested much effort into mainstreaming transfer and articulation is Arizona. Arizona has adopted two strategies for facilitating transfer: the Arizona General Education Curriculum (AGEC) and Transfer Pathway Degrees. A recent evaluation of Arizona's approach to transfer has received much attention, in particular for reporting that over the five cohorts studied, students from each succeeding year graduated with almost 2.5 fewer credits, leading to a 12-credit difference over five years.[36] This is a remarkable accomplishment. But it is not apparent what caused this reduction in credits to degree, since the same pattern was observed for all transfer groups (those with AGEC, those with transfer degrees, and those with just transfer credits). It is also not evident whether this decrease in credits to degree is a consequence of policy interventions, a reflection of changes in student characteristics, or the result of other factors (e.g., whether demographic and academic preparation profiles for Arizona students changed over this time period). AGEC is not likely to be solely responsible for this change because almost half of students interviewed were either unfamiliar with or unclear about AGEC requirements.

Students who complete AGEC graduate with about 3.5 fewer credits than students who enter with transfer credits only. This difference is relatively small and likely to be at least in part related to academic preparation. The report notes, for example, that AGEC students had significantly higher GPAs two and four semesters after transfer than students with just transfer credits. Since academic performance tends to be correlated over time, these students were probably performing at higher levels in high school and community college as well. Additionally, students who completed transfer degrees before transitioning to four-year institutions had a similar GPA and completed a similar number of credits to degree as did students who entered with transfer credits only. Since the analysis of credits to degree presented in the report does not control for prior academic preparation, it is not clear whether academic preparation explains the difference between AGEC and other transfer students. Moreover, the evaluation report focused on comparing different groups of students who transferred to four-year institutions, and thus did not include a discussion of transfer rates. Whether transfer rates have changed following the implementation of specific policies is a crucial question that needs to be addressed.

Articulation Polices and Transfer Reconsidered

This brief discussion of specific state efforts, coupled with the presentation of findings from a nationally representative dataset, highlights one key issue: transfer. After students transfer from two-year to four-year institutions, they seem to do as well as their four-year counterparts with respect to degree completion, and even credits to degree. However, average transfer rates are quite low. Moreover, low transfer rates in states that have invested much energy in articulation and little evidence of change over time (where available) suggest that articulation policies do not increase transfer rates. At the core, they are not intended to: articulation policies are intended to preserve credits for students *who transfer*.

There seems to be an expectation that articulation policies will have a "spillover" effect and increase transfer, but the available evidence does not support this expectation. It is thus not clear that adopting articulation policies can contribute substantially to increasing the production of bachelor's degrees. This does not imply that articulation policies are not needed or that they should not be developed to make the transfer process easier and more transparent. They may be of particular relevance in certain fields in which students have lower probabilities of transfer.[37] However, available evidence indicates that articulation policies do not represent a compelling strategy for improving overall bachelor's degree completion.

Extensive research on transfer identifies myriad factors associated with whether students make the transition from community colleges to four-year institutions.[38] One insight from this research—one that is obvious but seems to be often neglected in discussions of transfer—is that the same factors that facilitate or hinder educational success and degree completion more broadly are the factors that are related to transfer. For example, students who are well prepared academically and have high educational expectations are more likely to transfer, while those who transition into roles typically associated with adulthood, such as employment and parenthood, are less likely to make this educational transition. Moreover, students' socioeconomic background is strongly related to all educational outcomes, including transfer, even after controlling for other factors. This may at least in part reflect socioeconomic differences in students' "know-how" about the higher education system.[39] Recognizing that transfer is akin to other educational transitions and addressing these common factors would probably contribute more to increasing transfer rates than focusing on the unique aspects of this transition (such as articulation policies).

Alternative Ways of Earning Credits

If improving credit transfer among higher education institutions is not likely to lead to an increase in bachelor's degree attainment, considering other ways of accumulating credits may be productive. Credit transfer among higher education institutions typically rests on "content similarity": courses are deemed equivalent if their content (usually gleaned from course syllabi) is deemed equivalent. Another strategy for awarding credits would be to focus on what students can do—that is, credits (or even entire degrees) can be awarded to students who can demonstrate specific knowledge and skills; this approach is exemplified by initiatives such as prior learning assessment (PLA) and competency-based programs.

A number of different strategies are subsumed under the general PLA category. Perhaps two of the most common are PLA credits awarded by individual institutions (assessed through methods such as standardized examinations or portfolios) and PLA credits recognized by the American Council for Education (ACE). ACE began evaluating military training and recommending its acceptance for college credit following World War I and today also evaluates many corporate training programs.[40] Rigorous evaluations of whether these strategies enhance degree completion or reduce time to degree (and credits to degree) are absent to date. Analyses of PLAs usually focus on only one or a few institutions and have virtually no controls for students' characteristics. A recent large-scale study including 48 institutions led by the Council for Adult and Experiential Learning (CAEL) reported that adult students who completed PLA credits had higher graduation rates and shorter times to degree. However, the study could not adjust these estimates for a range of confounding factors or student selection, making the results largely suggestive.[41] Given the current state of knowledge, it is difficult to discern whether PLAs could play an important role in increasing bachelor's degree completion.

Instead of awarding a few credits to students for prior learning, some initiatives have aimed to organize entire degree programs around what students know and can do. Several institutions have adopted this competency-based approach, with perhaps the best-known being the Western Governors University (WGU). WGU is an online university founded in 1997 with a mission to expand access to higher education by "providing a means for individuals to learn independent of time and place and to earn competency-based degrees and other credentials that are credible to both academic institutions and employers."[42] Students can demonstrate competencies through a range of different strategies, from standardized exams to problem-solving assignments, special projects, and research papers. WGU focuses on nontraditional students (with an average age of 36), two-thirds of whom are working full-time. According to its website, WGU graduates over 2,200 students each year in more than 50 degree programs.

It is difficult to assess the contribution of WGU (or similar competency-based programs) to the national degree attainment rate. Independent evaluations of the program are not available. Comparisons of metrics such as graduation rates and time to degree between competency-based institutions and traditional higher education institutions are needed to begin the process of understanding whether, under what conditions, and for whom different contexts could provide effective pathways toward a degree. Without these comparisons, it is not clear whether expanding competency-based programs would contribute to increasing the overall bachelor's degree production rate any more than expanding access to traditional colleges and universities.

Conclusion

The disconnect between students' pathways through higher education and institutional practices focusing on institutional autonomy is obvious to even a casual observer of higher education. Students who change institutions go through a complex set of often opaque processes that vary across institutions if they wish to transfer credits earned at different colleges and universities.[43] Transfer procedures often seem arcane, and almost everyone knows of students who lost credits in the transfer process. These observations would suggest that credit portability is a key hindrance to degree attainment. While intuitive, this expectation is not supported by currently available research: there is no empirical evidence to date to suggest that credit portability is a primary hindrance to bachelor's degree attainment.

Students who attend multiple four-year institutions (i.e., who transfer laterally) do not have a lower likelihood of degree attainment (nor do they take longer or earn more credits) than students who attend only one four-year institution. Students who start at two-year institutions and subsequently transfer to four-year institutions have similar educational outcomes to students who begin in four-year institutions, after adjusting for individual differences. Moreover, statewide articulation policies do not seem to increase either the likelihood of transfer or the likelihood of degree completion for transfer students. This does not mean that articulation policies should be abandoned. They introduce some degree of standardization into the transfer process and thus may benefit both students and institutions.[44] However, efforts to improve credit transfer, including articulation policies, are not likely to make a substantial contribution to increasing the overall bachelor's degree attainment rate.

This does not mean that all is well in higher education. A large proportion of students who start in four-year institutions are not graduating; the majority of those who begin in two-year institutions with an intention to transfer do not actually make a transition to four-year institutions; and even when students complete degrees, they are taking an increasing amount of time to graduate. Moreover, students, regardless of the pathway traveled through higher education, are completing many more than the 120 credits typically thought to be required for a bachelor's degree. Even when they attend only one four-year institution, they seem to accumulate over 130 credits (and more in some systems).[45] This could reflect a number of underlying issues, from course availability and poor advising to what has recently been described as a "motivated but directionless" generation: students entering higher education today are very motivated and have high ambitions, but many of them have few if any concrete plans for realizing those ambitions and thus spend a certain amount of time floundering through higher education.[46] Changing programs or majors, or taking classes without adequate knowledge of whether and how those classes count toward the degree, could all contribute to the high credit accumulation even among students who do not change institutions.

It is also possible that students are not as focused on earning degrees efficiently as policymakers and academics would like to think. In the sample analyzed in this chapter, students who earned credits by examination—including Advanced Placement (AP), the College-Level Examination Program (CLEP), and institutional challenge examinations—did not maximize the use of those credits. By the time they graduated with a bachelor's degree, they still earned 130 credits through enrollment and 142 credits total. Students without examination credits earned a total of 138 toward their bachelor's degrees. Much additional research is needed to examine why students are completing more credits than appears necessary on their path toward a bachelor's degree.

One set of factors worthy of scrutiny pertains to contemporary campus culture. Many recent (as well as historical) descriptions of residential four-year colleges emphasize the importance of social life as opposed to academics.[47] College is also considered a component of transition to adulthood, not just a place to earn a degree.[48] Recent changes in financing of higher education may increase pressures toward efficiency, although for many four-year students, having a "college experience" is crucial, and they often go into debt to finance it.[49] Another area deserving careful consideration is students' lives outside of school. An increasing proportion of students attending higher education are "nontraditional." Most students today are not 18- to 22-year-olds focusing exclusively on their studies, but individuals of all ages who are often juggling multiple demands of work, marriage, and parenthood.[50] A policy that targets only one issue (transfer of credits) and does not consider the complexity of students' lives, in which credits are only one (and perhaps not even the primary) concern on a journey toward a degree, may not have much of an impact on degree attainment. Untangling these issues awaits future research, but the existing evidence suggests that credit transfer is not a major hindrance to degree attainment.

NOTES

1. Barack Obama, remarks prepared for the Joint Session of Congress, Feb. 24, 2009, White House Press Office, Washington, DC.

2. Lumina Foundation for Education, *Lumina Foundation's Strategic Plan: Goal 2025* (Indianapolis: Lumina Foundation, 2010).

3. John Bound, Michael Lovenheim, and Sarah Turner, "Why Have College Completion Rates Declined?" (NBER Working Paper no. 15566, National Bureau of Economic Research, Cambridge, MA, 2009).

4. Sarah Turner, "Going to College and Finishing College," in *College Choices: The Economics of Where to Go, When to Go, and How to Pay for It*, ed. Caroline Hoxby (Chicago: University of Chicago Press, 2004).

5. Sara Lipka, "Academic Credit: Colleges' Common Currency Has No Set Value," *Chronicle of Higher Education*, Oct. 17, 2010, available at http://chronicle .com/article/Academic-Credit-Colleges/124973.

6. Two-year institutions include both community colleges (i.e., public two-year) and private two-year institutions. Private two-year institutions are a small proportion of the total enrollment (less than 3%) and approximately 6% of the total two-year enrollment in the sample examined. The results do not change substantively if presented analyses focus only on students attending community colleges.

7. For more information on the National Educational Longitudinal Study (NELS, 1988–2000) and associated Postsecondary Education Transcript Study (PETS), see http://nces.ed.gov/surveys/nels88.

8. For recent descriptions of possible pathways through higher education and definitional challenges, see Clifford Adelman, *The Toolbox Revisited* (Washington, DC: U.S. Department of Education, 2006); Clifford Adelman, *Moving into Town—and Moving On* (Washington, DC: U.S. Department of Education, 2005); and Alexander C. McCormick, "Swirling and Double-Dipping: New Patterns of Student Attendance and Their Impacts for Higher Education," *New Directions for Higher Education*, no. 121 (Spring 2003).

9. While some community colleges are allowed to grant bachelor's degrees in specific fields, the majority of students need to transfer to complete their bachelor's degrees at a four-year institution.

10. If a more restrictive definition of transfer were to be used—for example, requiring students to complete a certain number of credits at two-year and/or four-year institutions—transfer rates would be higher. At the same time, the sample in this study is focusing on traditional-age students. If all students entering higher education were considered, the transfer rates would be lower.

11. Tatiana Melguizo, Gregory Kienzl, and Mariana Alfonso, "Comparing the Educational Attainment of Community College Transfer Students and Four-Year Rising Juniors Using Propensity Score Matching Methods," *Journal of Higher Education* 82 (May/June 2011): 265–91.

12. Sara Goldrick-Rab and Fabian T. Pfeffer, "Beyond Access: Explaining Socioeconomic Differences in College Transfer," *Sociology of Education* 82 (April 2009): 101–25.

13. Ibid.

14. Sara Goldrick-Rab, and Fabian T. Pfeffer, "Does Changing Colleges Matter? The Equity Implications of Student Mobility" (paper presented at annual meeting of the American Sociological Association, New York, Aug. 2007).

15. The results are similar across the two groups because students who interrupt enrollment are much less likely to complete their degrees. Among those who finish, interrupted enrollment does not seem to be a major factor in prolonging time to degree.

16. U.S. Government Accountability Office, *Transfer Students: Postsecondary Institutions Could Promote More Consistent Consideration of Coursework by Not Basing Determinations on Accreditation* (Washington, DC: GAO, October 2005); Lipka, "Academic Credit." This gap is usually referred to as a 10-point difference, a figure that emerges if both numbers are rounded. Moreover, the gap equals 10 credits if only credits earned through enrollment are considered.

17. Minnesota State Colleges and Universities, Office of Internal Auditing, *Summary of Student Credit Transfer Testing* (May 2010), available at www.internal auditing.mnscu.edu/committee/2010/1005-transfertestingsummary.pdf, accessed Dec. 5, 2011; Maryland Higher Education Commission, *Follow-Up Survey of the 2007–2008 Community College Graduates* (March 2010), available at www .mhec.state.md.us/publications/research/AnnualReports/FY2010CCFollowUp SurveywTables.pdf, accessed Dec. 6, 2011.

18. Colleen Moore, Nancy Shulock, and Cristy Jensen, *Crafting a Student-Centered Transfer Process in California: Lessons from Other States* (Sacramento, CA: Institute for Higher Education Leadership and Policy, Aug. 2009).

19. Academic Affairs Committee of the Academic Senate, California State University, available at http://rhet.csustan.edu/aa/docs/QAfor45-15.pdf, accessed Dec. 5, 2011.

20. Florida Department of Education, *"2+2" in Florida* (Tallahassee: Florida Department of Education, Dec. 2003).

21. Melguizo, Kienzl, and Alfonso, "Comparing the Educational Attainment of Community College Transfer Students."

22. Ann E. Person and James E. Rosenbaum, "Student Information Problems with College Procedures," in *After Admission: From College Access to College Success*, ed. James E. Rosenbaum, Regina Deil-Amen, and Ann E. Person (New York: Russell Sage Foundation, 2009).

23. Josipa Roksa, "Building Bridges for Student Success: Are Higher Education Articulation Policies Effective?" *Teachers College Record* 111 (2009): 2444–78.

24. Gregory M. Anderson, Jeffrey C. Sun, and Mariana Alfonso Anderson, "Effectiveness of Statewide Articulation Agreements on the Probability of Transfer: A Preliminary Policy Analysis," *Review of Higher Education* 29 (2006): 261–91; Betheny Gross and Dan Goldhaber, "Community College Transfer and Articulation Policies: Looking Beneath the Surface" (Working Paper no. 2009_1R, University of Washington–Bothell, Center on Reinventing Public Education, April 2009); Roksa, "Building Bridges for Student Success."

25. Josipa Roksa and Bruce Keith, "Credits, Time, and Attainment: Articulation Policies and Success after Transfer," *Educational Evaluation and Policy Analysis* 30 (2008): 236–54.

26. California Postsecondary Education Commission (CPEC), *Student Transfer in California Postsecondary Education* (Sacramento, CA: CPEC, 2005).

27. Moore, Shulock, and Jensen, *Crafting a Student-Centered Transfer Process in California.*

28. The percentages vary slightly (between 18% and 22%) across studies, depending on the definitions used.

29. Josipa Roksa, Eric Grodsky, and Willard Hom, "The Role of Community Colleges in Promoting Student Diversity in California," in *Equal Opportunity in Higher Education: The Past and Future of California's Proposition 209*, ed. Eric Grodsky and Michal Kurlaender (Cambridge: Harvard Education Press, 2010).

30. Florida Department of Education, *"2+2" in Florida.*

31. Florida Department of Education, "Statewide Articulation Agreement—Effective and Comprehensive," *Zoom* (newsletter), www.fldoe.org/cc/OSAS/Evaluations.

32. Florida Department of Education, Table II-2, Retention and Graduation Rates for All First Time in College (FTIC) and Community College AA Transfer Students (1988–2008), www.ir.ufl.edu/factbook/degree.htm.

33. Florida Department of Education, *"2+2" in Florida.*

34. Josipa Roksa, and Juan Carlos Calcagno, "Catching Up in Community Colleges: Academic Preparation and Transfer to Four-Year Institutions," *Teachers College Record* 112 (2010): 260–88.

35. See Roksa, "Building Bridges for Student Success."

36. Hezel Associates, *Evaluation of Arizona's Transfer Articulation System* (Syracuse, NY: Hazel Associates, 2007).

37. Kevin J. Dougherty, and Gregory S. Kienzl, "It's Not Enough to Get Through the Open Door: Inequalities by Social Background in Transfer from Community Colleges to Four-Year Colleges," *Teachers College Record* 3 (2006): 452–87.

38. For a recent study that examines the predictors of transfer as well as adeptly summarizes previous research, see ibid.

39. See Regina Deil-Amen, and James E. Rosenbaum, "The Social Prerequisites of Success: Can College Structure Reduce the Need for Social Know-How?" *Annals of the American Academy of Political and Social Science* 586 (2003): 120–43.

40. "College Credit Recommendation Service," American Council on Education website, www.acenet.edu/Content/NavigationMenu/ProgramsServices/CCRS/index.htm.

41. Center for Adult and Experiential Learning, *Fueling the Race to Postsecondary Success: A 48-Institution Study of Prior Learning Assessment and Adult Student Outcomes* (March 2010), available at www.cael.org/pdf/PLA_Fueling-the-Race.pdf. The study relies mostly on descriptives. The authors examine whether remedial courses affect students' outcomes. Although a step in the right direction, this analysis omits a host of factors that are likely to vary between PLA and non-PLA students.

42. "About WGU," Western Governors University website, www.wgu.edu/about_WGU/overview.

43. GAO, *Transfer Students.*

44. Betheny Gross and Dan Goldhaber, "Can Transfer and Articulation Policies Propel Community College Students to a Bachelor's Degree—and Is This the Only Goal?" (Policy Brief, University of Washington–Bothell, Center on Reinventing Public Education, May 2009).

45. Some of these "excess" credits seem to be related to college major; however, all majors in the NELS dataset earn on average more than 120 credits.

46. Barbara Schneider and David Stevenson, *The Ambitious Generation: America's Teenagers, Motivated but Directionless* (New Haven, CT: Yale University Press, 1999).

47. For a recent example, see Richard Arum and Josipa Roksa, *Academically Adrift: Limited Learning on College Campuses* (Chicago: University of Chicago Press, 2011).

48. Jeffrey Jensen Arnett, *Emerging Adulthood: The Winding Path from the Late Teens through the Twenties* (New York: Oxford University Press, 2004).

49. Steven Brint and Mathew Baron Rotondi, "Student Debt, the College Experience, and Transitions to Adulthood" (paper presented at the annual meeting for the American Sociological Association, Boston, Aug. 2008).

50. Josipa Roksa, "Work, Marriage, and Parenthood: Life Course Transitions and Inequality in Higher Education" (paper presented at the annual meeting of the Research Committee on Social Stratification and Mobility [RC28], International Sociological Association, New Haven, CT, Aug. 2009).

PART FOUR

The Lessons from Three States

CHAPTER NINE

The Challenge of Scaling Successful Policy Innovations

A Case Study of Three Colorado Community College System Grants

ELAINE DELOTT BAKER

The relationship between educational attainment and economic competitiveness is a familiar topic in the national discourse, one that has taken on a new sense of urgency within the context of the growth in global competition, the widening gap between the educational level of the U.S. population and that of populations in other industrialized nations, and recent disappointing data on college completion. Only 37 percent of U.S. adults aged 25–64 have an associate's degree or higher, as compared with 55 percent of adults in the highest performing countries.[1] In the United States, fewer than 20 percent of community college students will graduate within three years, and fewer than half of students enrolling in a four-year institution will graduate within six years.[2]

The response to the challenge of low educational attainment—from the research community to private foundations to the president—has been dramatic and has led to an array of ambitious college completion goals, such as doubling the numbers of certificates and degrees by 2025 or increasing the level of high-quality college degrees and credentials to 60 percent by 2025.[3] The cumulative effect of this focus can be felt in policy discussions and in allocation of new resources, in a renewed focus on effective practice, and in fundamental questions about the structure and delivery of postsecondary education.

Within this context, the phrase "initiative fatigue" has surfaced, a reflection of the frustration felt by many whose efforts to improve the access and success rate of at-risk postsecondary students have failed to yield systemic change.[4] Initiative fatigue is a worrisome term for the leadership and innovators of community colleges, coming as it does amid the intense focus on the low completion rates of community colleges students, the limited resources to support change, and the heavy pressures being brought to bear by state and national policymakers to double the numbers of certificates and degrees by 2025.[5]

The case study in this chapter addresses the question of why efforts to scale successful, grant-funded innovations for high-risk community college populations across institutions and states have met with limited success. To answer this question, I examine the trajectory of three grants awarded to the Colorado Community College System (CCCS) from 2004 to 2010: the Colorado Lumina Initiative for Performance, the Ford Foundation's Community College Bridges to Opportunity Project, and a U.S. Department of Education, Office of Vocational and Adult Education (OVAE) "Ready for College" grant.

The chapter identifies a series of challenges that community colleges face in their efforts to bring successful innovations to scale, including state funding formulas, the logistical and cultural barriers of scaling within an institution, the lack of effective mechanisms to bring innovations to scale across institutions, the dysfunction of grant timelines, the challenge of maintaining the fidelity of program models in the cycle of replication, and the absence of long-term evaluations of grant-funded innovations.

The Context

Profile of the Colorado Community College System

The Colorado Community College System (CCCS) is a highly centralized system of 13 community colleges, serving 38 percent of all Colorado resident undergraduates and 45 percent of the state's minority undergraduates. In 2008–9, CCCS served over 117,000 students, 26 percent of whom were classified as minorities and 41 percent of whom were certified as Pell-eligible. Of the certificates and degrees awarded in 2008–9, one-year certificates accounted for 40 percent, two-year certificates for 13 percent, and associate degrees in applied science (AAS) for 22 percent. Associate of general studies (AGS), associate of arts (AA), and associate of science (AS) degrees, which are transfer-oriented, accounted for the remaining 25 percent. The three-year transfer rate for first-time students in the fall 2005 cohort (2005–8) was 15.6 percent, with 89 percent of transfer students entering four-year institutions. Of CCCS transfers, 82 percent were part-time students and 18 percent were full-time students.[6] The overall three-year graduation rate in 2009 was 22.5 percent; the minority graduate rate was 17.4 percent.[7]

The Remedial Challenge

Academically underprepared students present a significant challenge in any effort to raise educational attainment. In Colorado, remedial course enrollments constituted 21 percent of CCCS's total student headcount in 2009, with 64 percent of incoming students testing into at least one remedial course and 16 percent into all three remedial subjects (mathematics, English, and reading).[8] Remedial need is more pronounced in urban regions with high minority populations and struggling school districts such as Denver, where 30 percent of first-time students tested into all three remedial areas, a rate nearly twice that of the overall population. CCCS remedial students are also more heavily minority and female as well as younger than the overall student population, characteristics that are associated with lower rates of college completion.[9]

The high numbers of recent high school graduates who test into remedial courses is disconcerting, not only for what it says about academic rigor in high school, but also for what it portends for student retention and attainment. Fall-to-fall retention for first-time students who tested into remedial courses in 2008–9 was 45.5 percent, 5 percentage points below the 50.7 percent retention rate of students who tested into college-level work.[10]

Fiscal and Policy Climate

Since fiscal year 1989–90, state support for higher education in Colorado has decreased from 20.3 percent to 9 percent of the state's general fund. Relative to other state services, higher education's share of the general fund has been reduced by 55 percent. Cuts to higher education became more pronounced with the decrease in discretionary spending during the recent recession. Community colleges saw a 35.3 percent reduction in general fund appropriations in fiscal year 2004–5, dropping from $3,565 per resident full-time equivalent (FTE) in 2001–2 to $2,306 per resident FTE in 2004–5.[11] A 28 percent increase in tuition and a variety of cost-saving measures—such as administrative cuts, greater reliance on adjunct faculty, and reduction in student services—were put in place to counter the impact on services from reduced general fund revenues, but the positive effects of these measures were offset by an 18 percent increase in enrollment during the same period, adding new stresses to the already strained capacity of the CCCS.

A modicum of relief came from the American Reinvestment and Recovery Act (ARRA) and from a state constitutional amendment that directed a portion of gaming proceeds to community colleges. Despite these efforts to restore funding, 2010 FTE funding for community colleges now stands at the 1993 level, at a little over $2,000 per resident FTE, with another significant drop anticipated with the sunset of ARRA funds in 2012.

Looking ahead to the pending shortfall in higher education funding, the 2010 state legislature passed a bill giving institutions of higher education the authority to raise tuition above the legislatively mandated 9 percent cap, subject to the approval of financial accountability plans that, among other requirements, ensure protection for low- and middle-income students.[12]

The Three Community College Initiatives

From 2004 through 2010, three statewide initiatives brought the issues of low academic skills to the attention of the state's higher education and economic development communities. The discussion that follows looks at the interplay of these initiatives from the perspective of implementation, the scaling of successful innovations within and across colleges, and the role of policy in efforts to sustain successful innovations.

The Ford Foundation's Community College Bridges to Opportunity Initiative

In 2004, Colorado was selected to participate in the Ford Foundation's Community College Bridges to Opportunity (Bridges) project, a five-year, six-state initiative focused on creating community college and career pathways for disadvantaged students. Participating states were awarded $100,000 to $200,000 per year and were provided with technical assistance in the four focus areas of the grant: integration of the workforce and academic missions of the colleges, strengthening stakeholder engagement, increased use of data to inform decision making, and policy innovation to support systemic change.

Bridges had a modest impact on the development of career pathways through input and refinements to the Career and Technical Education division of the system, but it had other significant impacts. The nationally designed communication strategy helped position community colleges as the engine of economic development for communities and as the road to opportunity for individuals. A series of high-profile reports on remediation helped raise awareness of the interrelationship between remediation and low educational attainment; the development of a longitudinal tracking system contributed to the capacity for data-driven decision making at the college, system, and state policy levels. The Colorado Bridges grant also financed the development of a cost-benefit analysis to evaluate the relative cost-effectiveness of different innovations.

The Bridges communication strategy helped garner public support for two legislative measures that averted catastrophic revenue cuts to higher education. A series of remedial reports produced by the system's Office of Institutional Research also had additional public policy impacts. The annual reports focused attention on the remedial needs of the state's workforce and the implications of low educational attainment on the state's economic future, prompting the State Board of Community Colleges to look for ways to improve remedial outcomes.[13]

The use of data to inform policy gained momentum with the development of a longitudinal tracking system, funded in part through the grant. The dismal completion rates made apparent in the ensuing study of remedial math outcomes were remarkably similar to the findings of the Community College Research Center's longitudinal tracking of Achieving the Dream remedial math cohorts, a study that was completed at approximately the same time.[14] These discouraging remedial math outcomes, coupled with a national study showing similar negative outcomes, further reinforced the importance of addressing remediation in the overall strategy to raise educational attainment.

The reports did not result in immediate action, but they brought the issue of remediation into policy discussions at both the system and state level. By 2010, improving remedial outcomes was incorporated into the Colorado Community College System's strategic plan, and the remedial agenda was listed in the recommendations of the Colorado Department of Higher Education to the governor.[15] In spring 2010, the CCCS math chairs met with the provost of the community college system to discuss the issues generated by the longitudinal remedial math study. As a follow-up to the meeting, each college was asked to design a two-year pilot to improve remedial math outcomes. The focus on improving developmental education outcomes continued with the Colorado's submission of a successful application to Complete College America, a significant player in the legislative landscape.[16]

Bridges resources also funded the development of a simplified student unit cost-benefit template that could be used by college staff to evaluate the fiscal implications of grant-funded innovations.[17] The template calculated the break-even point and the projected revenues of different strategies on the basis of retention rates and course-taking patterns of students in intervention and matched comparison groups. The tool was used in internal evaluations of strategies developed under the Lumina grant, was included as a resource on the Bridges website (Community College Central), and was featured in a 2010 webinar sponsored by the Joyce Foundation's Shifting Gears project.

The Colorado Lumina Initiative for Performance

Understanding the importance of leveraged funding, the Bridges program officers encouraged CCCS to apply for a Lumina Foundation grant to meet the objective of "developing models of effective institutional classroom and administrative practices for use by policymakers, college administrators and advocacy coalitions."[18] The program that resulted— the Colorado Lumina Initiative for Performance: Costs and Strategies for Serving Academically Under-Prepared Students—was funded in 2004 with a two-year, $650,000 grant, followed by a two-year supplemental grant of $324,000. Yearly grants to the three participating colleges, based on the scope of the colleges' projects, ranged from $30,000 to $86,000. The goal of the initiative was to support the development and implementation of innovation at the college level and to calculate the cost-effectiveness of different grant-funded strategies for serving academically under-prepared students.[19]

The Colorado initiative was structured as a centrally coordinated, bottom-up effort, with college teams choosing the strategies they would implement through an internal assessment of their practices in relationship to evidence-based practices.[20] These assessments allowed each college to determine its own needs, resources, and capacity and to identify strategies. Ongoing data collection was used to evaluate and adapt programmatic design. At the end of the first year of implementation, all three colleges had modified their initial strategies after examining student outcomes and faculty feedback.

Front Range Community College chose a hybrid accelerated developmental education format as its initial strategy, with one class session delivered on campus and two class sessions delivered online. In the second year the college added two learning community formats, one that paired developmental English and math with a college-level sociology course and a second one that paired developmental English with a single college-level course. Students in both formats were supported by a dedicated case manager who monitored their academic progress and assisted them in negotiating college processes and accessing support services.

Preliminary outcomes after three semesters were positive, with the learning community interventions showing higher gains than the hybrid format. Students in the learning community that paired developmental English with a single college-level course performed the best, with higher GPAs, a 45.7 percent higher completion rate, and a 33.4 percent higher retention rate than students in the comparison groups.[21]

A cost-benefit analysis of the paired developmental English / college-level strategy showed a net revenue on an average per-student basis of $408 over four terms.[22] As a result of the preliminary student outcomes, the positive revenue outlook provided by the cost-benefit analysis, and the feedback from faculty and staff, Front Range focused its strategy on expanding developmental English / college-level pairings and began shifting costs from grant funds to the general fund.[23] New paired learning communities were added, and the strategy was replicated at two additional Front Range campuses. Student numbers increased from an initial population of 20 students a semester to over 200 students a semester.

The Community College of Denver implemented two strategies. The first was an English as a Second Language (ESL) learning community that combined three upper-level, stand-alone ESL courses in reading, writing, and speaking in a block format; the second was an accelerated developmental learning community, FastStart@CCD, which compressed two or more levels of developmental courses into a single semester. With both formats, an educational case manager recruited, screened, and supported students and also monitored student progress. The Fast Start strategy included study groups, faculty professional development, and a mandatory student success course organized around career exploration.

Initial ESL outcomes demonstrated significantly higher retention and course completion rates for students in the intervention than for students in a matched comparison.[24] Cost-benefit analysis showed an average per student net revenue of $472 at scale after two terms, with the project reaching the break-even point in the first semester. Net per student revenue after two semesters was $912.[25] Armed with preliminary evidence of positive student outcomes and positive revenue projections, program staff successfully advocated for institutionalization of ESL Learning Communities using the college's strategic planning process. The program was fully institutionalized in 2009 with the transition of the ESL case manager from grant funds to the general fund. From 2007 to 2010, the college expanded the ESL learning community strategy to intermediate level ESL learners. An additional case manager was added and the number of program participants increased fivefold.

The second Community College of Denver strategy, FastStart@CCD, implemented a form of acceleration called "compression," which combines two or more levels of developmental courses in a single semester. First-semester Fast Start outcomes showed a significantly higher course completion rate (47% versus 24%) and a 50 percent higher semester-to-semester retention rate for students who took accelerated pairings in English, reading, and mathematics, as compared with students in a matched comparison taking a single course in the traditional format.[26]

In addition to breaking even in the first term, the program generated an average additional per student net revenue of $460 after two terms; this figure was calculated by comparing the retention rates and course-taking patterns of students in the intervention and those in a matched comparison. The cumulative average per student net revenue after two terms was $912, with a subsequent analysis over nine terms showing an average per student net revenue of $1,898.[27] On the basis of these strong outcomes and positive revenue projections, the college began the shift from grant funds to the general fund. Continued development and expansion from 2006 to 2010 was provided through two additional grants, Breaking Through and Scaling Up.[28]

From 2005 to 2010, the community college added six new course combinations to Fast Start, including pairings of developmental courses with college level courses, for a total of eleven course combinations. The number of classes and number of students doubled in each of the last three semesters of this period, expanding from a single cohort of 22 students in the first semester to 26 learning community cohorts. Enrollment in spring 2011 topped 450 students, boosting the cumulative number of students served to over 2,400. Student support continues to be provided by educational case managers and work-study students. Coaching to maintain program quality during rapid expansion and curriculum development for new course pairings is funded through a combination of grant carryover and support from the college's Teaching and Learning Center.

Colorado SUN: The OVAE Ready for College Initiative

In 2007, the U.S. Department of Education's Office of Vocational and Adult Education (OVAE) awarded an $875,000 two-year grant to CCCS under its Ready for College initiative. The goal of the project—called Colorado Success Unlimited (Colorado SUN)—was to provide transition services to GED completers and out-of-school youth at seven community colleges. The program design replicated the Community College of Denver's successful bridge program, College Connection, piloted in 2007 under the college's Breaking Through grant.[29] The College Connection model incorporated the key components of Fast Start: accelerated learning communities, case management, career exploration, and professional development. In the second year, several of the colleges moved to a credit-bearing format, making the program Pell-eligible and moving it toward sustainability. College Connection was offered in an eight-week summer intensive as well as in the first half of the traditional semester, allowing students the opportunity to enroll in late-start college classes during the second half of the semester.

Evaluation data showed that 65 percent of Ready for College students advanced one or two adult education levels in developmental math, 60 percent in developmental reading, and 47 percent in developmental English. Enrollment in college-level courses was high, with 80.3 percent of Ready for College learners enrolling in college-level courses and earning an average of 10 college credits.[30] While it is too early to know the extent to which College Connection will be sustained at either the college or the system level, at least one college is continuing the program through a new source of grant funds, while others are adopting program components. Another outgrowth of Colorado SUN is the CCCS College Career Navigation Initiative, a collaboration of community colleges and partnering workforce systems, funded through a U.S. Department of Labor incentive grant. The goal of the Career Navigation Initiative is to facilitate the successful transition of students who are referred from the workforce systems to postsecondary education.

The Ford, Lumina, and OVAE grants impacted CCCS in several positive ways: elevating the public perception of community colleges, promoting the development and implementation of new approaches for addressing high-risk populations, and positioning the system to take a leadership role in completion efforts. The grants also increased the capacity of the system and the colleges to measure outcomes and financed the development of a data-driven means to demonstrate the financial viability of innovations to a fiscal-oriented audience of decision makers.

Implementing Effective Approaches
Achieving Scale at the Institutional Level

Despite the early successes of these initiatives, the extent to which Colorado's community college system will sustain or scale these strategies remains an open question All levels of college leadership must be involved to move an innovation to scale: the president, who identifies an innovation as a priority for the institution and ensures that it appears in the college's strategic plan; the vice president, who must lead the charge to change rules and procedures in academic standards or staffing patterns; fiscal leaders, who must reconcile the fiscal benefits of scaling innovations with immediate budget concerns; faculty and deans, who must facilitate the logistics of change (in classes, schedules, faculty loads, etc.); and faculty, whose creativity and commitment are vital to the success of an initiative.

As critical as college leadership and college-wide buy-in are, institutional commitment to a strategy alone is not enough to move an innovation to scale. In assessing scale, the key criterion is the number of students served by the practice in relationship to the potential number of students who would benefit from the strategy.

At Front Range Community College the benchmark for reaching scale was to enroll 80 percent of students who tested at the highest level of developmental English into a developmental English / college-level course pairing. The college successfully resolved procedural and logistical issues, the courses were gaining in reputation with faculty and students, the cost-benefit analysis was positive, and the strategy was supported at all levels of leadership. Despite this, the movement toward scaling stalled as grant funds ended, state funding continued to decline, and the number of FTE students soared.

The first fiscal impact was the elimination of the case manager, the staff member who advised students on the expectations and pace of the learning community; assisted students with logistical issues, such as applying for financial aid; and followed up on instructor referrals for students who were struggling with academic or nonacademic issues. The loss of the case manager position coincided with a drop in course completion rates, which program staff felt was a direct result of the elimination of the position.[31]

The second fiscal impact was a hiatus in program expansion. As of this writing, the ongoing instructional costs of paired learning communities (one credit hour per instructor per learning community) continue to be supported by the general fund, but the goal of reaching scale has receded into the background. With increasing fiscal pressure, it is unclear how long Front Range will sustain the additional per-student cost of paired learning communities, despite strong evidence of the strategy's ability to deliver a lower cost per outcome and higher per student revenue over time.

The trajectory of the Front Range learning community initiative is a familiar one. A program begins with grant funding, achieves success, and remains a feature of the college—but at a limited scale. This is what is often spoken of as a "boutique program," the connotation being that it is both expensive and limited in the number of students served. Often, the colleges that pilot these strategies will continue them after a grant has ended for a particular segment of the population, such as first-generation students. In other cases, a college might expand the program to all students because of a passionate belief in the program's importance to the college mission. In these cases, going to scale means that colleges must find other ways to support program costs by reallocating general funds or by securing external funding, a process that continues from grant cycle to grant cycle.

The Community College of Denver has made greater progress in expanding innovations to scale than has Front Range, partly because a succession of grants gave the college time to develop leadership, support professional development, expand the program, and collect longitudinal data on the program's cost-effectiveness, thus bolstering the case for institutionalization.

Another difference in the progress of these two community colleges in reaching scale is the relative expense of the paired learning communities at Front Range as compared with that of Denver's compressed learning communities. Paired learning communities, which are team taught, incur one-third more instructional costs than the costs of delivering classes in a traditional format, without generating additional revenue.

By comparison, compressed courses, which are taught by one instructor, incur some additional instructional costs for the added preparation time, but to compensate, they garner more revenue from tuition and FTE reimbursement than traditional instruction. The reason for the reduced instructional costs lies in the efficiency of compression, which allows students to master material in less "seat time" than do traditional formats. Because tuition for Fast Start students is based on the number of credit hours, while pay for Fast Start instructors is based on a mix of credit hours and instructional time, the program-wide net result is cost neutral.[32]

Compressed course pairings, with their lower costs and higher revenues, provide the rationale for program continuation, but the outlook is less positive for team-taught learning communities. Despite the evidence of stronger student outcomes and higher cumulative revenues per student over the long term, the additional short-term costs of team-taught learning communities leave them vulnerable in a fiscal climate focused on inputs rather than outputs.

Using Dissemination as a Tool for Replication across Colleges

As difficult as it is to reach scale within an institution, the challenge of replicating, or scaling across institutions, is even more difficult. One of the lessons of the Colorado Lumina project was that innovations that are developed by a single college in a consortium are not easily implemented across colleges without intentional strategies to promote replication.

The Lumina initiative structured multiple opportunities for cross-college communication as part of its three-college project design, including quarterly meetings of project directors, presentations to the CCCS Council of Vice Presidents of Instruction, and a statewide basic skills summit to highlight best practices developed over the course of the initiative. Despite this, the only replication of successful strategies from one college to another from 2005 to 2011 was Denver's adoption of the Front Range developmental English / college-level pairings.

The implicit expectation that dissemination will lead to replication was not borne out in reality. Dissemination plays an important role in informing the field, but reliance on it as a means of replication is based on the assumption that conference presentations, forums, summits, reports, and briefs will lead to implementation of best practices. This assumption ignores the difficulty of translating what appears to work in one context to a different context, particularly when pilots are developed and put into place with generous grant funds.

While dissemination is an important part of introducing new ideas, hearing or reading about successful programs does not translate into the ability to successfully carry out practices. An awareness of the limitations of dissemination practices and of the importance of linking policy and implementation efforts is becoming a more significant part of the dialogue on scaling innovation. Several new strategies that address the challenge of replication are beginning to emerge in multicollege efforts, including practitioner-based technical assistance, peer coaching, and web-based collaboration. Legislative or system-wide initiatives to promote innovation present another avenue of promise, combining accountability with new resources; but without buy-in from all levels of leadership, as well as structured mechanisms for replication of effective practices across colleges, they are unlikely to achieve the elusive goal of scale.

Let a Thousand Flowers Bloom

Another example of the challenges of replication can be seen in how the individual colleges in the Lumina initiative responded to the CCCS request to design and implement two-year remedial math pilots. During the development period for the pilots, there was no formal attempt and minimal informal effort to draw on the lessons of the Lumina project. Competition between colleges may have played a role in the "go it alone" approach, but another likely factor is the commonly held belief that what will work in one college is different from what will work at another college, fueling the result that is sometimes referred to as "Let a thousand flowers bloom." While this approach honors the differences in college contexts and allows each college to choose the most effective way to implement a strategy in its own specific setting, the dissimilarity between strategies makes it more difficult for evaluators to identify the common elements of effective practice, a critical element in successful replication and, ultimately, in widespread system reform.

Maintaining the Fidelity of the Model

Ensuring the fidelity of a program is another challenge in moving to scale. College cultures vary widely, from the way departments are organized, to the strength of leadership, to beliefs about how students learn, to the ability of faculty and staff to learn new ways of thinking about how to efficiently and effectively serve students. All of these differences play out when a college attempts to replicate a practice that was developed in a different academic context.

The challenge of context was evident in the Ready for College initiative, where seven colleges committed to replicate the College Connection bridge program. The variation in the ways that the program was implemented—which was driven by the different capacities, overall goals, and cultures of the different colleges—was significant. While overall, student outcomes for the project were impressive, there was considerable variation in outcomes, with the strongest outcomes posted by those programs that exhibited the greatest fidelity to the model.[33]

Strengthening the Impact of Evaluation

Evaluation is a critical tool for identifying effective practices, but issues of institutional research capacity and the time frame of the evaluation cycles limit the usefulness of grant evaluations in providing a robust argument for scale. Even when there are adequate resources for a rigorous evaluation, the duration of most grants is not long enough to collect the longitudinal data needed for anything but a preliminary assessment of an innovation's effectiveness. In addition, once the formal lines of communication between grantor and grantee no longer exist, and even assuming that a college has the capacity to continue to collect and analyze data, there is no central vehicle to capture the ongoing quantitative and qualitative lessons learned. The granting agency has moved on to the next initiative, with all but the most prominent and well-publicized innovations receding into the landscape. There is no repository for continued evidence. Grant funds are no longer available to send innovators to conference where they can interact with colleagues. In terms of ongoing impact, innovations and the lessons that have been learned from them fade into the background and ultimately disappear from the discourse.

Achieving Scale and Sustainability

Perhaps the most difficult aspect of reaching scale is the challenge of moving from grant funds to institutionalization. In their discussion of scale, Rachel Christina and Jo Victoria Nicholson-Goodman define sustainability as "policy and infrastructure systems that support continued improvement and impact over time."[34] In the context of scaling innovation in community colleges, these critical systems include the curricular and internal sets of policies and procedures that support or inhibit the scaling of initiatives, as well as the legislative policies that determine governance, funding, and accountability.

The interplay of the three statewide initiatives in Colorado highlights the power of parallel and coordinated efforts in policy and implementation. The Ford Foundation's Community College Bridges to Opportunity project played a significant role in the development of innovations for academically underprepared students. It aided the system in leveraging the Colorado Lumina Initiative funding; helped make the public case for the importance of community colleges to the economic well-being of the state; connected remedial success to college completion; and contributed resources to the longitudinal tracking system, thereby strengthening the capacity of the system to make data-driven decisions. The Lumina and OVAE initiatives provided the content; the Bridges project influenced the policy climate and supported the development of strategic tools that brought a modicum of recognition to the initiatives in the short term, and the possibility of long-term impact. The timing of these three initiatives, coming as they did in the five-year period directly preceding the current focus on completion, was fortuitous, providing continuity to the system's efforts to strengthen developmental education outcomes.

As important a role as policy plays in supporting innovation, the development of policy without the reality check of implementation is both inefficient and ultimately counterproductive in the promotion of systemic change. While bottom-up efforts are unlikely to move beyond a particular institution, policy-driven efforts that fail to include the expertise of educators in the development of policy are likely to fail because the policies do not anticipate and respond to challenges on the ground.

Colleges differ from one another in critical ways: in their governance, in their funding, in their internal organization, in their leadership, and in the populations that they serve. The importance of policy in promoting systemic change cannot be underestimated, but rushing to embrace new strategies while ignoring the importance of working with multiple stakeholders within a real context presents its own dangers. Imposing top-down solutions to the challenges of postsecondary attainment without authentic and deep engagement with the field is likely to lead to wasted opportunities and a new round of recriminations that could sour the public, the government, and the foundation community on the ability of community colleges to fulfill the multiple missions of educating and training the nation's citizens.

Conclusions and Recommendations

The experience gained from these three Colorado initiatives suggests that replicating innovation at scale will require changes in both policy and implementation: changes in policies and procedures at the institutional level, changes in state and federal policy, changes in the way that grants and other initiatives are structured, and changes in the ways that we approach and support the replication of successful practice.

Policy Changes

There are two broad categories of policy change: changes at the institutional and system levels in the curricular, regulatory, and administrative policies that create barriers to efficient functioning, and changes in formulas that determine how state funds are awarded. Rethinking curricular and alignment issues and streamlining the labyrinth of administrative policies that govern community colleges are necessary steps in a broad change agenda, but the key driver of institutional policy and ultimately of college practices is how community colleges are funded.

A detailed consideration of the broad challenge of assuring sustained and adequate funding streams for higher education is beyond the scope of this chapter, but changes in how colleges are financed are central to the challenges of innovation and scale. What is measured is what is rewarded. The way in which we fund colleges—based on rewarding credit hours, without regard to student outcomes—creates a disincentive for colleges to do anything other than maximize enrollment and reduce operating costs. Gregory Bateson, a pioneer in systems theory, described an organization's capacity for change as its "budget of flexibility," defined as the uncommitted resources of an organization.[35] From this perspective, the uncommitted resources of community colleges are scant, resting often on the creativity and commitment of their staff and faculty. Without incentives that reward innovation or changes in funding formulas, it is difficult to see where innovations will come from, let alone be sustained, no matter how small the short-term costs or how strong the evidence that specific strategies will yield higher outcomes.

Accountability and costs drive community college policy. Cost-per-outcome over time has little meaning if the benefit is in the future and the fiscal crisis is in the present. Increased revenue over time is not a strong argument for scaling innovation in a period of over-enrollment and cost containment. In an environment of shrinking resources, the policy driver is the ability to generate the maximum revenue at the lowest cost in the shortest amount of time.

RECOMMENDATION: Move toward performance funding by instituting a system of targeted incentives that reward effective practice in areas that have been identified as the critical loss and momentum points in the educational continuum, with particular emphasis on lower-skilled and under-represented minorities.[36] As the knowledge base of effective practice matures, incorporate outcomes into accountability and funding formulas, with careful safeguards to discourage colleges from excluding under-represented or lower-skilled students, populations that have been identified as critical to achieving the goals of the completion agenda.

Grant Structure

The traditional structure of grants does not promote replication or scalability. Defined grant periods, even when accompanied by efforts in dissemination, do not allow for an adequate time frame for the collection of longitudinal data or adequate mechanisms to facilitate replication.

RECOMMENDATION: Structure grants in two phases—the first phase as an implementation period of two to three years, followed by a three-year period of program replication. In the first phase, a primary grantee would be responsible for program development; in the second phase, the primary grantee would serve as a coach or mentor to a second tier of colleges. The primary grantee would receive reduced funding during the second phase to support continued data collection and program expansion, with the bulk of funds going to the second tier of colleges for program replication. Colleges, departments, and programs would need to "opt-in" to replication efforts and agree to basic elements that would ensure the fidelity of the replication.

Second, strengthen evaluation by establishing and funding a central collection point for ongoing, post-grant data collection and analysis that would be readily available to both practitioners and researchers.

Scaling Innovation

Traditional means of replication do not provide the type of guidance that is necessary to promote scale. Top-down mandates for change that are prescriptive in approach without consideration of the local context are likely to be met with resistance by professionals whose buy-in is critical to success, while bottom-up strategies are difficult to evaluate and replicate.

RECOMMENDATION: Include practitioner-based technical assistance as a key feature in replication across colleges. Practitioners with a detailed understanding of community college culture and practice would be an essential part of planning and implementation, including coaching and web-based collaboration for critical stakeholders: leadership, staff, faculty, and institutional research, technology, and student services.

Community colleges are at an important juncture in their development, moving front and center in efforts to create the workforce of the future. At the same time, the numbers of students earning credentials, as well as the rate of certificate and degree attainment, are inadequate to maintain the nation's economic competitiveness. Innovation is one avenue to pioneering systemic solutions, but without an understanding of how to move from innovation to widespread adoption, the promise of innovation will be unrealized. The political will to provide adequate and sustained funding is a necessary part of the solution, but political will often comes with political pressure to achieve results in an unrealistic time frame, creating new obstacles to the ability of the education community to meet the challenge of the completion agenda. Overcoming these obstacles will be critical in the success or failure of this important and ambitious goal.

ACKNOWLEDGMENT

This chapter was written from the perspective of a participant-observer. The author was the principal investigator of the Colorado Lumina Initiative for Performance, a member of the Ford Foundation's Colorado Bridges team, designer and initial project director of the Colorado Community College System's "Ready for College" initiative, and co-developer and director of FastStart@CCD.

1. National Center for Higher Education Management Systems, "Linking Higher Education with Workforce and Economic Development" (National Forum, Education Commission of the States, Denver, April 2009).

2. Alexandria Walton Radford et al., *Persistence Rates among 2003–04 Entering Students: After 6 Years* (Washington, DC: U.S. Department of Education, National Center for Educational Statistics, 2010).

3. Bill and Melinda Gates Foundation, *Postsecondary Success: Focusing on Completion* (Seattle, WA: Bill and Melinda Gates Foundation, 2010), available at www.gatesfoundation.org/learning/Documents/postsecondary-education-success-plan-executive-summary.pdf; Lumina Foundation for Education, "Goal 2025," www.luminafoundation.org/goal_2025.

4. Eric Kelderman, "Lumina Foundation Will Shift Away from New Projects, State Leaders Are Told," *Chronicle of Higher Education*, July 14, 2011.

5. American Association of Community Colleges, "College Completion Challenge: A Call to Action," 2010, www.aacc.nche.edu/About/completionchallenge/Pages/default.aspx.

6. Colorado Community College System, *Fall 2008 Transfer Report*, 2010, www.cccs.edu/Docs/Research/2008FallTransferReport.pdf.

7. Colorado Department of Higher Education, *Graduation Counts for Two-Year Public and Community Colleges*, Higher Education Summary (Denver, 2010), http://highered.colorado.gov.

8. Colorado Commission on Higher Education, *2009 Legislative Report on Remedial Education* (Denver, Feb. 2010), available at http://highered.colorado.gov/Publications/Reports/Remedial/FY2009/2009_Remedial_relfeb10.pdf.

9. Kerri King Nawrocki, Elaine DeLott Baker, and Kristin Corash, *Success of Remedial Math Students in the Colorado Community College System: A Longitudinal Study* (Denver: Colorado Community College System, 2009), available at www.cccs.edu/Docs/Research/Success of Remedial Math Students.pdf.

10. Colorado Commission on Higher Education, *2009 Legislative Report on Remedial Education*.

11. *Colorado Community College Source Book* (Denver: Colorado Community College System, 2010), available at www.cccs.edu/Docs/Communication/sb/Funding.pdf.

12. Colorado Senate Bill 10-03 is summarized on the Colorado Commission on Higher Education website, at http://highered.colorado.gov/CCHE/Meetings/2010/oct/oct10_vic.pdf.

13. Kristin Corash, Elaine DeLott Baker, and Kerri Nawrocki, *The Colorado Remedial Challenge* (Denver: Colorado Community College System, Feb. 2008), available at www.cccs.edu/Docs/Research/TheColoradoRemedialChallenge.pdf.

14. Nawrocki et al., *Success of Remedial Math Students in the Colorado Community College System*; Thomas Bailey, Dong Wook Jeong, and Sung-Woo Cho, "Referral, Enrollment, and Completion in Developmental Education Sequences

in Community Colleges" (CCRC Working Paper no. 15, Community College Research Center, Teachers College, Columbia University, New York, 2008).

15. Colorado Community College System, *Colorado Community College System Strategic Plan*, 2010, available at www.cccs.edu/Docs/About/StrategicPlan .pdf.

16. Colorado Proposal Narrative Statements, "Completion Innovation Challenge," Complete College America website, www.completecollege.org/docs/Colorado Proposal Narrative Statements.pdf.

17. Kristin Corash and Elaine Baker, *Calculating the Productivity of Innovation: Using a Simplified Cost-Benefit Analysis to Promote Effective Practice* (Denver: Colorado Community College System, 2009), available at www.cccs.edu/ Research/costeffect.html.

18. "Evaluating the Community College Bridges to Opportunity Initiative," Community College Research Center website, www.ccrc.tc.columbia.edu/Collec tion.asp?cid=14.

19. Hunter Boylan and D. Patrick Saxon, *What Works in Remediation: Lessons from Thirty Years of Research* (Boone, NC: National Center for Developmental Education, Appalachian State University, 2002).

20. To address the long term for sustained funding, the governors' Higher Education Strategic Planning Group identified a number of potential revenue-generating strategies that could create a sustained funding source for higher education, including restoring the income and sales tax rates to 5.0% and 3.0%, respectively; expanding sales tax to specific services; implementing a 1.0% surcharge on extraction; implementing a statewide 4.0% mill levy; and implementing a 4.0% mill levy in counties where an institution of higher education is located.

21. Laura Jensen, "Front Range Community College Project Methodology and Analysis" (internal report to the Colorado Lumina Initiative for Performance, 2007).

22. Kristin Corash and S. Jackson, "Cost-Benefit Analysis of Front Range Community College Learning Communities" (internal report to the Colorado Lumina Initiative for Performance, Dec. 2007).

23. Debra Bragg, *Ready for College in Colorado: Evaluation of the Colorado SUN and the College Connection Program* (Champaign, IL: University of Illinois, Office of Community College Research and Leadership, Dec. 2010).

24. Ruth Brancard, Elaine Baker, and Laura Jensen, "Accelerated Developmental Education Project Research Report: Community College of Denver," available at www.mdrc.org/publications/601/execsum.pdf.

25. Kristin Corash and Elaine Baker, *Calculating the Productivity of Innovation: Using a Simplified Cost-Benefit Analysis to Promote Effective Practice* (Denver: Colorado Community College System, 2009).

26. Ruth Brancard, Elaine Baker, and Laura Jensen, "Accelerated Developmental Education Project Research Report: Community College of Denver," available at http://inpathways.net/accelerated-dev-ed.pdf.

27. Kristin Corash and Elaine Baker, "Linking Outcomes and Cost Effective-

ness in Strategic Planning: Using a Simplified Cost-Benefit Analysis to Promote Effective Practice" (presentation at National Institute for Staff and Organizational Development [NISOD] conference, Austin, TX, Spring 2009).

28. The Community College of Denver was awarded a total of $330,000 over the course of five years as part of Breaking Through and Scaling Up, joint projects of the National Council of Workforce education and Jobs for the Future, funded by the Charles Stewart Mott (2006–9) and the Bill and Melinda Gates Foundations (2010).

29. Breaking Through was a four-year project of the National Council of Workforce Education and Jobs for the Future, funded by the Charles Stewart Mott Foundation.

30. Bragg, *Ready for College in Colorado*.

31. Phone interview with Shanna Jan, chair of Developmental English, Front Range Community College, Larimer Campus, and director of the Front Range Community College Lumina Initiative, Dec. 13, 2010.

32. In some course combinations, such as the compressed combination of medium and advanced levels in developmental English and reading, students pay for nine credit hours of instruction, while instructors are paid the equivalent of seven credit hours. In the case of the compressed sequence that combines the low and medium levels of developmental math, students pay for five credits, while instructors are paid the equivalent of six credits.

33. Bragg, *Ready for College in Colorado*.

34. Rachel Christina and Jo Victoria Nicholson-Goodman, *Going to Scale with High-Quality Early Education: Choices and Consequences in Universal Pre-Kindergarten Efforts* (Santa Monica, CA: Rand Corporation, 2010).

35. Gregory Bateson, *Steps to an Ecology of Mind: Collected Essays in Anthropology, Psychiatry, Evolution, and Epistemology* (Chicago: University of Chicago Press, 1972).

36. Vicki Choitz, *Getting What We Pay For: State Community College Funding Strategies that Benefit Low-Income, Low-Skilled Students* (Center for Law and Social Policy, Nov. 2010), available at www.clasp.org/postsecondary/publica tion?id=0829&list=publications.

CHAPTER TEN

Efforts to Improve Productivity

The Impact of Higher Education Reform in Texas

GERI HOCKFIELD MALANDRA

Texas is a reform-minded and action-oriented state where change occurs on a very large scale: today, Texas is home to 1 in every 12 U.S. residents.[1] In 2010, there were over 1.4 million postsecondary students enrolled in the state's colleges and universities, 40 percent more than in 2000. A decade ago, anticipating this rapid growth, the state of Texas embarked on a targeted strategy to improve the diversity, quality, and productivity of higher education through the implementation and updating of its "Closing the Gaps by 2015" higher education plan. Within this policy framework, the efforts of higher education reformers, coupled with strategic initiatives and investments, have led to significant and more diverse enrollment growth, improved persistence and completion rates, and increased degree production. Between 2000 and 2009, the number of degrees awarded increased 42 percent—to nearly 210,000— and more minority students are enrolled than ever before. The results have been tracked and, some might argue, amplified by a noteworthy statewide higher education accountability system that shines a bright light on results.

These efforts to improve Texas's system of higher education are both ongoing and subject to regular enhancements. Currently, higher education reform is becoming increasingly focused on the productivity of higher education. In a recent update, the Texas Higher Education Coordinating Board noted that despite positive results over the last 10 years, the state "has a long way to go to meet other targets by 2015."[2] Updated targets are designed to help drive Texas toward higher levels of overall participation and success, including higher rates of enrollment and degree completion among African American men and Hispanic students. Meeting these targets will also contribute to the nationwide goals laid out by the Obama administration to increase postsecondary credentials.[3] In light of the tough economic times, considerable attention has also been paid to cost-effectiveness; in September 2009, Texas Governor Rick Perry issued an executive order that called for a comprehensive review of higher education cost efficiencies and laid out numerous specific recommendations to enhance the productivity of higher education in Texas.[4]

The experience of policymakers and higher education leaders suggests that this progress can be attributed to a combination of three elements: reform-oriented leadership; a robust and flexible statewide planning framework; and persistence in pursuing a goal-oriented agenda via decision-making processes that engage state, system, and institution leaders. Underlying these factors is Texas's distinctive political culture of low taxes, light regulation, and openness to new business, which encourages innovation and participation in change.[5]

The Driving Force: 10 Years of "Closing the Gaps"

Since its adoption in 2000, the Closing the Gaps plan has served as the framework underlying the strategic expansion of higher education in Texas. The framework has been adjusted and enhanced, leading the state to continued improvements in access, success, and quality. The persistent effort to reach the plan's goals and the related, highly transparent reporting framework led to Texas's very high scores in a recent study of higher education accountability systems.[6]

Closing the Gaps was intended to close gaps in participation within Texas, and also between Texas and other leading states. The plan emphasized four broad areas: participation (adding 630,000 higher education students), success, excellence, and research. Statewide benchmarks and goals for enrollment growth, diversity, and degrees conferred were set in each area; and these goals were then customized for the specific mission of each institution. The legislative funding formula provided incentives for enrollment growth, tying increases in funding to gains in enrollments. Campuses must also report their progress under rigorous reporting requirements, and these data make progress and results tangible, transparent, and accessible.[7]

The Higher Education Coordinating Board functions as an agency of Texas government, and it was this body that proposed the Closing the Gaps plan that was adopted by the legislature. Closing the Gaps became the state's higher education master plan, laying out official, specific ideas and goals.[8] The Texas plan has been flexible enough to evolve in light of new developments, and its goals are periodically adjusted to reflect changes in population projections and institutional progress in achieving targets. It gained quick support from education, business, and policy leaders; and it has sustained visibility and support as results have emerged from the first decade of implementation.

Growth in Enrollment and Improved Outcomes

Texas serves an increasingly large and diverse number of postsecondary students at 146 public and private institutions of higher education.[9] The complex systems of higher education include 50 public community college districts, 38 public universities and upper-division centers, 4 technical colleges, 9 public health–related institutions, 3 public two-year lower-division colleges, 39 independent four-year colleges and universities, 1 independent medical school, and 2 independent junior colleges.

The size and growth of postsecondary education in Texas is extreme. In fall 2010, Texas colleges and universities enrolled 1,464,081 students.[10] Between 2000 and 2009, higher education enrollment increased by nearly 40 percent, adding 401,500 students. In one year (2008–9), Texas higher education enrollment (including enrollment in career colleges) increased by nearly 122,000 students—the largest jump in state history. Impressive increases in degrees awarded accompanied these massive increases in enrollment. The number of degrees awarded grew by 42 percent between 2000 and 2009, and the absolute number of degrees awarded (209,600) was quite close to the state's 2015 goal of awarding 210,000 undergraduate degrees and certificates.[11] In addition, Texas has achieved a 50 percent increase in allied health and nursing awards and a 40 percent increase in doctoral degrees; and the state more than doubled research and development expenditures, to $3.3 billion (the 2015 R&D target was reached seven years early).

The growth in enrollment and degrees completed has been particularly impressive among minority students. In 2009, 42 percent of the students enrolled in postsecondary institutions in Texas were African American or Hispanic; those two groups make up just over 55 percent of the state's entire population of 15- to 34-year-olds. In fall 2009, African American students were proportionally the best represented among major ethnicities, with a 6.5 percent participation rate (above the 2010 and the 2015 targets). While Hispanic enrollment grew 74 percent from

2000 to 2009, the overall participation rate in 2009 was 4.4 percent. Rates of success (measured in degrees awarded) also increased for these traditionally underrepresented groups by about 85 percent for Hispanics and 54 percent for African Americans from 2000 to 2009.

In addition, financial support for higher education has not flagged, reflecting both political priorities and the comparative strength of the state's economy. For the 2010–11 biennium, funding increased by 8.4 percent over the previous biennium. A modest proportion of the $22 billion appropriated ($178 million) was designated for performance or incentive funding to promote and reward degree completion. This sustained investment, guided by the state master plan, has enabled Texas to focus on key priorities over the past decade.

By any metric, the state's higher education system has become more productive over this period. More students are attending college, more degrees are being awarded, and the diversity of graduates is increasing. Texas was able to achieve this progress because Closing the Gaps has provided a clear, unified, and flexible framework for systematic goal-setting, actions, and investments, and measurement of progress. The Higher Education Coordinating Board is viewed as asking the right questions, measuring progress effectively, putting pressure on institutions of higher education to think about results, and understanding that the goal line for postsecondary education is a credential.[12]

The Sources of Higher Education Reform in Texas

How has Texas been able to create, implement, sustain, and direct these reforms over the past 10 years? Discussions with policymakers and higher education leaders in Texas reveal some key areas of consensus regarding the sources of reform ideas, how implementation proceeded, the impact of reforms, and the potential for replication and scalability. Observers generally attribute the track record of success to the persistence of individual leaders and of the state's Higher Education Coordinating Board, but there is more to the story.

Texas's outcomes-focused higher education reform agenda developed against a backdrop of ambitious K–12 reform. Like the K–12 movement in Texas, the push for higher education reform was fueled by concerns about demographic change and economic competitiveness and has been increasingly focused on data and accountability. The process has been both top-down and bottom-up: work by the governor's office and the state legislature was complemented by efforts of business leaders and key policymakers in higher education agencies. And the work of individual policymakers and higher education leaders had a particularly strong impact at key points in the reform process. Many claim a role in these efforts, but these same individuals also have concerns that more still needs to be done. Thus, despite Texas's apparent accomplishments, there is not universal agreement that this is a success story yet.

Demographic and Economic Imperatives

At the core of higher education reform in Texas was growing awareness of population changes coupled with concerns about economic prosperity. By 2000, demographers were drawing attention to the massive demographic shifts under way in Texas, and gradually people began to pay attention.[13] Of great concern to the business and policy community was the disconnect between demographic trends and the need for the state to become more competitive by improving education. These two phenomena appeared incompatible—"something had to give," according to Diana Natalicio, president of the University of Texas at El Paso (UTEP).[14]

Leaders in the University of Texas System and in other systems were, at the same time, also beginning to become more aware of diversity within higher education institutions. Policymakers were gathering finer-grained data that helped to build an understanding of the different kinds of institutions and the students that they were serving—and the data served to clarify just how much work there was to be done. In the UT System, for example, the flagship campus in Austin is best known, but the other eight universities under the UT umbrella were actually quite different from UT–Austin and from one another. The four border and south Texas campuses served a largely first-generation, low-income Hispanic population; and their leaders voiced strong concerns about the impact of demographic trends. Through their advocacy, awareness of these different missions grew: the Coordinating Board took on the Closing the Gaps initiative, and although their metrics have been questioned, there is some consensus that the board set the right targets and understood the unique issues facing individual campuses.[15]

Awareness of demographic growth trends was soon coupled with concerns about postsecondary education success and completion, as leaders came to recognize that the "goal line" for higher education is not enrollment but a credential. The key question was, How do we know that once students begin an education that they will be successful, where, and how? A focus on success was driven by the Coordinating Board, but it was also a "ground movement" begun by some postsecondary leaders even before Closing the Gaps was official policy.[16]

The initial steps in higher education reform occurred before the state's more recent financial bind. Raymund A. Paredes, commissioner of higher education, observed that Texas was in better economic shape than other states in the early 2000s and so was able to put ideas on the table that were not feasible in places like California.[17] Texas A&M chancellor Mike McKinney observed that Texas has had both flush and hard times. In his view, a lot of the impetus for higher education reform came from industry, which was concerned about Texas's supply of skilled workers, given demographic trends. For example, in 2001–2, the Greater Houston Partnership announced that the top economic issue facing Texas was the Hispanic dropout rate. This group came to the Governor's Business Council with ideas about how to address this problem in the face of shifting demographics and the resistance of the education system to change.[18]

K–12 and Higher Education Accountability

The past decade of higher education reform in Texas was heavily influenced by Governor George W. Bush's focus on promoting accountability in K–12 education: outcomes-based accountability was the single driving force in every education policy discussion. While accountability has become part of the vernacular in contemporary education policy, it was not a widely discussed concept at the time that Bush took office as governor.[19]

At the institutional level, the link to K–12 reform was an important ingredient in changing the focus of the universities. As UTEP President Diana Natalicio observes, it was Texas's strong commitment to K–12 accountability that provided a context for the spotlight on higher education accountability spawned by Closing the Gaps. At UTEP, she built on the compatibility between the push for accountability at the K–12 level and the promotion of such ideas in higher education; because of the earlier push for K–12 accountability, there was not the kind of discomfort with outcomes-based reform that might have occurred in other states. The local effort of the El Paso Collaborative for Educational Excellence, which pushed to raise the aspirations and achievement of K–12 students, laid a foundation for the higher education reforms that came later.

Texas education reformers Sandy Kress and Beth Ann Bryan observe that, simultaneously, some ideas about accountability in higher education preceded the political push for a statewide accountability system. They highlight the influential role played by Charles Miller, then chair of the University of Texas System Board of Regents. Under Miller's leadership, accountability measures were developed by individual systems before they were required by state policy. Miller, who served as chairman of the education committee of the Governor's Business Council, had the authority and responsibility to develop the reform agenda through contacts in major Texas cities and in discussions about education on the council. According to this view, higher education accountability followed on the heels of institutional work to improve outcomes and provided a mechanism to measure what was accomplished in the pursuit of both institutional and state goals. The concrete work on accountability (and on the importance of the pipeline between K–12 and postsecondary education) that the UT System began under Chancellor Mark G. Yudof is also a big part of this story.[20]

According to Charles Miller, Governor Bush was not interested at first in higher education and did not hold it in high regard. He viewed higher education leaders as asking for money and then to be left alone. At that time, the Higher Education Coordinating Board did not coordinate with the governor or consult with him about appointments. Governor Bush's appointment of Pamela Willeford to the Coordinating Board in 1997 launched a transformation in the board from a regulatory to a more policy-oriented agency. As chair from 1999 to 2003, Willeford spearheaded the work that led to the Closing the Gaps blueprint. Her efforts also led to a changed atmosphere in Texas higher education, to one of openness for reform, which also served to change the relationship between the regulators and higher education institutions.

Miller recalls that a number of events occurred simultaneously. Governor Bush asked Miller to become chairman of the Board of Regents of the University of Texas System. In this role, one of his first actions, even as a "freshman" board member, was to start talking about accountability. In 2002, Mark G. Yudof was appointed chancellor of the UT System; under Yudof's leadership, an accountability framework was created, and he was tasked with figuring out how to implement it. Early on, it was hard to get academics to support the accountability plan, and the business community was, in Miller's terms, "kind of ho-hum." The accountability measures were subsequently connected to the proposal to expand the authority of the Board of Regents to set tuition, which gained support of prominent political leaders, including the lieutenant governor and the state comptroller.

Miller argues that the two elements—"freedom to operate" and accountability—were always connected: "Everyone had to be serious on both." Chancellor Yudof helped push these ideas through the UT System, facilitating academic engagement in the process and leading the first steps toward an accountability system. The Texas legislature did expand the power of the Board of Regents to set tuition in 2003. That same year, Governor Perry issued an executive order calling on all systems of higher education in Texas, and the Coordinating Board, to establish systems of accountability.

Texas leaders aspired to more than statewide scaling of reform ideas. In addition, they sought national leadership on both K–12 and higher education reform. While there was no intention to create a "no child left behind" policy for higher education, Texas's leadership on higher education accountability gradually gained national momentum. In 2003, Miller testified for a U.S. House committee (chaired by Congressman John Boehner) on affordability, accountability, access, and quality.[21] And, when Secretary of Education Margaret Spellings established the Commission on the Future of Higher Education in 2005, she chose Miller as the chair. As a result, after some debate, accountability became a focal point of the commission's deliberations and report.[22]

Implementation

The factors that help explain the success of Texas in implementing this ambitious slate of higher education reforms fall into three general categories: a common strategic vision (provided by the Closing the Gaps plan), engaged stakeholders, and a robust, data-driven, and outcomes-focused accountability system.

Common Strategic Vision

Commissioner Paredes argues that a sense of common purpose has been key to the continued implementation of reforms at the state level. Closing the Gaps has focused on the right issues and sensible goals, even though the state has not made as much progress as it would have liked. In addition, because the common vision set priorities for the entire state but was flexible enough to reflect distinct campus missions and needs, it helped to mobilize stakeholders across the spectrum of institutions.

Engaged Stakeholders

A strong and persistent theme in the story of Texas higher education reform is has been the clear sense of shared responsibility among stakeholders and pride in the changes among state-level, system, and institutional leaders. The Texas policy environment has supported a freedom to innovate that seems to have reinforced a deep and widespread sense of ownership in the process and results of reform.

For instance, Sandy Kress and Beth Ann Bryan note the importance of actively engaged college and university presidents who became supportive of legislative involvement in higher education policy. Equally important, in their view, was the Governor's Business Council, which had a strong interest in accountability. Charles Miller's ability to "shake things up" was significant, particularly at the beginning of the movement. These civic and business leaders have been able to "keep the fire burning," although it might not be strong enough to deepen implementation.

From an institutional point of view, a key to implementation was the level of collaboration among institutional leaders and policymakers. University of Texas System associate vice chancellor Martha Ellis served as a community college president during this period. She observed that looking at issues of student success and accountability typically led to the divisive question of "whom do you blame?" In Texas, however, there were some policy and campus leaders who decided to go beyond worrying about blame and, instead, tried to "take students where they are now and figure out how to assist them to be successful, as defined by the institution." This also required developing partnerships between those that provide higher education and those at the K–12 level. These institutional and regional collaborations were fueled by systematic thinking about the postsecondary pipeline. which began to focus on college readiness, the college-going culture, transfer policies, a standardized core curriculum, and common course numbering. Many local and regional reforms were developed with this pipeline in mind, and some went on to influence statewide reforms. In the case of developmental education, for instance, everyone from presidents to provosts, faculty, and student services leaders began to see the data about gatekeeper and developmental courses; and successful local projects evolved to become part of a state-wide agenda.

A Robust and "True" Accountability System

Charles Miller recalls that publishing the UT System's first accountability report in 2003 created attention in the community and nationally. When the system began using the Collegiate Learning Assessment, the accountability report was able to report aggregate data on student learning outcomes, a level of transparency that is rare in higher education. The focus on student outcomes remains a cornerstone of ongoing state policy and goals. As Miller observes, "Some of the things the UT System developed are still alive and working."

Commissioner Paredes believes Texas has "the best accountability system" in the country and that its impact has been sustained by continued investment in collecting timely data and using those data to make further improvements. Texas recently received a $12 million federal grant to link K–12 and postsecondary data and is replicating a successful model that California has used to link its educational data.

From an institutional point of view, Guy Bailey, who was provost at UT–San Antonio from 1999 to 2005, observed that for him, as the "implementer of the university," Closing the Gaps worked quite well because it coincided with what the campus wanted to achieve. As provost, his biggest challenge was selling the plan on campus, but changes to the way higher education money was doled out helped to build support for the reforms among campus leaders. While the baseline funding formula was based on enrollments, and the rapid growth of UT-San Antonio meant that that institution received a larger slice of the pie, the new financial incentives to improve student success (with higher reimbursements for students who persisted to higher levels of study) also motivated institutional change. In particular, the incentive funding for degrees awarded, for degrees in critical fields, and for degrees to underrepresented students also benefited the campus.

These benefits made the accountability plan easier to sell. In Bailey's view, this direct link of goals and financial rewards is true accountability and is at the heart of what makes the Texas system work. Once faculty, chairs, and deans understood the incentives in the funding formula, it was easier to sell the goals because there were real dollars behind them.

As Bailey puts it, "Showing the connection between funding and actions makes decision-making much easier."

The Impact of Reforms on Ways of Doing Business
An Outcomes Focus

The accountability component of Closing the Gaps helped instill a focus on outcomes across the higher education system. Commissioner Paredes pointed to Texas's increased focus on student success as the strongest evidence of this impact, a change the Coordinating Board has achieved through its emphasis on accountability data reporting and its emphasis on student outcomes data. In addition, the state has made student advising mandatory, has reduced the number of courses students are allowed to drop, and has programs to support faculty training designed to promote student success. Moreover, the Coordinating Board is close to implementing common metrics for learning outcomes, going beyond what individual systems and institutions currently use.

Martha Ellis emphasizes that an important characteristic of higher education reform in Texas is that much of the impact begins at institutions and is moved forward by proponents, often in parallel with official political and policy actions. For example, in 2009, Texas faced huge dual credit issues between community colleges and higher education institutions. In what may have seemed a somewhat informal process, the chancellor of the UT System led a voluntary effort to bring all stakeholders together; they developed a collective position, speaking with the same voice on common principles for dual credit. As the policy was implemented, all affected parties were engaged in discussion and trouble-shooting. The Coordinating Board's transfer advisory committee was disbanded, while the associations of community college and public university presidents have joined to advise the legislature on policies to promote and improve transfer.

The University of Texas at El Paso provides a noteworthy illustration of the impact of these reforms: over the past decade, UTEP has increased the number of undergraduate degrees awarded by nearly 100 percent while enrollments have increased 30 percent.[23] President Natalicio underscores the campus's focus and hard work in fostering student success, first by supporting efforts at the precollege level to promote higher aspirations and academic preparation among El Paso high school students, and then by addressing the obstacles that may affect students who enroll in higher education, whether at UTEP or El Paso Community College. The implementation of accountability reinforced the need for data to strategically plan interventions. Using these data, the institutions have become much more efficient in helping students accelerate progress to degrees through advising, scheduling, and pruning required hours. UTEP has implemented "a whole host of interventions" (including such tactics as financial literacy coaching and special loan programs); the institution studies the impact very closely through data gathering. As a result, it knows much more about its students and their issues than was the case 10 years ago and is better at helping them succeed. UTEP has achieved dramatic change because it can "figure out a whole lot of things by understanding students and regularly studying data."[24]

This focus on student outcome data has not been without controversy. For UTEP president Natalicio, the debate over graduation rates has been a major distraction. In her experience, most people have not understood the basis for low graduation rates at UTEP and similar schools that serve at-risk students. During the first half of this decade, she devoted considerable time to responding to critiques about low graduation rates and then explaining how they are calculated—excluding most nontraditional students, who are the majority at UTEP. Yet, here again, Texas has demonstrated its ability to focus on evidence and goals and to reform its practices. Now, the state's incentive program is moving to a focus on the number of degrees awarded rather than on graduation rates. Natalicio considers this a success, achieved through "sheer tenacity and continued effort" because traditional graduation rates are deeply etched in the minds of policy leaders and the public. Her achievement has been getting people to understand that there has to be a better way to understand the success of individual students and institutions.

In this, she has demonstrated one of the unique characteristics of Texas higher education reform: although it is driven from top-level political and policy leadership, determined institutional leaders have also contributed significantly to fostering new policy directions and adjusting goals when necessary.

Economic Pressure to Increase Efficiencies

In contrast to its economic strength 10 years ago, Texas now is facing a budget crisis. For Sandy Kress and Beth Ann Bryan, this may be the most important factor in moving higher education toward more substantive reform. Higher education is vulnerable now, and they are seeing a sudden increase in interest about how institutions might do things differently—particularly with respect to operating more efficiently. These measures might include looking at course selections that lead to a degree or at low-enrollment courses. But such changes would need to be forced through budget pressures, not a reformist motivation to operate "right." There is also the risk that with large economic problems, and with redistricting on the table, the status quo may prevail and make for "rough sailing for anything controversial."

These uncertainties are causing some leaders to be less optimistic about the future of Texas higher education reform. Board of Regents chair Charles Miller believes that there is momentum for operational change among higher education institutions that creates a culture focused on productivity and results, rather than just inputs. But this kind of change, he observes, is "glacial" and may not be possible without external pressure.

These pressures are shaping new priorities for postsecondary reform that will also have significant impact on how institutions do business, according to Commissioner Paredes. For example, Texas is in the process of ensuring that there is a common course numbering system across community colleges and universities to promote smoother transfers. With support from the Lumina Foundation, Texas is working on this course alignment initiative, beginning with development of common course metrics and a common template, which will be extended first to the 40–50 most popular lower-division undergraduate courses, and then will be aligned with upper-division courses. Paredes also cites the Coordinating Board's continued work to reduce and avoid duplication of programs and redundant administrative structures—a challenge because of the many entrenched system structures.

Replicable and Scalable Lessons from the Texas Experience

The scaling of reform in Texas was possible because of the clear and widely accepted vision of the goals for the system. Higher education leaders could and did use this framework to drive change at the system and campus-level. They had the freedom to innovate and contribute to these reforms within the statewide conversation; and this interplay of ideas, in turn, created a sense of shared ownership of the reform process and enthusiasm to do even more. This spirit is exemplified by Texas A&M Chancellor McKinney, who believes that the practice of transparency can and should be applied more broadly, to syllabi, the cost of assigned books, student evaluations, and more: "Disclosing information in an understandable format . . . makes a wonderful story."

The Texas reform experience may provide significant lessons about how to reform higher education elsewhere. For instance, was Texas successful in its attempts to bring its reform ideas to scale across the state system? And more broadly, are the roots of Texas's successful reforms replicable elsewhere? Or was this success contingent on the particular constellation of political and cultural conditions that prevailed in Texas during the late 1990s and 2000s?

Scalability in Texas

In terms of scaling reform ideas across institutions within the state system, observers generally agree that Texas was quite successful, largely because policymakers focused on linking institutional and state goals and engaging stakeholders in setting and adjusting policy. For instance, Guy Bailey concludes that it is critical to align internal decision making with broad institutional and state goals. His practice now, as president of Texas Tech University, is to allocate funding at his institution as the state does, using the same formula, with allocations based on student credit hours and research funding. If an internal budgeting process is parallel to the state process (assuming it is a good one), it is possible generate a lot of momentum. At the same time, the challenges are always political, because that approach always produces winners and losers.

UT System associate vice chancellor Martha Ellis observed that a great deal of input was gathered from college presidents and provosts, and that this engagement was critical to success.[25] The Coordinating Board adopted a participatory approach, resulting in a broad and flexible range of accountability measures.

Ellis observes that the emphasis on "freedom to operate" also gave rise to numerous "pockets of innovation" to improve participation and success, addressing topics from developmental education to degree completion to the growth of doctoral programs. These local efforts generated many ideas that were first used in individual schools. These ideas are now being shared across institutions as part of major initiatives like Achieving the Dream, but they had their roots in the initial accountability work that accompanied Closing the Gaps. Texas has made great progress in aligning the work of community colleges with broader higher education objectives. The new web portal set up to facilitate transfers from community colleges to four-year institutions, Transfer101.org, exemplifies these collaborative relationships: it was developed quickly and, in Ellis's view, is already making a huge difference.

Replicability beyond Texas?

In considering whether what was accomplished in Texas is replicable elsewhere, Charles Miller believes that Texas's culture was a key prerequisite, particularly in contrast with other states that have a history of absorbing large immigrant populations. Texas culture, he believes, is more civil, open to opportunity, and hospitable; all populations have grown and performed, and it has not become an entitlement state. Higher education institutions are connected to their communities, and support for higher education is not just about the institutions but about a broad culture of commitment to education. This commitment, together with the openness to opportunity, are, in his view, essential if other states wish to replicate Texas's approach to higher education reform.

For Bryan and Kress, 2000 to 2009 were "golden years" in Texas for higher education reform. Replicating the Texas experience elsewhere requires the "right set of people with the right passion," high-level leaders who really understand what the goal is. This means a governor who is "blood-religion" committed to reform, a supportive legislature, and proponents in the academic world. Without that support, "it doesn't matter how full of fire the movement is" because others will "pour water on it." Moreover, reform is not a one-time event that fixes everything; it is ongoing and requires constant vigilance. According to Bryan and Kress, reformers must also establish a succession of leadership, or the work will not move forward.

Commissioner Paredes observed that determining what to do differently is not the most difficult aspect of reform. In all institutions, not just in higher education, the key is figuring out how to implement the change Leaders must determine "how hard you can push the structure of higher education to reform without having a huge backlash." Yet, if reform moves too slowly, the state loses economic competitiveness and students fall through the cracks. These efforts require a persistent, long-term strategy; he predicts that it will take two to three sessions in the Texas legislature, which meets biennially, to achieve changes in formula funding and financial aid allocation policies.

In Diana Natalicio's view, Texas is now a doing a tremendous amount of dissemination of its ideas and successes; she and her colleagues emphasize the need to continue to build awareness locally and nationally to provoke thinking and dialogue because a tremendous amount of attitude shaping still needs to occur. UTEP is involved in model projects sponsored by the Lumina Foundation and has partnered with Texas A&M International to adapt a database that UTEP uses to monitor students. In other words, the El Paso campus is trying to transfer its "technology" to other campuses. Her goal is for the campus to be a beta site, a proof of concept that low-income Hispanic students can achieve like any other students if they are given the opportunity. UTEP is not trying to keep its strategy a secret; rather, it would like to help every higher education institution to ensure that underrepresented populations can be contributors to our future competitiveness.

The Future of Higher Education Reform in Texas

In the big picture, the experiences recounted here illustrate an extraordinary confluence of policy and action. But, there is not universal agreement—even among the reformers themselves—that Texas has been as successful as it could have been. There is, instead, a sense of "unfinished business" and of new horizons for reform.

For example, Sandy Kress gives these reforms a grade of incomplete "because it is not clear where Texas is headed despite some legislative support for new reforms." Despite a foundation to do more, there are "plenty of ways" in which Texas falls short: for instance, it is not clear how committed the University of Texas at Austin, the flagship university in the system, is to accountability—and its actions have a lot of influence.

Miller is disappointed that Texas's accountability system has not yet been used to focus on how institutions teach, or used by faculty to figure out how to teach the needed workforce skills. Developing these aspects has been, in his view, very slow. He also believes that to have an effective, full accountability system, Texas needs a student unit record system, with data covering early childhood education, K–12, college, and workforce needs, to measure the real outcomes of education in the workforce. Without it, "we are limited in what we can do on accountability."

Perhaps more telling is the conclusion that Commissioner Paredes draws: in his view, higher education in Texas has not really changed significantly in the past 25–30 years. Costs continue to go up, and even though more attention is being paid to higher education, public institutions are doing about the same as they always have done. The top schools have always tended to take their superiority for granted, while the institutions that serve the vast majority of students—those below the top 100–150 in the world—have received insufficient attention. Paredes's analysis is that because the top schools are among the world elite, Texas continues to be complacent about the lack of progress for all institutions.

Accelerating Closing the Gaps

In spite of the state's successes, higher education policymakers have concluded that Texas still has a great deal more to accomplish to meet other 2015 targets. For example, even though the gap in total enrollments is narrowing, Hispanic students are still underrepresented: 4.4% of Texas's Hispanic population participated in higher education in 2009. To achieve faster progress in these and other areas, in 2009 the state adopted a second iteration of Closing the Gaps that calls for "accelerated" pursuit of a subset of goals.[26] The key areas for acceleration are African American male and Hispanic participation, Hispanic and African American degrees and awards, STEM degrees and awards, and teacher certifications. Like the original plan, this new initiative calls on a broad network of partners to promote the acceleration, from the Texas Higher Education Coordinating Board, the state legislature, and the Texas Education Agency, to third-party stakeholders like the business and philanthropic communities.

The accelerated plan highlights a set of specific policy levers to aid in the acceleration, including improving the effectiveness of developmental education, aligning finance policy with success goals (for example, funding granted on the basis of student course completion rather than student enrollment), developing comprehensive transfer agreements and learning outcome frameworks, placing more emphasis on community colleges, and using data to instigate change. However, according to Paredes, behind the scenes the Coordinating Board has encountered opposition to more recent, aggressive reform ideas, particularly a performance funding formula that would reward completion, not just attendance.

Moving Beyond Closing the Gaps

Even with these caveats, catching up with Texas may prove difficult. Sandy Kress observed that the "fire is still burning, the flame is still there," but efforts may move forward in fits and starts.

While the Closing the Gaps plan has produced notable improvements, the recent work of the Higher Education Coordinating Board and the governor's office to plan beyond 2015 is even more significant. In 2009, Governor Rick Perry issued Executive Order RP73, which set in motion an in-depth and broad-based study of systematic opportunities for cost efficiencies in higher education. Motivating this study was the realization that if Texas is to achieve not just parity with its peers in the United States but also a position of global leadership, funds in excess of those available from the state legislature would be needed. Thus, institutions will have to become more efficient and effective and align their work more closely with state goals and needs. The recommendations are grouped in five "big ideas." Two continue from Closing the Gaps: "funding results—paying for performance" and "creating clear pathways for successful student outcomes." But three go further in terms of funding structures and institutional performance: "meeting demand with new approaches to delivery"; "making capital financing make sense"; and "making productivity and continuous improvement a cultural change."[27]

A distinctive characteristic of Texas higher education reform is that some leaders operate ahead of the pack. Texas A&M Chancellor Mike McKinney illustrates well the role of system leaders in pushing the boundaries of higher education reform. Following a 2007 summit on higher education reform convened by Governor Perry, McKinney moved quickly to develop initiatives that are changing the views of faculty about accountability. For example, the Texas A&M board passed a policy to give up to five-year rolling appointments to nontenured faculty, making it possible to retain faculty who are good at teaching without locking them (and the institution) into tenured positions. In his view, this policy actually strengthens the meaning and use of tenure, which is conferred on faculty who are what he describes as "triple threats"—strong in teaching, research, and service.

Conclusion

Three distinctive traits stand out in this story: the sense of pride and shared ownership at every level in the state's reform directions and accomplishments; the mutual impact of top-level political and policy decisions together with tenacious institutional leadership and influence; and an ongoing restless desire to accomplish even more, with the fear that the pace of change for the next round of operational reforms is too slow. And while Texas's postsecondary institutions do compete for re-sources, over the past eight years system and institutional leaders have sometimes taken the lead and often collaborated to pursue high-priority reform goals that are mutually beneficial. Texas's open, innovative, and participative culture might be difficult to replicate elsewhere. For policy-makers and higher education leaders around the country, the big ques-tion is whether and how it would be possible to create the specific com-bination of conditions that have made Texas's efforts successful.

Since spring 2011, events in Texas have confirmed the chief charac-teristics of higher education reform discussed above: the role of state leaders in setting bold goals, the role of system and campus leaders in pushing the boundaries on change, and the sense that reform is never complete. The particulars of the topics—a cheap degree and a challenge on faculty productivity—cut to the heart of the dichotomy between Tex-as's reform goals (access and massification of postsecondary education for tens of thousands more Texans) and the need for faculty-driven re-search and technology transfer to fuel the state's competitive economic advantage. In contrast to the environment a decade ago, Texas now has tighter budgets and tougher economic times. These are not likely to be barriers to continued success; instead, they are fueling a new generation of reform ideas.

In his February 2011 State of the State address, Texas Governor Rick Perry challenged four-year institutions to develop a $10,000 baccalaure-ate degree, what he termed "a bold, Texas-style solution" to the inexora-ble increases in college costs.[28] An advisor to Perry noted that "reaching $10,000 is a challenge, as opposed to a directive."[29] Coordinating Board commissioner Raymund Paredes took up the charge, presenting strate-gies to achieve this goal at the board meeting in April 2011. Paredes said a $10,000 degree is "not as far-fetched as it seems." He suggested that "Texas should embrace the challenge and become a national leader."[30]

Proponents of the $10,000 degree pointed out that such an approach would work only for some types of degrees and would depend on credit-transfer articulations with community colleges, faculty buy-in, use of tech-nology, online degree programs, open-source textbooks, and a rigorous structure based on proven competency levels. This type of degree would not be for every student and every degree, according to Paredes.[31] These would be virtual degrees: economical and fast-track, aimed at working parents, young adults caring for family, or traditional-age students who want a degree without all the amenities of an on-campus experience.[32]

Not surprisingly, faculty questioned the viability of the challenge. The Faculty Council chair at UT–Austin, Dean P. Neikirk, observed: "I can't imagine we could deliver the same quality of education that we currently do here at the University of Texas at such a price point. . . . I don't see how it could be done."[33] Texas Tech president Guy Bailey, a supporter of other higher education reform ideas, asked, "Will the ten thousand dollar degree produce what we actually need or is it just a degree?" He commented that "you'd be very constrained in the majors, and you'd have to ask yourself, 'do we just need people to have a college degree or do we need more engineers and more nurses?'"[34]

At the same time, the issue of productivity in higher education is playing out at the University of Texas, as it did at Texas A&M in 2010. A&M chancellor Mike McKinney's most controversial reform was the development of a methodology intended to document faculty productivity by comparing the funds faculty bring into the university (through tuition and grants, primarily) with their cost in terms of salary and benefits.[35] His purpose was to prove that faculty more than pay their way; the nine-month study showed, among other things, that liberal arts faculty contribute far more than they cost the university. McKinney, who announced his retirement in May 2011,[36] said his larger point is that a university, by definition, must teach "the universe of knowledge" from undergraduate-level to doctoral-level courses in all subjects. Some faculty are needed to teach many undergraduates so that others can teach fewer students in upper-level and graduate courses. The analogy he made was to a football team; linemen rarely score touchdowns, but without them, no one would.

UT System officials have generated a large data set on faculty salaries, course enrollments, course loads, grant money, grades awarded, student evaluations, and more. While the University of Texas did not intend to produce a report like Texas A&M's, the data were requested by a newly formed task force on productivity and excellence, suggesting that the issue of faculty productivity will be on the table in the foreseeable future. In December 2011, UT System officials announced the launch of a web-based productivity dashboard.[37]

These challenges illustrate the continued Texas penchant for addressing big issues at the state, system, and institution level that have the potential to reform higher education. Not to be outdone by the governor, in early May 2011 Lieutenant Governor David Dewhurst and House Speaker Joe Straus created a new legislative committee to consider profound changes in Texas universities. The committee would consider the governor's call for a $10,000 degree and the suggestion by UT Board of Regents' chair Gene Powell that enrollment at UT–Austin increase by 10 percent a year for four years while reducing tuition 50 percent.[38]

While the spirit of collaboration may be less evident in these directions than it was a decade ago, there has been no diminution in the shared concern to make Texas higher education the highest quality and the most accessible. It appears that Texas is remaining true to its heritage as the reform state.

NOTES

1. Michael Barone, "The Great Lone Star Migration," *Wall Street Journal*, Jan. 8–9, 2011, p. A13.

2. Texas Higher Education Coordinating Board, *Closing the Gaps Progress Report*, June 2010, p. iii, available at www.thecb.state.tx.us/reports/pdf/2045.pdf ?cfid=13631048&cftoken=90386355.

3. Texas Higher Education Coordinating Board, *Accelerated Plan for Closing the Gaps by 2015*, April 29, 2010, available at www.thecb.state.tx.us/reports/ pdf/2005.pdf?cfid=13631048&cftoken=90386355.

4. Texas Higher Education Coordinating Board, *Report of the Texas Higher Education Coordinating Board on Higher Education Cost Efficiencies to the Governor*, Nov. 1, 2010, available at www.thecb.state.tx.us/files//dmfile/CostEfficiencies11.19.2010.pdf.

5. Barone, "Great Lone Star Migration."

6. Chad Aldeman and Kevin Carey, *Ready to Assemble: Grading State Higher Education Accountability Systems*, Education Sector Report, June 30, 2009, available at www.educationsector.org/sites/default/files/publications/HigherEd Accountability.pdf.

7. The state-wide accountability system is described at "Texas Higher Education Accountability System," www.txhighereddata.org/Interactive/Accountability/ default.cfm.

8. Texas Tech president Guy Bailey interview, Oct. 18, 2010. The interviews used in the writing of this chapter are generally cited only the first time the interviewee is mentioned. Unless otherwise indicated, subsequent information attributed to these interviewees in the text derives from these conversations.

9. Texas Higher Education Quick Facts 2010, available at www.thecb.state.tx .us/reports/pdf/1096.pdf.

10. Texas Higher Education Data, available at www.txhighereddata.org.

11. *Closing the Gaps Progress Report*, June 2010. The *Closing the Gaps* report and follow-up studies are available at www.thecb.state.tx.us/index.cfm ?objectid=fbe1507f-c5d0-fc95-369ef7ac883b5f24.

12. Beth Ann Bryan and Sandy Kress, attorneys at the law firm Akin Gump, interview, Oct. 20, 2010.

13. Dr. Diana Natalicio, president of the University of Texas at El Paso, mentioned the extensive and influential demographic studies by Stephen Murdoch, who was at Texas A&M and then at UT—San Antonio's Texas State Data Center during these years. For archival material, see http://txsdc.utsa.edu/greet.php.

14. Dr. Diana Natalicio, president, University of Texas at El Paso, interview Nov. 24, 2010.

15. Ibid.

16. Martha Ellis interview, Nov. 4, 2010.

17. Commissioner Raymund A. Paredes interview, Oct. 7, 2010. Dr. Paredes was at UCLA during this period, assuming his current position in Texas in 2004.

18. Chancellor Mike McKinney interview, Nov. 24, 2010.

19. Charles Miller interview, Sept. 23, 2010.

20. Bryan and Kress interview, Oct. 20, 2010. For early editions of the UT System accountability reports, see www.utsystem.edu/osm/accountability/home page.htm.

21. House Education and Workforce Committee, Hearing entitled "The State of American Higher Education: What Are Parents, Students, and Taxpayers Getting for Their Money," May 13, 2003, available at http://frwebgate.access.gpo .gov/cgi-bin/getdoc.cgi?dbname=108_house_hearings&docid=f:87721.wais.

22. U.S. Department of Education, *A Test of Leadership: Charting the Future of U.S. Higher Education* (Washington, DC: Government Printing Office, 2006), available at http://www2.ed.gov/about/bdscomm/list/hiedfuture/reports/final -report.pdf.

23. Natalicio interview, Nov. 24, 2010.

24. Ibid.

25. Ellis was president of Lee College in Baytown from 2002 to 2008, when she joined the UT System.

26. Texas Higher Education Coordinating Board, *Accelerated Plan for Closing the Gaps by 2015*.

27. Texas Higher Education Coordinating Board, *Higher Education Cost Efficiencies*, pp. 9–10.

28. Gov. Rick Perry, "We Must Reform, Streamline State Government," State of the State Address, Feb. 8, 2011, available at http://governor.state.tx.us/news/ speech/15673.

29. Reeve Hamilton, "Raymund Paredes: $10,000 Degrees 'Entirely Feasible,'" *Texas Tribune*, April 27, 2011.

30. Katherine Mangan, "Texas Could Offer a Stripped-Down Degree for Just $10,000, Commissioner Says," *Houston Chronicle*, April 27, 2011.

31. Ibid.

32. Melissa Ludwig, "Board Embraces Challenge to Create $10K Degree," *Houston Chronicle*, April 28, 2011.

33. Ibid.

34. "Texas Tech's Bailey Doesn't See $10,000 Degree Cutting It," Fox 34 News, Lubbock, Texas, June 13, 2011, www.myfoxlubbock.com.

35. See Katherine Mangan, "Texas A&M's Bottom Line Ratings of Professors Find That Most Are Cost-Effective," *Chronicle of Higher Education*, Sept. 15, 2010, for an example of the wide news coverage of this initiative.

36. Ralph K. M. Haurwitz, "A&M Chancellor Mike MCKinney to retire," *Austin-American Statesman*, May 11, 2010.

37. Audrey Williams June, "Release of Faculty-Productivity Data Roils U. of Texas," *Chronicle of Higher Education*, May 6, 2011; "U. of Texas System Posts 'Productivity Dashboard,'" *Chronicle of Higher Education*, Dec. 15, 2011.

38. "Texas Panel Will Review Proposed Changes at State Universities," *Chronicle of Higher Education*, May 7, 2011.

CHAPTER ELEVEN

The Ohio Experience with Outcomes-Based Funding

RICHARD PETRICK

National, state, and institutional leaders are setting goals for higher education to improve productivity, promote student success, and ensure accountability.[1] These recurring and now consistent calls for change tend to direct attention to the sources and consequences of successful policy innovation at the state level. Ohio is generally perceived as a somewhat conservative, middle-of-the-road midwestern state. Despite this general reputation, Ohio is increasingly known as a state that has had numerous creative and relatively successful policy innovations in higher education, especially in the area of outcomes-based, or performance-based, funding. Why? After providing a brief review of Ohio's history of state funding and recent policy innovations, I argue that Ohio's successful implementation of performance funding is a function of five factors:

1. participation, authorization, or direction by state executive or legislative policymakers, which both legitimized and authorized initiatives;
2. an institutionalized practice of bringing stakeholders together to craft and evaluate new funding policies, a practice that increased participation, communication, mutual respect and trust, and buy-in among affected parties, and built an explicit sensitivity to diverse campus missions and campus financial circumstances;
3. a robust data system capable of quickly modeling funding ideas and scenarios and producing trustworthy funding allocations;
4. commitment to systematic evaluation of programs and policies; and
5. additional money.

From the Outset: A Data-Based Foundation

The Ohio Board of Regents was created in the mid-1960s to coordinate higher education policy for the state. Shortly after its creation, the board's first chancellor, John Millett, developed a methodology for allocating state support through a cost and student enrollment–based formula. Chancellor Millett was already an expert in higher education finance and had been the president of Miami University of Ohio.[2] His appointment as chancellor gave him an opportunity to put his financial expertise into practice at the state level. The subsidy allocation methodology that Millett developed for Ohio's public institutions, based on a single formula for all campuses, required the routine collection by the Regents of detailed student, faculty, finance, facilities, and course data from all campuses; this data system came to be known as the Uniform Information System.[3] While the original purpose of the Uniform Information System was to determine state subsidy shares on the basis of enrollments and cost allocations, over time the data in the system came to be used for other purposes, including the development of alternative funding approaches, many of which could be classified as performance based.

The use of data in this manner this early in the history of the Board of Regents established a number of important precedents, including the rejection of a simple "base-plus" funding system and of a politicized approach to allocating resources. Most importantly, the data-driven funding model was premised on a recognition of the need for, and acceptance of the consequences of, an empirically based funding system that would produce variable allocations from year to year, tied to results valued by the state—namely, student enrollments categorized by level and costs. As one former senior vice chancellor of the Board of Regents observed, the state's enrollment-based subsidy system was in fact a performance-based funding system: it valued and funded the campus performance known as enrolling students, and it did so with great precision.

The subsidy allocation proposals were not made unilaterally by the Regents or its staff. At least biennially, the Regents would convene a series of consultations of campus financial and academic leaders and representatives of selected state agencies to revisit the funding system's data and methodology. These consultations were used to update the data in the Uniform Information System, to revise the formula to correct for unintended or perverse effects or to reflect new priorities and realities, and ultimately to recommend to the Regents changes in the formula, the level of funding that should be requested of the state, and when appropriate, tuition levels as well.[4] This process of consultation became institutionalized in Ohio; technical issues would be handled by mid-level campus and Board staff, while major changes in policies and potential conflicts would trigger the collective attention of the chancellor, vice chancellors, institutional presidents, legislators, leaders of other state agencies, and members of the Regents themselves. In addition to the formally invited members, the meetings were open to the public, and the number of nonmembers sometimes equaled the number of members at many consultations.

The 1980s: Seeking Excellence during an Economic Boom

Ohio's first major experiment with a non-enrollment performance-based funding occurred in the mid-1980s, as Ohio's economy came roaring out of the early 1980s recession. State tax revenues began to exceed projected collections by hundreds of millions of dollars, giving state policymakers significant additional resources to allocate for public purposes. In higher education, some of those additional state funds were directed to a new program, called "Selective Excellence," which was intended to foster excellence and change among Ohio's arguably underfunded public campuses. While it maintained its base subsidy allocation, Ohio experimented with a number of alternative funding schemes to achieve new goals.

Funds from four of these programs—called Academic Challenge, Program Excellence, Productivity Improvement, and Eminent Scholars— were either competitively awarded or were "bolt-on" additions to the base funding formula. A fifth program, called Research Challenge, provided for a distribution of state funds proportionate to each university's share of total third-party research grant revenues generated annually. By providing a partial state match for past research success, Research Challenge became the first true performance-based funding mechanism created in Ohio and is the only Selective Excellence program that has continuously persisted over the years. An evaluation of the Selective Excellence program conducted by the National Center for Higher Education Management Systems (NCHEMS) endorsed the use of incentive-based funding streams as an effective funding tool and concluded that the programs did change institutional allocation decisions in desired directions.[5] The NCHEMS report lauded the fact that the goals were jointly developed by the Board of Regents and campus leaders but criticized the programs as being underfunded and too focused on campus, rather than state, goals.

The Early 1990s: Recession, Retrenchment, and the Managing for the Future Initiative

Following the economic recovery of the late 1980s, the recession of the early 1990s put Ohio's state finances back on its heels. Limited resources resulted in the abandonment of a number of the Selective Excellence programs and the creation by a new governor of a management improvement commission for state agencies. Higher education was granted its own management improvement commission, which came to be known as the "Managing for the Future" commission, and its final report was titled "Securing the Future of Higher Education."[6] The broadly representative commission included senior academic and financial leaders from higher education and state agency directors who met over an extended period of time, and wrestled with a number of governance, coordination, quality, and access issues. Among this commission's recommendations was a proposal to rationalize Ohio's kaleidoscope of two-year campuses by converting most two-year campuses into community colleges.

At the time, largely because higher education had "evolved" in the state over hundreds of years, Ohio had five types of two-year public campuses. This multiplicity of two-year campus types caused confusion among state decision makers, resulted in poor coordination of higher education programs, and produced uneven access and service delivery throughout the state. University branch campuses served a variety of two-year, four-year, and even graduate purposes and generally charged higher fees than other two-year campuses. State technical colleges provided career education but had no authority to offer transferable associate of arts degrees. State community colleges could transfer degrees but lacked the resources to ensure access because they did not have taxing authority from their communities and had to survive on the combination of state and student funds. A few fully funded community colleges—those with local levies—benefited from the additional resources provided by local tax revenues and generally served a broader array of two-year campus programs at more affordable prices, but they were the exception to the rule. Finally, four universities had embedded "Comm-Techs" which offered a mix of two-year services, generally at significantly higher prices than those charged by the community colleges.

The Managing for the Future Task Force recommended that Ohio create a statewide system of community colleges by transforming all technical colleges and regional campuses into true community colleges. A battle ensued, and opposition to the proposed changes—primarily from the regional campuses—was successful. A substitute proposal emerged in the final recommendations which required that all two-year campuses meet uniform service expectations. The final proposal thereby avoided the sticky structural and governance issues by focusing instead on the functions to be performed by the two-year campuses. The "service expectations" laid out by the "Securing the Future" report represent the first explicit linkage of funding to performance. In the report, the Board of Regents argued that service, not organizational structure, was the defining characteristic of an institution of higher education:

> The Board also sees much merit in the argument of the report's critics that the concept of a two-year college system should be based on a service principle, not an organizational one. The Board is principally concerned about what two-year campuses should do—their institutional behavior—and has interest in their administrative structures only when they fail to serve effectively. Although in the long run it will be helpful to adopt a single term to strengthen public understanding of the consistency of services provided, it is not important from the Board's perspective whether the campuses are administered as university branches, or as community colleges. The goals of all of these campuses must be one of full service at an affordable price.[7]

On the basis of this reasoning, the Regents set nine service expectations that two-year campuses were expected to meet. These included developing an array of technical and career programs to prepare individuals for the workforce, offering developmental education with an eye toward building academic skills, maintaining college transfer programs for those students who sought a bachelor's degree from a four-year college, and offering all of these things at an affordable price and in a convenient fashion. The report also emphasized the need for collaboration among institutions, the community, and local industry to make decisions about course offerings, fees, and other operational issues.

In the FY 1993–95 state appropriations act, the General Assembly supported the Regents' recommendations with the following provision: "In conducting its biennial . . . consultation for the 1995–1997 biennium, the Board of Regents shall examine methods to tie a significant and growing portion of the funding distributed to two-year campuses to the performance records of those campuses beginning during the 1993–1995 biennium against the nine service expectations established by the Board of Regents' report *Securing the Future* of December 1992."[8]

Although Research Challenge had introduced the idea of performance-based funding to Ohio's campuses in the 1980s, the implementation of the two-year campus service expectations first introduced Ohio to the explicit use of the term "performance" in a funding allocation. The Regents requested, and the General Assembly provided, about $3 million per year to support the implementation of the two-year campus service expectations. Each of the nine expectations was defined and weighted for funding, and data were collected from all campuses regarding their ability to deliver the services. All two-year campuses quickly demonstrated that they met the service expectations, and funding for the program was eliminated after two biennia, in the late 1990s.

The Late 1990s: The Four Challenges Supported during an Economic Surge

In the 1990s, surging enrollments at the community colleges and relatively flat state funding caused increasing shares of the base state subsidy to be driven to the community colleges, often at the expense of university main campuses.[9] Ostensibly concerned about the loss of state support and the prospect of future losses, university representatives asked the General Assembly to direct the Board of Regents to examine and recommend ways to distribute portions of state subsidy on the basis of performance instead of enrollments. Specifically, the appropriations act for FY 1995–97 stipulated: "A review of the . . . subsidy formula shall begin by October 1, 1995 and be completed by July 1, 1996. The actual review process shall be determined jointly between the Board of Regents and the state-assisted colleges and universities. The review shall address how the state can provide base funding for its institutions of higher education while allocating a higher share of funding according to measures of performance and quality."[10] Recognizing the significance of such a charge, Chancellor Elaine Hairston convened a new senior-level commission, called the Higher Education Funding Commission, to develop recommendations, which were completed in 1996.[11]

Given additional administrative resources in the form of an appropriation line item, and assisted by the insights and guidance of a very able consultant, the Funding Commission recommended that Ohio cre-

TABLE 11.1. Ohio "Challenge" programs established in 1996

Challenge program	Goal	Basis of distribution of funds	Primary recipient of funds
1. Access	Reward access campuses for enrolling more students; use funds to lower student fees	Campus shares of total lower-division students enrolled	Two-year campuses
2. Success	Reward university main campuses for academic success of undergraduates	33% for timely completion of any in-state undergraduate baccalaureate degree; 67% for baccalaureate degree completion of at-risk students at any time	Four-year campuses
3. Jobs	Reward primarily two-year campuses for noncredit job-related training	Campus shares of job training revenues obtained from businesses and industry; some funds reserved for capacity building	Two-year campuses
4. Research	Reward university main campuses for research competitiveness	Campus shares of third-party-sponsored research	Four-year campuses and stand-alone medical colleges
5. School Success	Reward all campuses for K–12 linkages	Categorical and competitive grant (rejected by General Assembly)	All campuses
6. Technology	Reward all campuses for IT investments	Categorical and competitive grant (partially funded by General Assembly)	All campuses

ate five new programs—in addition to Research Challenge—that were mission-driven and performance-based.[12] The final forms of these "Challenge" line items are described in table 11.1.

In the remainder of this section, I examine Challenge programs 1–4, which were largely adopted by the General Assembly as recommended by the Funding Commission, with the notable exception that the assembly's appropriations for Access Challenge actually exceeded Board-recommended levels. These four Challenge programs were perceived as reasonably balanced among four-year and two-year missions and targeted on Ohio's needs, and the distribution of funds were performance-based in a manner that was not highly correlated with the distribution of the base enrollment subsidy.

Because the Challenge line items were universally supported by all the stakeholders—campuses, the Funding Commission, the Regents, newly appointed chancellor Roderick G. W. Chu, and the General Assembly—and were created during a time of economic growth in the state, funding was generous up through the recession of 2002, as shown in table 11.2. Funding was maintained during and after the recession with relatively minor reductions.

The Challenge line items were successful politically, financially, and programmatically. Legislators embraced the idea of focusing new state funds on specific programs whose outcomes could be systematically tracked. Financially, Challenge funding quickly grew to an amount equal to 8 to 10 percent of base state funding (fig. 11.1)—an almost unheard of proportion relative to that in most other states. Most importantly, the line items quickly demonstrated successful outcomes. By the late 1990s, Ohio had embraced the idea of performance funding, which was promoted, at least initially, by campuses concerned that a simple enrollment-based formula would work to the disadvantage of "mature" or at-capacity campuses.

Implementation of the Challenge Line Items

Implementation of the Challenge line items at the state level was relatively easy to accomplish. The information needed to determine allocations for Access Challenge and Success Challenge were already collected in the Board's higher education data system.[13] Likewise, the data needed to continue the Research Challenge allocations had been collected for years and were gradually incorporated into the more comprehensive state data system. Only Jobs Challenge required the collection of new data, on noncredit job-related training revenues, but again, those data were relatively easily collected and put into use in the existing data system.

As one might expect, implementation of the Challenges at the campus level varied by the goal of the program. Access campuses were required to use new incremental amounts of Access Challenge funding to restrain or reduce tuition; compliance, as well as the consequences of compliance in terms of enrollment growth, was relatively easily monitored by

TABLE 11.2.   State funding for Challenges 1–4 during FY 1998–2009

Fiscal year	Access Challenge	Success Challenge	Jobs Challenge	Research Challenge	Total
1998	$12,000,000	$2,000,000	$500,000	$12,764,600	$27,264,600
1999	16,000,000	4,000,000	2,500,000	14,756,861	37,256,861
2000	35,313,691	20,068,104	8,743,864	19,436,382	83,562,041
2001	65,268,000	48,741,000	10,979,694	21,568,440	146,557,134
2002	58,531,920	44,218,540	9,494,000	18,800,000	131,044,460
2003	57,068,622	43,113,077	9,348,300	18,255,000	127,784,999
2004	64,711,966	48,952,126	9,348,300	17,555,047	140,567,439
2005	63,340,676	52,601,934	9,348,300	17,183,044	142,473,954
2006	63,340,676	52,601,934	9,348,300	20,343,097	145,634,007
2007	63,340,676	52,601,934	9,348,300	23,186,194	148,477,104
2008	66,585,769	53,653,973	9,348,300	17,186,194	146,774,236
2009	66,585,769	53,653,973	9,348,300	17,186,194	146,774,236
All years	$632,087,764	$476,206,595	$97,665,659	$344,159,638	$1,550,109,656

SOURCE: Ohio Board of Regents, *An Assessment of the Four Challenge Line Items* (Columbus, OH: May 2008).

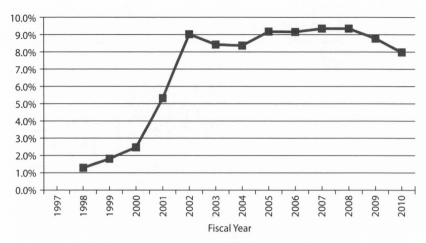

FIGURE 11.1. Challenge funding as a portion of base funding.

Regents' staff. University main campuses were required to submit a biennial report on the outcomes of their Success Challenge–funded programs to assist at-risk students.[14] These individual campus reports were summarized and compiled into a single state report for submission to the General Assembly and use by all campuses. Jobs Challenge funds were partitioned into two or three components, one being restricted to capacity-building in campus Business and Industry offices, while another was devoted to an initiative called the Targeted Industry Training Program, which provided subsidized training assistance to small- to medium-sized firms in manufacturing, information technology, and a few other fields. Research Challenge funds were used largely as they had been used in the past—for example, to make strategic investments to reduce teaching loads for selected faculty (either promising young faculty or senior faculty) to free up their time to work on research and grant applications.

Ultimately, all the campuses that received Challenge funds shared one goal—*to do more of what they had been doing in the past* in order to obtain more state funds, or at least a largest possible share of available funds. These funds were sought after because they allowed institutions to enroll more lower-division students, help more in-state undergraduates achieve baccalaureate degrees, train more employees and assist more businesses with noncredit training, and successfully compete for more third-party research. The state had little interest in how campuses achieved these goals and therefore did not micromanage the implementation of the programs.

The Effects of the Challenges

In the short run, two-year campuses—especially community colleges—experienced extraordinary enrollment growth as Access Challenge appropriations allowed them to freeze and then reduce student fees. University main campuses biennially reported their Success Challenge plans and programs to serve at-risk students, and this information was shared both on the web and in a number of new campus-initiated statewide consultations on student success. Evaluations of Research Challenge continued to report annual returns of about $10 for every $1 invested; and small business owners and managers would often testify before occasional Regents meetings and legislative committees that the training subsidized by Jobs Challenge helped make their businesses more competitive and profitable.

All of these initial reports and outcomes persisted and were documented in a 2008 report mandated by the General Assembly.[15] For Success Challenge, the report found the following results for time to degree:

1. The median time to degree for in-state bachelor's degree graduates at university main campuses decreased from 4.7 years in FY 1999 to 4.3 years in FY 2003, and has stayed at this level through FY 2006;
2. The percent of in-state bachelor's degree graduates who earned their degrees in 4 years or less increased from 34 percent in 1999 to 43 percent in 2006; and conversely,
3. The percent of in-state bachelor's degree graduates who took longer than 6 years to earn their degree decreased from 18 percent in 1999 to 14 percent in 2006.

Success Challenge funding also had positive effects on at-risk students:

1. . . . the number of at-risk students who received bachelor's degree increased by 13 percent;
2. The at-risk student share of total in-state bachelor's degree graduates stayed fairly constant at around 30.5 percent;
3. The median time-to-degree of in-state, at-risk, bachelor's degree graduates decreased from 1998 to 2006, from 5.0 to 4.8 years; and
4. The percent of in-state, at-risk degree graduates who earned their

degree in 4 years or less increased from 20 percent in 1999 to 26 percent in 2006.

Regarding Access Challenge, the evaluation concluded that the funds were indeed used to restrain or reduce in-state tuition: tuition at two-year campuses actually dropped an average of about 6 percent from FY 2000 to FY 2001. As a result, enrollments at access campuses had increased by over 37,000 students in a seven-year period, and the increased enrollments at the two-year campuses had not come at the expense of Ohio's four-year campuses.

Jobs Challenge funding was successfully used to build campus capacity to offer more noncredit training and market campus noncredit offerings and to deliver specialized training programs throughout the state. Over 190,000 employees at small to medium-sized firms benefited from the training, and a survey of participating companies concluded:

> Companies reported that Jobs Challenge generated an average ROI of
> $372 million per year in the six-year period from FY 2002 to FY 2007.
> The reported ROI ranged from a high of $641.6 million in FY 2002 to a
> low of $210.7 million in FY 2006. According to the survey responses, the
> ROI occurred through: increased efficiency, reduced cycle time, reduced
> turnover, achievement of certification, increased quality, increased busi-
> ness, better job succession, improved safety performance, and decreased
> waste—all contributing to improved worker wages and increased profits.

The Research Challenge program demonstrated its continuing effectiveness in increasing the competitiveness of Ohio's research universities. The dollar volume of third-party sponsored research increased continuously and significantly year over year, and Ohio's per capita share of such research increased from a low of about 60 percent of the national average in the late 1980s to nearly 90 percent of the national average toward the end of the period studied. One external report to the Board of Regents in 1996 indicated that Research Challenge funds had resulted in a leverage of $14 in external funding for every $1 in Research Challenge funds provided by the state.[16]

In the Twenty-First Century

Four major events in the twenty-first century have had the cumulative effect of accelerating and broadening Ohio's use of performance-based funding. Each has reaffirmed general support for performance-based funding and extended the principles far beyond the status quo that was established by the Higher Education Funding Commission.

The Governor's Commission on Higher Education and the Economy

Primarily at the urging of the Board of Regents, in 2003 Governor Bob Taft created the Governor's Commission on Higher Education and the Economy, which came to be known by its acronym, CHEE. This commission engaged college and university presidents, business leaders, legislators, executive staff, and others in a year-long analysis of the significance of higher education to Ohio's economy. The final report provided a framework and a charge for increasing academic and administrative efficiency among Ohio's public institutions, formally engaged Ohio's business community in higher education policy and practice through the creation of an organization known as the Business Alliance for Higher Education and the Economy, and reaffirmed the significance and popularity of Research Challenge by recommending increases in funding for the program and, less directly, endorsing the other Challenge line items.[17]

The Higher Education Funding Study Council

Shortly after the issuance of the CHEE report, a new entity, the Higher Education Funding Study Council, started its work. Established by the legislature and chaired by a legislator, the council worked in 2006 and 2007 under what was arguably too broad a mandate, as stated in the appropriations act: "The Council shall review all aspects of higher education funding contained in this act, including all appropriation items and shall recommend any changes it determines are necessary."[18]

Coming 10 years after the work of the Higher Education Funding Commission and hard on the heels of the work of CHEE, the council's work also coincided with another technical but major revision of the state's base enrollment subsidy formula. In addition, the council's final report was accompanied by a dissenting minority report, authored by members of the minority party in the House and Senate.[19] The combination of these factors no doubt weakened the impact of the council's recommendations. However, in regard to performance-based funding, the council

- directed decision makers' attention to the idea of using degree and certificate completions in the base subsidy formula;
- recommended the creation of a new "challenge" to promote certificate and associate degree completion; and
- reaffirmed support for the Access Challenge.[20]

The TANF Educational Awards Program

In 2006, Ohio began to experiment with outcomes-based student financial aid with the creation of the TANF Educational Awards Program, or TEAP. The state had a surplus of Temporary Assistance for Needy Families (TANF) appropriations, and the governor's office invited proposals from the Regents to create an outcomes-based student financial aid pilot.

The TEAP program was created by an executive order, effective July 1, 2006. The executive order provided that up to $30 million could be used in one year for the program and that all public and private not-for-profit campuses were eligible to participate. Student eligibility was limited to independent students with dependents who had an "expected family contribution" of $0, had already completed 15 credits of college work, and were enrolled in at least three credit hours.

These criteria targeted the funds to very-low-income single parents who had demonstrated their ability to overcome some of their life circumstances by completing one-half year of college without extraordinary support from the state.

The TEAP grants were structured to supplement, not supplant, existing student financial aid, were sizable, and were contingent on performance. The maximum grant was $1,200 per semester for a full-time student and $600 for a part-time student; one-third of the grant was distributed at the beginning of the term, and two-thirds at the end of the term; the student had to successfully complete his or her courses to receive the full end-of-term portion. Students were permitted to use the grant funds for a wide variety of uses, including books and materials, equipment, transportation, and child care.

An evaluation of the FY 2007 program by agency staff concluded that the program appeared to be successful in achieving its goals.[21] Compared with the TANF students who did not participate in the program, the TEAP students had a higher course completion rate, higher GPAs, higher "persistence + graduation" rates, and a higher full-time attendance rate.

TABLE 11.3. FY 2007 outcomes for TANF Educational Awards Program (TEAP)

Evaluation measure	TEAP grant recipients	Non-TEAP TANF students
Number	7,439	18,488
Course completion rate	82%	70%
GPA	2.79	2.54
Persistence + graduation rate	82%	60%
Full-time attendance	52%	26%

SOURCE: Andy Lechler, *Draft Evaluation of the TANF Educational Awards Program: Student Outcomes Fall 2006 and Spring 2007* (Columbus: Ohio Board of Regents, March 2009).

NOTE: Quasi-experimental design with no random assignment of students.

Table 11.3 summarizes some major findings from the agency study. These results were further buttressed in the evaluation by an analysis of TEAP and non-TEAP student cohort performance in the academic terms *before* the implementation of the TEAP program. The two groups were then virtually identical in terms of their academic performance; the differential performance between the two cohorts occurred only after TEAP was implemented.

Following the creation of the 2007 TEAP program, a second, smaller, and more focused iteration of the program was created through the leadership of the research organization MDRC. The 2009 program used a true experimental design and assigned students randomly to treatment and control groups at three community colleges. The initial evaluation of the MDRC-led program showed results similar to, but less substantial than, those of the 2007 program.[22] The final MDRC evaluation of the 2009 program is expected in 2013, at which time the MDRC analysts would have had an opportunity to assess the longer-term effects of the one-time "treatment" on student persistence and success, and also will attempt to provide an assessment of the cost-effectiveness of the program.

Change in Governors and Governance

The election of Governor Ted Strickland in 2006 ushered in a major change in the governance of higher education. Campaigning on a pledge to reverse Ohio's economic decline, and using higher education as a major instrument for doing so, Strickland advocated for and enacted a change in state law that made the chancellor of higher education both a gubernatorial appointee and a member of the Cabinet, and that made the Board of Regents an advisory board to the chancellor.[23] The powers and duties previously held by the Regents were transferred to the chancellor, and one of the first new major responsibilities mandated in law to the new chancellor was the creation of a 10-year strategic plan for higher education. In addition, Governor Strickland supported higher education both rhetorically and financially, providing in his first biennial operating budget significant increases in state aid to campuses—and frozen fees for students—during tight fiscal conditions for the state.

The strategic plan for higher education was issued by Chancellor Eric D. Fingerhut in May 2008. Among its recommendations and goals was one that would result in a transformation of the state's enrollment-based funding formula into one even more focused on state goals, much like the Challenges.[24] The section of the strategic plan entitled "Aligning Funding Formulas and State Priorities" argued that the funding formula needed to be revised such that the interests of colleges and universities were more "systematically aligned" with the interests of the state. The plan explicitly suggested that "increases in enrollments or degrees granted, or improvements in other activities or outcomes that advance state goals" should be rewarded with "appropriate" increases in funding; that these criteria be designed to reflect differences in institutional missions; and that the funding formula recognize differences in the cost of delivery and encourage cost efficiency. (See the appendix to this chapter for the text of this section of the strategic plan.)

A consultation was launched to revise the formula along the lines required by the strategic plan. Following about nine months of discussion and review, and with the strong support and leadership of Ohio's public higher education institutions and their associations—the Inter-University Council and the Ohio Association of Community Colleges—a new approach emerged for consideration in the upcoming FY 2010–11 state budget bill.[25] The allocations are described in table 11.4.

The single base subsidy formula was separated into three separate formulas, one for each major sector: community colleges, regional campuses, and university main campuses. The creation of separate formulas enabled each formula to better link the sectors' different missions to their funding streams. One size did not fit all.

The formula for community colleges relies heavily on the previous enrollment-based formula, in large part because community college enrollments can surge and decline very rapidly—much more so than en-

TABLE 11.4. FY 2011 subsidy allocations (millions of dollars) in Ohio, by purpose and sector

	Community colleges		Regional campuses		University main campuses			
	Allocation	% of total CC funds	Allocation	% of total RC funds	Allocation	% of total UM funds	Total allocation	% of total
Enrollment	$370.20	84.2	$0.00	0.0	$0.00	0.0	$370.20	18.5
Success Points	18.60	4.2	0.00	0.0	0.00	0.0	18.60	0.9
Course completions	0.00	0.0	116.30	87.8	964.20	67.7	1,080.50	54.1
At-risk course completions	0.00	0.0	4.20	3.2	13.10	0.9	17.30	0.9
Degree completions	0.00	0.0	0.00	0.0	128.80	9.0	128.80	6.4
At-risk degree completions	0.00	0.0	0.00	0.0	9.20	0.6	9.20	0.5
Medical and doctoral funding	0.00	0.0	0.00	0.0	306.00	21.5	306.00	15.3
Tuition subsidy	50.70	11.5	12.00	9.1	3.70	0.3	66.40	3.3
All funding sources	$439.50	100.0	$132.50	100.0	$1,425.00	100.0	$1,997.00	100.0

SOURCE: Prepared for the author by the Ohio Board of Regents.

rollments at regional campuses or universities. The new formula, however, adds to the enrollment base a component for performance relying heavily on the concept of "momentum points" (called Success Points in Ohio).[26] In addition, the community colleges and the other two sectors receive their historical share of a state allocation that helped restrain or buy down tuition. Success Points constituted a little under 5 percent of the total subsidy for community colleges in FY 2011, but the expectation was that the share will grow over time to become about 20 percent of total subsidy.

Regional campus funding is no longer based on enrollments, but instead is based on course completions, weighted by cost of course. An additional adjustment is made to provide an increment of funding for the successful course completion of at-risk students, defined in the FY 2010–11 biennium as any student who is eligible for state need-based aid.[27]

University main campus funding has a number of components, most of which are performance-based. Set-asides that had been established for doctoral funding and medical education remain, but their distribution among eligible campuses will change to reflect the use of more dynamic and performance-related indicators, including degrees awarded, grant revenues, and indicators of quality. A little over 15 percent of the university main campus funding, or $306 million, is reserved for this portion.

Of the remaining core subsidy, 95 percent initially was allocated on the basis of course completions, and 5 percent on the basis of degree completions in FY 2010. The portion allocated to degree completions was increased to 10 percent in FY 2011 and is expected to grow over time. Like the adjustment made for course completions at the regional campuses, the course and degree completions for at-risk students are weighted to reflect the challenges that campuses experience in serving these students. The adjustment is based on the difference between the completion rates of non-at-risk and at-risk students. The purpose of the adjustment is not to provide access campuses with a bonus for serving at-risk students, but rather, to ensure that these campuses do not lose funds, as they would if the state formulas rewarded student success without such an adjustment. *Without an adjustment of this nature, success-based formulas will reward campuses with more selective admissions policies and penalize those campuses that are less selective.*

Annually, all three formulas are run and the unadjusted outcomes are shared. This information lets each campus know how it is performing vis-à-vis its peers. However, a "stop-loss" provision is included for the initial years to ensure that campuses have more time to adjust their policies and programs to respond to the new performance metrics and to ensure that no campus experiences a precipitous loss of state subsidy. The stop loss was 1 percent in FY 2010 and 2 percent in FY 2011 and is expected to increase by one percentage point per year for the next biennia or two, as the effects of the new formulas are, in effect, phased in over time.[28]

Conclusion

In a span of about 25 years, state funding for higher education in Ohio has evolved from a system that almost exclusively rewarded campuses for enrolling more students to one that focuses about 64 percent of total funding on outcomes, or performance. It is instructive to review the factors that contributed to these initiatives and to understand that no single factor played a predominant role.[29]

Executive and legislative participation, direction, and leadership obviously were evident and significant in every stage in this long process. In many cases, not only did members of these decision-making bodies formally authorize or direct the examination or adoption of certain studies or policies, but they or their staff also personally participated in many of the formal and informal consultations, councils, and commissions, joining higher education representatives and others to identify problems, consider options, and make recommendations. In general, and across many legislative and executive administrations, state policymakers were successful in skillfully prodding and supporting change in higher education without forcing policies on a recalcitrant system.

The more technical consultations took advantage of the data available through Ohio's data system and the analytical capacity of its staff to generate more concrete ideas for implementation and consider a multiplicity of funding scenarios. Importantly, these analyses allowed decision makers to collectively identify, discuss, and address the more sensitive issue of mission differentiation.[30] This sensitivity to mission was apparent early on. For example, the various components of the Selective Excellence programs were designed in part to ensure that state policies and programs equitably supported all public campuses in their missions. The creation of the Challenge programs in the late 1960s explicitly and directly funded two-year and four-year campuses in a manner that was sensitive to their missions and that promoted state goals.[31]

Program evaluations provided critical examinations of the programs and policies, helped fine-tune some, eliminate others that were no longer needed (such as the Two-Year Campus Service Expectations), and generally legitimize Ohio's culture of experimentation. While external studies—such as the evaluation by NCHEMS of the Selective Excellence programs and MDRC's evaluation of TEAP—arguably provided more disinterested analyses and are preferable, they are also more expensive than in-house evaluations. These internal evaluations played an important role, both in a formative and summative sense.

Finally, in most cases the availability of new money was a significant factor. New state funds were made available for Selective Excellence, Two-Year Campus Performance Expectations, the Four Challenges, and TEAP, although the most recent action—the creation of the Strategic Plan formula—came when state funding for higher education was flat or declining.

While it is difficult to select the most critical factor in this mix, four factors seem to stand out. First, the early and sustained success of the Research Challenge provided both a model and an inspiration for almost all subsequent endeavors. In the absence of this initiative, performance funding in Ohio might have had a completely different history. Second, the existence and use of timely and reliable data seemed at times paramount.[32] Strong political leadership, collaboration among campuses, and even new money are all important; but without the ability to model new ideas quickly and precisely, implement those ideas, and evaluate them, attempts to innovate and experiment seem bound to flounder or fail. Third, sensitivity to the diverse missions of Ohio's campuses created proposals that were deemed by the participants to be equitable and thereby sustained the political support and goodwill needed to advance the programs to state decision makers.

Finally, the collaborative process of policymaking among all stakeholders established the communications, knowledge base, and trust so critical to the success of inducing change in large organizations and systems. This decision-making process, sometimes referred to as "problems down, solutions up," worked fairly well for Ohio, and for its campuses and citizens. Led by chancellors who were responsive to state policymakers and were willing to innovate *and* delegate, the consultations enabled campuses to speak with one voice, more or less, before legislative and executive bodies about major funding programs. That consensus helped sustain policies over time and minimize disruptions that could have occurred when new administrations and new legislative leaders took office.

APPENDIX

The text on aligning funding with state interests in Ohio's 2008 higher education strategic plan is as follows:[33]

> A core principle of higher education finance is that funding formulas must be systematically aligned with the goals and priorities of the state in order for colleges and universities to have the incentives and resources they need to achieve the targets set for them.
>
> The state's basic funding formula, the State Share of Instruction, is currently designed to reward enrollment growth and penalize enrollment decline. This formula, as much as any other factor, has contributed to the wasteful competition among state institutions. A new funding formula will be recommended to the Governor and the General Assembly in the next biennial budget that will be aligned with the goals of this plan. The funding that is currently provided through the "Challenges"— Jobs Challenge, Access Challenge, Success Challenge and Economic Growth Challenge—will be incorporated into the new formula to better incentivize the goals of this plan.
>
> The formula itself will be developed in consultation with legislators and university officials who will be convened immediately after the release of this report. The following principles, adapted from lists of principles developed by the members of the Inter-University Council and the Ohio Association of Community Colleges, will guide the decision-making process as this plan becomes a reality.
>
> 1. The funding formula should only reward those educational outcomes that align with Ohio's priorities.
> 2. The funding formula should be designed to continuously support and improve systematic, cost-effective collaboration among state colleges and universities in the achievement of state goals.
> 3. The outcomes that are rewarded should take into consideration differences in institutional missions, including differences between community colleges and universities, and provide appropriate levels of state support for each mission, including not only the teaching

mission of all colleges and universities, but other relevant contributions such as research, technology transfer, workforce development, globalization, and community revitalization.

4. Increases in enrollments or degrees granted, or improvements in other activities or outcomes that advance state goals, should be supported by appropriate increases in state funding. To determine what is an "appropriate" level of funding, the funding formula should be informed by systematic comparisons of Ohio institutions versus their peers across the nation, with the goal of making Ohio competitive with its peer states or peer-state institutions.

5. The funding formula should harmonize and integrate state policies regarding institutional subsidy, student tuition, student financial aid and institutional capital funding.

6. The funding formula should be designed to provide some level of predictability and financial stability for institutions.

7. The funding formula should include an incentive for each campus to develop excellence in academic programs and disciplines significant to its mission, region, and state priorities and goals.

8. The funding formula should recognize differences in academic program cost and should encourage cost efficiency among similar programs.

9. The details of the funding formula should be the outcome of an open consultative process with broad participation.

NOTES

1. Recent examples include the Lumina Foundation–funded Productivity Initiative, the Bill and Melinda Gates Foundation's Complete College America effort, and the Voluntary System of Accountability, sponsored by the Association of Public and Land-Grant Universities and the American Association of State Colleges and Universities.

2. John D. Millett, *Financing Higher Education in the United States* (New York: Columbia University Press, 1952).

3. Ralph R. Gutowski, "Higher Education Finance: An Analysis of Ohio's Budget Formula" (doctoral diss., Miami University, Oxford, OH, 1984).

4. For a partial list of these consultations and committees, see http://regents .ohio.gov/financial/index.php.

5. National Center for Higher Education Management Systems, *An Evaluation of the Ohio Selective Excellence Program* (Boulder, CO: NCHEMS, Oct. 13, 1992).

6. Ohio Board of Regents, "Securing the Future of Higher Education," Columbus, Dec. 1992, available at http://regents.ohio.gov/news/plandocs/secure.html.

7. Ibid.

8. Ohio General Assembly, Am. Sub. H.B. 152, 120th General Assembly, Biennial Operating Appropriations for FY 1993–FY 1995, sec. 84.01.

9. With flat funding and a bimodal pattern of enrollment growth, the formula would leverage money away from the more slowly growing university main campuses and toward the faster-growing community colleges.

10. Ohio General Assembly, Am. Sub. H.B. 117, 121st General Assembly.

11. Higher Education Funding Commission of the Ohio Board of Regents, "Final Report and Recommendations," Columbus, Nov. 15, 1996, available at www .rpia.ohio-state.edu/bplan/docs/archive/highered.pdf.

12. The Higher Education Funding Commission's work was greatly assisted by the expertise of an external consultant, Brenda Albright. The contributions of external facilitators such as Ms. Albright are probably understated and underappreciated by readers who are not directly familiar with the process of consultation.

13. In the late 1990s, the Regents' data system was completely reviewed, revised, and renamed.

14. See for example, Ohio University, "Success Challenge At-Risk and Timely Degree Completion Report," Athens, OH, Sept. 30, 1999, available at http://regents .ohio.gov/hei/success/ousc99.pdf.

15. Ohio Board of Regents, "An Assessment of the Four Challenge Line Items," Columbus, May 2008.

16. "Research Challenge: The Results of a Decade of Investment in University Research," Report to the Ohio Board of Regents, June 1996.

17. Governor's Commission on Higher Education and the Economy, *Building on Knowledge, Investing in People: Higher Education and the Future of Ohio's Economy* (Columbus, April 29, 2004), available at http://regents.ohio.gov/ financial/hefsc/publications/CHEE_4_22.pdf.

18. Ohio General Assembly, Am. Sub. H.B. 66, 126th General Assembly.

19. Ohio General Assembly, *The State of Higher Education Minority Report* (Columbus, May 2006), available at http://regents.ohio.gov/financial/hefsc/ publications/HEFSC Minority Report 5-31-06.pdf.

20. Ohio General Assembly, *Higher Education Funding Study Council Report* (Columbus, May 2006), available at http://regents.ohio.gov/financial/ hefsc/publications/HEFSC Final report 5-31-06.pdf.

21. Andy Lechler, "Draft Evaluation of the TANF Educational Awards Program: Student Outcomes Fall 2006 and Spring 2007" (Ohio Board of Regents, Columbus, March 2009).

22. Paulette Cha and Reshma Patel, *Rewarding Progress, Reducing Debt: Early Results from Ohio's Performance-Based Scholarship Demonstration for Low-Income Parents* (New York: MDRC, Oct. 2010), available at www.mdrc.org/ publications/568/full.pdf.

23. Ohio General Assembly, Am. Sub. H.B. 2, 127th General Assembly.

24. University System of Ohio and Ohio Board of Regents, *The Strategic Plan for Higher Education 2008–2017* (Columbus, May 2008), available at www.uso .edu/strategicplan.

25. Much of the following description is taken from Ohio Board of Regents, *Ohio's Performance-Based Subsidy Formula for Higher Education: Fact Sheet for the New State Share of Instruction Formula* (Columbus, 2010).

26. D. Timothy Leinbach and Davis Jenkins, *Using Longitudinal Data to Increase Community College Student Success: A Guide to Measuring Milestone and Momentum Point Attainment* (New York: Community College Research Center, Teachers College, Columbia University, January 2008), available at http://ccrc .tc.columbia.edu/Publication.asp?uid=570.

27. The use of this measure of financial status as the sole indicator of an at-risk student was adopted primarily because it was the one indicator for which nearly universal and current data were available. Consultation members recognized that this single metric was an incomplete measure and subsequently developed and adopted a more comprehensive measure which also included age, academic preparation, and race/ethnicity. The use of the more complex measure has the effect of driving more money to campuses that successfully serve more at-risk students.

28. That is to say, no campus would experience a loss of more than 1% of its previous year's support in year one, no more than 2% of its previous year's support in year two, and so on.

29. It is worth noting that a number of the factors that contributed to success in Ohio—especially strong leadership and broad collaboration—played an important role in Texas as well, as described in chapter 10.

30. These analytical activities are not fully fleshed out in this analysis, but plenty of evidence is available on Board of Regents' websites. See, for example, http://regents.ohio.gov/financial/hefc/index.php.

31. National Center for Higher Education Management Systems, *An Evaluation of the Ohio Selective Excellence Program* (Boulder, CO, Oct. 13, 1992).

32. The processes included in the higher education information system also minimized, but probably did not eliminate, the opportunities for any campus to "game" the system. All data submitted by campuses are subject to internal automated logical edits as well as staff review, and the state conducted periodic enrollment and financial aid audits, as well as annual financial audits, of all campuses. In addition, some data sources, such as those used in Research Challenge distributions, came from unimpeachable national sources like the National Science Foundation. Finally, the structure of programs designed to respect campus missions—for example, by providing additional funding to at-risk students— minimized any incentive for less selective campuses to become more selective.

33. University System of Ohio and Ohio Board of Regents, *The Strategic Plan for Higher Education 2008-2017*.

Conclusion

ANDREW P. KELLY AND MARK SCHNEIDER

Two years after President Obama announced his ambitious plans for higher education, a "completion agenda" has taken root in state governments, foundations, and colleges across the country, all of which have made large financial investments in service of increasing the number of adults in the nation with postsecondary credentials. This undertaking presents an unprecedented opportunity to learn more about the strengths and weaknesses of our higher education system and to use that knowledge to reform the system. Because these investments are usually attached to concrete attainment goals—a 60 percent attainment rate, doubling the numbers of low-income degree-holders, and so on—they have also raised the stakes for success. Any verdict as to whether American higher education has met the challenges of the completion agenda will be based largely on how much measurable progress we make on these goals.

Say what you will about whether focusing on completion rates is the best strategy—and many of the contributors to this volume voice concerns in this regard—the rhetorical shift from an access agenda to a success agenda has been remarkable. As we stated in the opening of this volume, however, shifting the rhetoric is the easy part. Sought-after results will require significant policy change, a cultural shift in the way institutions think about their work, far better metrics for measuring success, and serious commitment on the part of policymakers to demand more of a system that has rested on its laurels as the world's best. Even more important, policymakers and institutional leaders must have a "playbook" of strategies that can promote student success and improve institutional performance, as well as a strategy for scaling up reforms that do prove successful. The current fiscal crisis in the states has further complicated matters, as these reform strategies must be not only effective, but also cost-effective. We have entered an era where continuing to conduct business as usual will be increasingly difficult, if not impossible.

We began this volume with a set of seemingly simple questions: Where does the United States currently stand when it comes to postsecondary attainment, and how much would productivity have to improve in order to make progress on these new higher education goals? Are the goals feasible? What do we know about how to dramatically raise the proportion of Americans who hold a college degree, and which types of programs are likely to provide the most bang for our reform buck? Finally, what might policymakers learn from states and institutions that have embarked on ambitious higher education reforms in the past?

We did not set out to deliver a hard and fast verdict on any of these questions—indeed, many of our contributors disagreed on the feasibility and appropriateness of the attainment goals. Instead, in this concluding essay we explore what we see as several recurrent themes that surface throughout the chapters. We begin by assessing the goals themselves vis-à-vis the status quo in higher education, then move on to discuss what we know about strategies to improve productivity and how to measure them. We then turn to examine potential game-changing developments in the sector and offer a few words on how to rethink what success looks like going forward.

Assessing the Goals

As many of our authors point out, the completion agenda actually consists of a series of distinct goals. The president has promised that by 2020, America will "once again" be the most highly educated nation in the world—a promise that he translated into a call for an additional eight million degrees, including five million at the sub-baccalaureate level. The Gates Foundation's goal is to double the number of low-income adults who earn a postsecondary credential that has labor market value by age 26. The Lumina Foundation for Education has set its sights on increasing the proportion of American adults with a postsecondary credential to 60 percent by the year 2025. The Georgetown Center for Education and the Workforce recently projected that the United States will need an additional 20 million degrees by the year 2025: 15 million bachelor's degrees, 4 million certificates, and 1 million associate's degrees.

Whether these goals are reasonable depends on how our participation, completion, and attainment rates look today and how they have changed over time. It is only with these data in hand that we can even begin to assess the extent of change that is required to fulfill the completion agenda. Arthur M. Hauptman has provided a detailed exploration of these topics, helping to sort through some of the competing claims about America's current attainment rates, our national ranking compared with other industrialized democracies, and the trends in these numbers over time. In addition to clarifying the crucial distinction between completion rates and attainment rates, Hauptman reminds us that some of the most often-cited justifications for the completion agenda are either a mischaracterization of the data or are flat-out incorrect.

Most importantly, Hauptman points out that, contrary to much of the conventional wisdom, our attainment rate has not been stagnant of late but has steadily grown over time, keeping pace with the average OECD country. The gist of his argument: the country is actually coming at these new attainment goals from a running, rather than a standing, start.

But even this running start will not make achieving the goals much easier, as many of our authors point out. Hauptman bluntly argues that "the likelihood of achieving a 60 percent attainment rate by 2020, or even 2025, is close to nil." Thomas Bailey argues that producing an additional five million degrees and certificates from the community college sector will require a year-over-year growth rate of 8.5 percent, more than triple the yearly growth rate over the past decade (2.5%). Without a 5 to 10 percent yearly increase in community college enrollments, meeting the goals will prove impossible. And as Bailey notes, the tight fiscal environment means that sizable increases in enrollment will be hard to come by.

Beneath this pessimism, however, many of the authors also highlight some opportunities. In general, there seems to be consensus that the sub-baccalaureate sector has the most room for improvement. The U.S. bachelor's degree attainment rate has been consistently high, and the nation compares favorably with our most high-performing international peers. On measures of sub-baccalaureate attainment, however, the United States lags. Given the large numbers of students who begin a two-year degree and fail to finish (three-year graduation rates in public community colleges typically hover below 25%), even incremental gains in completion rates could pay large dividends.

In particular, Brian Bosworth sees potential for certificate programs of more than one year to raise the proportion of people with a high-quality postsecondary credential. Bosworth shows that these types of programs have high completion rates and high labor market returns—rivaling the returns for associate's degrees in many cases. Unfortunately, these certificates do not currently "count" in the way the U.S. Census or the OECD measure attainment. Given their track record, Bosworth argues that these programs represent an opportunity to raise attainment rates and should be made a more prominent part of the nation's post-secondary portfolio. Diane Auer Jones's exploration of apprenticeships makes a similar argument, suggesting that formal apprenticeship programs are an underdeveloped and underutilized avenue to postsecondary credentials with labor market value.

In sum, on the feasibility question our contributors are generally doubtful that our system, as currently conceived, could produce the kind of short-term gains called for by the president and leading foundations. On the question of whether these goals are the "right" ones, most of our authors agree that shifting to a focus on completion was a move in the right direction, provided policymakers exercise appropriate caution in setting goals and priorities. While access questions continue to be important, Tom Bailey argues, "Given the large number of students already in college who do not finish a degree, increasing completion rates for those students is a more logical first step." However, some of our contributors rightly caution that an explicit focus on completion rates could unleash potentially perverse results.

One theme comes through in each of these early chapters: the recent flurry of reform energy has, for better or worse, sent the nation's higher education system into uncharted territory. Unfortunately, the same chapters make it clear that our playbook of proven strategies is not well developed.

What Do We Know about Increasing Attainment Rates?

Put simply, we do not know much about how institutions can improve the success of their students, let alone do so in a way that is cost-effective and scalable. As Matthew M. Chingos argues, although we know that some institutions do a better job than others in getting similar students over the finish line, we know very little about which policies, practices, or programs contribute to such success. To be sure, targeted interventions in financial aid and student services have occasionally proven successful in promoting gains in retention and credits completed. But the effects have generally been small—and far too limited to reach the ambitious goals set out for the nation. Moreover, such targeted programs are often simply grafted onto existing practices, leaving basic policies and structures untouched and potentially adding costs rather than saving money. At the community college level, even interventions that seem to "work" on a small scale are unlikely to promote the dramatic improvements in productivity we need. As Tom Bailey argues, popular reforms like learning communities and enhanced student services have produced no effects when submitted to a rigorous evaluation. While other "programmatic" interventions have had small positive effects on intermediate student outcomes like retention, it remains to be seen whether they have a positive effect on completion, and whether these benefits outweigh the costs. But even without considering costs, the vast majority of small-scale reforms simply do not have enough of an impact to produce dramatic gains in completion.

Moreover, the best evidence suggests that fixing the most frequently invoked policy issues—financial aid and credit portability—would not actually make much of a dent in our quest to raise attainment. Eric Bettinger's chapter shows that traditional financial aid programs are an inefficient and ineffective tool for promoting retention and completion. Bettinger estimates that using financial aid to drive a 10 percentage point increase in the retention rate would cost an additional $40 billion over what we already spend on Pell grants, more than doubling the current level of funding. Likewise, Josipa Roksa concludes that the vagaries of moving credits from one college to another—often seen as a barrier to completion—are not actually much of a culprit after all. Students who transfer appear to be just as likely to graduate as their peers, and the problem of "excessive" credit accumulation is as prevalent among students who stay at one institution as it is for students who transfer.

Issues of sustainability, scale, and cost-effectiveness are particularly challenging for community colleges. Even the most promising programs are difficult to export across institutions and states. Elaine DeLott Baker's chapter provides a cautionary tale to all who would assume that effective practices and interventions can be scaled up. The problem, according to Baker, is that attention and resources are often front-loaded to the development and implementation of the program, while questions of diffusion and scale receive less attention. As a result, successful programs blossom in some places, but knowledge about what works and how to implement it does not accumulate systematically, leaving institutions at a loss when trying to replicate best practices.

Put simply, incremental reforms, in isolation, are not likely to drive the kind of dramatic and lasting improvements in student success that the nation requires. As Bailey's chapter shows, the poor performance of current reforms reveals a need for more radical approaches to organizational change. Qualitative studies have found that successful community colleges have a number of cultural and structural elements in common: an explicit commitment to promoting student success, simplified programs and processes to help students navigate the system more easily, and innovative modes of teaching. While institutions can take steps to promote student success, Chingos reminds us that the evidence suggests "it is hard to imagine that tinkering at the margins is going to result in substantial increases in graduation rates," particularly when budgets are tight. The recipe for success may not be a mix of small, targeted interventions that solve particular problems, but a more comprehensive rethinking of entire organizations and systems.

Collectively, the chapters in this volume suggest that the country must think more imaginatively about higher education reform. We must also think differently about how we measure success, creating metrics that better reflect the increasingly diverse array of students, institutions, and models of delivery. But these challenges also raise questions without easy answers: What innovations are potential game changers in higher education? What mix of providers, programs, and policies will get us where we want to go without breaking the bank? And what measures of success will we need in order to assess whether new ideas are leading us in the right direction?

We see two intertwined avenues of improvement that can help us rise to this challenge. First, we are beginning to see innovations in the structure and delivery of higher education that have the potential to upend the high cost / low success model we now have in place.

Second, there is a growing consensus on what we need to measure to improve the productivity of the higher education system—so that we can in fact do more with less. A lack of good information about which policies and practices help students earn valuable postsecondary credentials, and which do so in a cost-effective manner, is a fundamental handicap to making progress. Moreover, many of our current measures of success are not well suited to the new models of postsecondary education that have come to serve increasing numbers of nontraditional students.

Potential Game Changers

We see three potential game changers on the horizon: online delivery of courses, competency-based models of education, and for-profit colleges and universities. We discuss each of these developments in turn before shifting to a discussion of how to rethink the way we measure higher education success in the years to come.

Online Delivery

In its purest form, online delivery renders the traditional limitations of geographic distance, physical capacity, and time moot. Students can take online courses from anywhere and at any time, instructors can teach far more students online than in a traditional format, and online courses can start any day of any week of the year. These attributes make online delivery particularly enticing in an era of tight public budgets. Because of space and resource constraints, traditional community colleges cannot meet the current demand from prospective students, and online programs have continued to grow apace. Moreover, the convenience offered by online courses and programs often appeals to nontraditional adult learners, a key target group in the push to increase the nation's attainment rate.

By any measure, the growth in online learning in higher education over the last 15 years has been remarkable. In 1995, just 7,000 students were pursuing degrees in online programs. By 2008 that number had grown to 1.8 million.[1] The Sloan Consortium, which tracks online learning in higher education, estimates that in 2009 more than 5.6 million students were taking at least one online course. That number represents almost 30 percent of all higher education enrollments, up from just 10 percent of students in 2002. Online enrollments grew at a rate of 21 percent from 2008 to 2009, more than 10 times the 2 percent growth rate in the rest of higher education.[2]

The prominence of online delivery has grown across the postsecondary sector. Among for-profit institutions, the University of Phoenix has developed an enormous online footprint. In the public sector, the University of Maryland–University College has carved out a niche as one of the largest online universities in the world. It currently has the highest enrollment of any college in the University of Maryland system. In 2009, it had over 196,000 online course enrollments, making it the public institution with the largest online presence.[3] At the community college level, Rio Salado College enrolls about 35,000 online students across the country in more than 500 online courses. Most online courses at Rio Salado start on 50 Mondays out of the year.[4]

Online courses and programs are already changing the way institutions of higher education operate, allowing unprecedented expansion and eliminating the constraints of geography. But are online courses any good? And does simply moving instruction online save money?

Research on the quality of online higher education is still in its infancy, but the results have been mixed. Recent studies have produced discouraging conclusions about the effects of online coursework, finding that students enrolled in online courses were more likely to fail and drop out than students in traditional courses.[5] Other studies have been more sanguine. A high-profile meta-analysis published by the U.S. Department of Education found that students learning online actually outperformed those in traditional courses, while hybrid models—in which course content is delivered partly in person and partly online—seem to outperform both traditional and online-only programs.[6] The work of the National Center for Academic Transformation (NCAT) and the Open Learning Initiative at Carnegie Mellon University suggests that students in hybrid introductory courses learn more and at a faster rate than their peers in traditional, lecture-based classes. In short, well-designed online courses, most probably mixed with some in-classroom experiences, can be highly effective.

The second question—whether online delivery can cut the cost of higher education—has received less attention. In many cases, colleges have simply grafted online courses and degree programs onto the existing structure, using the online program as a cash cow to keep the traditional college and departments flush with resources. But other efforts to implement online learning have realized cost savings over the traditional model. Evaluations of the course redesign experiments by NCAT have found that the hybrid models save an average of 35 percent over the traditional model, while producing student outcomes that are as good if not better.[7] The key to the NCAT model is deploying labor more efficiently: replacing expensive full-time faculty with lower-cost teaching assistants and peer tutors on tasks like grading and on-demand assistance. These results suggest that for online learning to reduce the cost of instruction, institutions must rethink their traditional way of doing business.

Online delivery can also present an opportunity for instructors and institutions to think about student learning, assessment, and course design and improvement in unprecedented ways. The Open Learning Initiative's courses are a case in point. The modules feature embedded assessments that students must pass through before moving on to subsequent content. The results from these assessments are all collected in real time, enabling instructors to understand which concepts their students have mastered and which students are still struggling with.[8] The technology allows for continuous improvement on the basis of student learning—a concept that is currently largely foreign to higher education. Measuring student learning and improving instruction are likely to become increasingly important as policymakers place more emphasis on accountability for student learning.

Competency-Based Models and Prior Learning

A second potentially transformative innovation is the competency-based model of higher education. In the simplest form, competency-based models allow students to move at their own pace through a course of study, progressing from one concept to the next only after proving mastery on an assessment aligned with the content. Because of their emphasis on learning outcomes rather than seat time, competency-based models also allow for the certification and credentialing of prior learning. As Robert Mendenhall, president of the competency-based Western Governors University (WGU), puts it, while traditional models "hold the time constant and let the learning vary," competency-based models "hold the learning constant and let the time vary."[9] The Council for Adult and Experiential Learning has developed a prior learning assessment designed to award adult learners with credit for the skills and knowledge they have acquired prior to enrolling in a college or university.

The highest-profile competency-based bachelor's degree program in the country is that of WGU, which serves students across the country. The WGU model is straightforward: students are awarded credits once they demonstrate competency on the learning outcomes attached to those credits. Students who already know a given subject can get credit for that prior learning by passing an assessment that tests their competencies. For those areas where students need to brush up, they are provided with course materials and guidance from mentors and allowed to move through the material at their own pace. WGU offers bachelor's and master's degrees in a few basic majors: business, education, healthcare, and information technology. WGU is specifically designed to serve adult learners, particularly those with some college credit but no degree. The typical student is clearly "nontraditional": the average age is 36, and many students work full or part time while enrolled. Tuition—which varies by program and ranges from about $3,000 to $4,250 per semester— is charged every six months. Students can amass as many competency-based credits in that six-month period as they can.

WGU was started in 1997 by 18 governors from western states and has since become a linchpin in the competency-based movement. Enrollment grew more than 350 percent between 2006 and 2011, going from 5,525 in 2006 to 25,000 in 2010.[10] Between 2010 and 2011, WGU was invited into Indiana and Washington to provide bachelor's degrees as part of each state's public university system. These state-based partnerships are likely to boost enrollments even further. They are also economically attractive: WGU–Indiana and WGU–Washington are both self-sufficient, operating on tuition and start-up grants from foundations and receiving no direct subsidy from the state.

What makes competency-based models an innovation to watch, though, is the ability to move students to degrees more quickly. Among WGU graduates, the average time to complete a bachelor's degree is just 2.5 years, about half what it is at a traditional four-year university.[11] Other measures of student success and satisfaction are also positive. For instance, WGU students report high levels of engagement, and 79 percent of employers who hired WGU graduates rated them as being as good as or better than graduates of other universities.[12]

In light of the current focus on time to degree, affordability, and non-traditional students, observers have promoted competency-based models like WGU as one of the most promising innovations on the higher education landscape. But questions remain as to the scalability of the WGU mode. While Western Governors' approach has shortened the time to degree for completers, there is some evidence that WGU struggles to graduate its "traditional" students. According to the U.S. Department of Education's Integrated Postsecondary Education Data System (IPEDS), just 22 percent of first-time, full-time WGU students graduated in 150 percent of the time of their program.[13] Though the standard first-time, full-time graduation rate applies only to a fraction of WGU's students, the lackluster completion rates among traditional students do raise concerns about the scalability of a competency-based model. It is also unclear how the cost structure would change if the average time to degree increased with an influx of less-qualified students. Despite these questions, competency-based models appear well designed to serve adult learners with some college experience but no degree, a high-value "target" of the completion agenda.

For-Profit Institutions

Dramatically increasing attainment in an era of declining public funding will require new capacity to serve students. Online delivery provides one route to building new space for prospective students, but colleges and universities themselves must have incentive to find ways to grow their enrollments.

Unfortunately, outside of some of the innovative colleges mentioned throughout this volume, most traditional institutions have little incentive to grow. Facing the high costs of bricks and mortar coupled with rapidly declining public dollars, the typical college or university is usually content to fill its seats with the best students it can find and then turn other students away. For instance, California's community colleges may have turned away as many as 140,000 prospective students in 2010.[14] At the highest levels of selectivity, limiting the size of the student body and rejecting more and more students actually helps institutions climb up the rankings.

In contrast, for-profit colleges and universities operate under a model in which growth is good. Proprietary colleges are rarely limited by physical capacity, and they can raise private capital to finance further expansion. For-profits are also leading the way in developing online learning platforms, further freeing them from any physical barriers to enrollment growth. This capacity for growth sets for-profit colleges up to be potential game changers in the effort to produce more college degrees.

The result of this incentive to grow, coupled with generous federal financial aid policies, has been a massive expansion in for-profit enrollments over the past decade. Between 2000 and 2009, enrollment in for-profit colleges almost quadrupled, moving from 400,000 students to 1.58 million.[15] Most of this growth has been in bachelor's degree programs, where enrollment increased more than 450 percent during that period (211,000 students in 2000; 1.2 million in 2009).[16] The University of Phoenix grew from serving 25,000 students in 1995 to more than 455,000 in 2010, making it the largest university system in the country. While the other publicly owned for-profit companies are not nearly as large, many still enroll 100,000 students or more, ranking them among the nation's largest in terms of size.[17]

Incentive to grow is not the only thing that sets for-profits apart; their approaches to instruction, program design, and labor market connections have also received considerable attention from observers.

The largest for-profit systems have a centralized model of curriculum development and faculty training that encourages uniformity in instruction across multiple sites and instructors. Faculty at institutions like the University of Phoenix, ITT Tech, and American Public University are evaluated on the basis of their students' learning outcomes, and promotion and salary decisions are based in part on these metrics. On the student service side, Guilbert Hentschke argues that for-profits have experimented with "client-centered" rather than "functionally-oriented" systems to more efficiently serve students' needs. Essentially, rather than dividing up student services like academic advising, career services, and financial aid into distinct departments, for-profit institutions merge these services, tasking student advising staff with a broader array of responsibilities. And when it comes to responding to labor market demand, for-profits are generally far more agile than their traditional peers. For instance, DeVry University works with local industry advisory councils at sites across the country to gauge labor market demand for particular programs and skills and then tailors its program offerings, and the curriculum within those programs, to fit regional employers' needs.[18] These aspects of for-profit organization—assessment of student learning, a student-centered outlook on service, and real-time connections to the labor market—stand in stark contrast to the concerns that preoccupy most traditional institutions.

The picture is far from rosy for for-profit colleges, however. Completion rates for four-year programs at for-profit colleges lag behind the national average. In for-profits, 22 percent of first-time, full-time students who started a four-year degree in 2002 had finished a degree at that institution by 2008; the national average is about 57 percent. High default rates also raise alarm bells. One-quarter of all for-profit graduates had defaulted on their student loans within three years of entering repayment; and although for-profits enroll only 10 to 15 percent of all students, their graduates make up about 47 percent of all three-year defaults.[19] While these high default rates are explained in part by the number of high-risk students for-profits are trying to educate, part of the explanation also lies in the high cost of many of their programs.

These troubling outcomes have not escaped the view of federal regulators. A series of high-profile congressional hearings, federal investigations, and Justice Department lawsuits have exposed recruiting abuses, false advertising, and financial aid fraud at for-profits. In spite of the bad press, for-profit institutions have developed a sizable foothold in the higher education market and are unlikely to fade from the scene anytime soon. Although growth rates have slowed in light of the poor economy and public criticism, the tight fiscal environment probably means that traditional colleges will continue to be strapped for seats, opening up market share for for-profit institutions. And their track record in graduating students is not all bad: graduation rates for two-year degree programs are much higher among for-profit institutions than at public community colleges (58% at for-profits, 21% at public community colleges, according to the latest data available).[20] Given the country's focus on sub-baccalaureate degree production, the for-profits' success in this sector is encouraging.

The big question going forward is whether for-profits can move "upmarket" to "disrupt" traditional institutions.[21] It seems just as likely that the most entrepreneurial of the traditional institutions will adopt some of the successful innovations pioneered by for-profits over the past decade. Regardless of the outcome, the for-profits will continue to push our understanding of how institutions of higher education can and should be organized and run.

Rethinking How We Measure Success

Innovation is essential, but we also need to rethink the way in which we measure success. Just as institutions and systems will have to change if we are to make progress on the completion agenda, our measures of quality and productivity must also evolve to reflect the changing student demographics and the nation's changing fiscal climate.

For instance, as noted throughout this volume, what many people call "traditional students"—full-time students between the ages of 18 and 24 who earn associate's degrees in two years and bachelor's degrees in four— are now the exception rather than the norm. Yet our current measures of success rarely cover these "nontraditional" students. There is also a need to measure student outcomes beyond retention and completion. To justify increasing debt levels and rising tuition, policymakers are also demanding concrete measures of student success in the labor market after graduating. There is also a growing concern that students are not learning enough while in college, so that even if we increase the number of graduates, college degrees might not be as valuable as we think. And in an era of fiscal crisis, it is also clear that we must be more mindful of the costs of producing degrees and promoting student success.

In light of these imperatives, a concern for better metrics has become part of the national dialogue about higher education. Policymakers, foundations, and researchers are all seeking to improve the ways in which we measure the efficiency and effectiveness of higher education. These efforts can be viewed as falling into four broad categories—student success, student learning, graduates' economic success, and the cost of degrees.

Student Success

Improving how we measure student success occupies center stage. There is a growing recognition that we need better and more comprehensive measures of student retention, progression, and completion.

To earn a credential, students have to stay enrolled (retention), they have to accumulate enough credits in a timely fashion (progression), and ultimately they have to finish their program (completion). Currently, the nation relies on the U.S. Department of Education's Integrated Postsecondary Education Data System (IPEDS) for these fundamental data. However, IPEDS is fatally flawed, since it concentrates on the performance of first-time, full-time students. This category of students currently comprises fewer than half of all postsecondary students in the country—and that proportion will continue to shrink in the years to come. And beyond its limited coverage, IPEDS fails to measure most aspects of student success. For example, we can turn to IPEDS to find out how many students on a campus return after their first year, but the data do not capture rates at which students drop out after that. IPEDS also has no information at all about student progression.

Slowly (and hopefully surely), the nation's governors (coordinated by the National Governors Association and Complete College America) are forging a new set of measures that will allow us to measure more accurately the success of all students enrolled in colleges and universities.[22] Better measurement matters but so does elevating the importance of those measures by tying public funding to institutional performance on those outcomes. Increasingly, states are doing just that: allocating increasing shares of their higher education budgets on the basis of how well their institutions are doing on more accurate measures of student success. About half of the states now have "performance budgeting systems" that reward campuses for student progress and success rather than simply for "seat time." We are slowly accumulating evidence on how performance budgeting systems might be more effectively fashioned to help the nation meet the completion agenda.

Student Learning

Higher education is about just that: educating students. Yet, measuring how much students have learned is a movement that is only now beginning to gain traction. Critics have long suspected that far too many colleges do not add much value—in terms of knowledge and skills—to their students. Richard Arum and Josipa Roksa's recent book, *Academically Adrift*, elevated that concern from a back-room parlor game to an issue on the front pages of newspapers across the country. Arum and Roksa show that during the first two years of college, 45 percent of students in their study did not improve in critical thinking, complex reasoning, and writing. Moreover, they show that students are distracted by socializing or working and that colleges and universities often put undergraduate learning close to the bottom of their priorities.[23]

One of the strengths of Arum and Roksa's study is its empirical base. Rather than asserting that students are not learning, these authors used the Collegiate Learning Assessment (CLA), one of a handful of new assessments developed to measure the cognitive skills of students. While the CLA has attracted the most attention (thanks in large part to *Academically Adrift*), other assessments are available (such as the College Board's Collegiate Assessment of Academic Proficiency or ETS's Proficiency Profile); and more are likely to emerge as policymakers demand measures of the value added by a college education.

The Economic Success of Graduates

Ultimately we need some assessment of the extent to which labor markets are validating the value of the skills college graduates possess. About half the states in the nation can now link student-level data that document graduates' experiences in college (e.g., major field of study) with unemployment insurance records that document salary, employment status, and industry of employment after leaving. With these data, we can compare the returns on the investment students and taxpayers have made in different degree programs and campuses. Perhaps even more importantly, these linked data can be used to measure the returns for students with the same credential from different campuses. Armed with these data, students and policymakers can compare how students with bachelor's degrees in materials science from one college fare in the labor market as compared with students with the same degree from another campus.

These objective data on student labor market success can be used to hold schools accountable for quality even as we press for more graduates. This idea has already taken hold in federal policymaking: witness the prolonged fight over what the Department of Education has called "gainful employment"—an attempt to make sure that campuses are producing degrees that allow students to find jobs with earnings that are sufficient to pay off their loans. Whether the move to measure gainful employment will blossom into a wider effort to link labor market outcomes to colleges and universities remains to be seen, but attention to measures of labor market success is likely to increase.

Cost of Degrees

Finally, reformers must take account of the cost of producing college degrees. We know that costs are driven by some fundamentals (the mix between upper-division students versus lower-division ones; the mix between majors—physics is far more expensive to teach than French). And there are some accounting issues that need to be considered. For example, how should we allocate spending on research and administrative support when it comes to the cost of producing degrees? Given these issues, it is perhaps not surprising that good metrics about how much college degrees cost are lacking.

There is also a fundamental problem in how people confuse the *price* and the *cost* of a college degree. Government subsidies can lead to little relationship between what we pay for something and what it costs to produce it. When we look at a highly subsidized service such as higher education, the divergence between price and cost can be substantial—a college diploma that carries a low price tag can cost far more than people realize. For example, taxpayers may contribute as much as $100,000 in subsidies for each bachelor's degree granted by the nation's public "flagship" research universities.[24]

We must also take a hard look at the cost-effectiveness of policies and practices that are designed to promote student success. In a provocative study, Douglas Harris and Sara Goldrick-Rab argue that colleges and universities rarely pay much attention to cost-effectiveness concerns and that many popular reforms—from lower student-faculty ratios to augmented student services—fail to pass a cost-effectiveness test. The authors conclude that the absence of this kind of thinking on college campuses suggests that there is room for institutions to become more cost-effective.[25]

There has been some improvement on measuring the costs of a degree, much of it done by the Delta Project on Postsecondary Education Costs, Productivity, and Accountability, a high-visibility effort to bring greater attention to college spending through better data and cost metrics.[26] In general, though, measuring college costs is still a difficult enterprise because the data are poor and accounting practices are byzantine. Until we can more accurately measure costs, we cannot hope to accurately measure cost-effectiveness.

Looking Forward

For years, American higher education was viewed as the best in the world. The nation was a pioneer in creating something that resembled a universal system of higher education open to most students who wanted to attend. Using federal programs, such as Pell grants and subsidized student loans, coupled with large state subsidies to public colleges and universities, the nation pursued an "access agenda" with remarkable success. As educational attainment increased in the latter half of the twentieth century, so too did the productivity of our economy. Thanks in part to the nation's commitment to higher education, America emerged as an economic power in what economists have labeled the "human capital century."[27]

However, the costs and inefficiencies of that open-access system have become ever more apparent—and the growing fiscal problems of both the federal and state governments have made this system unsustainable. At the same time, as other industries throughout the nation have faced restructuring and disruption, traditional institutions of higher education have proven resistant to large-scale changes in the way they operate.

The spotlight is now on higher education, and the appetite for reform is high.

But there are clearly tensions that the nation has to address as the access agenda runs squarely into the new completion agenda. Simply put, it is easier for an upper- or middle-class 18-year-old to attend and complete college in a reasonable time frame than for her low-income peer. And adults returning to college—coming with a more complicated life including a mortgage, a job, and a family—face greater hurdles. Even if these nontraditional students successfully complete college, they often accumulate large amounts of debt along the way as they try to finance the ever-increasing costs of college.

A dual commitment to access and success is critical to continued economic competitiveness, but it is not easy to manage. Nontraditional students are now the majority of Americans seeking postsecondary degrees, forcing the nation to take a fresh look at the structure of higher education. In the modern era, institutions modeled on a centuries-old tradition of elite education developed in Italy and Germany will become less and less able to meet these challenges. Policymakers, students, and taxpayers have begun to demand more radical changes.

There are many degrees of difficulty in reorganizing the higher education industry to meet these increasingly vocal demands:

- There is a high degree of difficulty in reconceiving higher education when two radically different agendas, one focused on access and the other on completion, run up against each other.
- There is a high degree of difficulty in creating postsecondary credentials that are cheaper but that still have high market value.
- And there is a high degree of difficulty in moving from the ivory-tower campus where bricks and mortar dominate to a virtual campus that operates 24/7.

But we cannot ignore these difficulties—because business as usual is a dead end.

NOTES

1. Peter Stokes, "What Online Learning Can Teach Us about Higher Education," in *Reinventing Higher Education: The Promise of Innovation*, ed. Ben Wildavsky, Andrew P. Kelly, and Kevin Carey (Cambridge: Harvard Education Press, 2011).

2. I. Elaine Allen and Jeff Seaman, *Class Differences: Online Education in the United States, 2010* (Boston: Sloan Consortium, 2010).

3. See University of Maryland, University College, "UMUC at a Glance," www.umuc.edu/visitors/about/ipra/glance.cfm.

4. See Rio Salado College's profile on "Transparency by Design," www.collegechoicesforadults.org/institutions/9.

5. Di Xu and Shanna S. Jaggars, "Online and Hybrid Course Enrollment and Performance in Washington State Community and Technical Colleges" (CCRC Working Paper no. 31, Community College Research Center, Teachers College, Columbia University, New York, 2011).

6. Barbara Means et al., *Evaluation of Evidence-based Practices in On-line Learning: A Meta-Analysis and Review of Online Learning Studies* (Washington, DC: U.S. Department of Education, Sept. 2010).

7. On costs, see National Center for Academic Transformation, "Program in Course Redesign (PCR): Outcomes Analysis," www.thencat.org/PCR/Outcomes.htm; on student outcomes, National Center for Academic Transformation, "Colleagues Committed to Redesign (C2R)," www.thencat.org/RedesignAlliance/C2R/C2R_SavingsSummary.html.

8. Open Learning Initiative, "Feedback Loops for Continuous Improvement," http://oli.web.cmu.edu/openlearning/initiative.

9. Robert Mendenhall, quoted in Kathy Witkowsky, "Indiana's 'Eighth University': Western Governors University Brings Its 'Competency-Based' Approach to the Hoosier State," *National Crosstalk*, Dec. 2010.

10. Western Governors University, *Annual Report, 2010*, www.wgu.edu/wgu/2010AnnualReport.pdf.

11. Western Governors University, "Western Governors University Enrollment Tops 25,000: Nonprofit, Online University, Now with More Than 10,000 Graduates, Has Grown by More Than 350% over the Past Five Years," www.wgu.edu/about_WGU/enrollment_tops_25000_5-17-11.

12. Western Governors University, *Annual Report, 2010*.

13. U.S. Department of Education, National Center for Education Statistics, IPEDS Data Center, http://nces.ed.gov/ipeds/datacenter/Snapshotx.aspx?unitId=afaeaeaeb3b2.

14. Erica Perez, "Community Colleges Consider Cutting of Repeat Course-Takers," *California Watch*, July 11, 2011.

15. U.S. Department of Education, National Center for Education Statistics, "The Condition of Education—Participation in Education: Undergraduate Education," table A-8-1 ("Number and percentage of actual and projected undergraduate enrollment in degree-granting postsecondary institutions . . . : Selected years, fall 1970–2020"), http://nces.ed.gov/programs/coe/tables/table-hep-1.asp.

16. Ibid., table A-8-2 ("Actual and projected undergraduate enrollment in degree-granting 4- and 2-year postsecondary institutions . . . : Selected years, fall 1970–2020"), http://nces.ed.gov/programs/coe/tables/table-hep-2.asp.

17. Robin Wilson, "For-Profit Colleges Change Higher Education's Land-

scape," *Chronicle of Higher Education*, Feb. 7, 2010. The year 2010 was a high point in for-profit enrollments. Faced with a drumbeat of criticisms and a tough economy, the largest for-profit systems have seen steep declines, with Kaplan and the University of Phoenix losing over a third of their enrollments. See, for example, Nicola Kean, "Enrollments Down at For-Profit Colleges," Portfolio.com website, www.portfolio.com/views/blogs/daily-brief/2011/08/23/devry-and-corin thian-report-declining-enrollments-and-profits.

18. For an exploration of how for-profit colleges are different from traditional institutions, see Guilbert Hentschke, "For-Profit Sector Innovations in Business Models and Organizational Cultures," in Wildavsky, Kelly, and Carey, eds., *Reinventing Higher Education*.

19. Goldie Blumenstyk, "Loan Default Rate at For-Profit Colleges Would Double under New Formula," *Chronicle of Higher Education*, Feb. 4, 2011.

20. U.S. Department of Education, National Center for Education Statistics, Digest of Education Statistics, table 341 ("Graduation rates of first-time postsecondary students who started as full-time degree-seeking students . . . : Selected cohort entry years, 1996 through 2005"), http://nces.ed.gov/programs/digest/d10/tables/dt10_341.asp.

21. See Clayton M. Christensen et al., *Disrupting College: How Disruptive Innovation Can Deliver Quality and Affordability in American Higher Education* (Washington, DC: Center for American Progress, 2011).

22. Complete College America's metrics for student success can be found at www.completecollege.org/path_forward/commonmetrics.

23. Richard Arum and Josipa Roksa, *Academically Adrift: Limited Learning on College Campuses* (Chicago: University of Chicago Press, 2011).

24. Jorge Klor de Alva and Mark Schneider, "Who Wins? Who Pays? The Economic Returns and Costs of a Bachelor's Degree," www.air.org/focus-area/education/index.cfm?fa=viewContent&content_id=1286&id=6.

25. Douglas Harris and Sara Goldrick-Rab, *The (Un)Productivity of American Higher Education: From "Cost Disease" to Cost-Effectiveness*, La Follette Working Paper no. 2010-023 (Madison, WI: Robert M. La Follette School of Public Affairs, University of Wisconsin, 2010).

26. The Delta Project's annual "Trends in Spending" report documents patterns in revenues and spending across public and nonprofit higher education. More can be found at www.deltacostproject.org.

27. Claudia Goldin and Lawrence F. Katz, *The Race between Education and Technology* (Cambridge: Harvard University Press, 2008).

THOMAS BAILEY is the George and Abby O'Neill Professor of Economics and Education at Teachers College, Columbia University. He is also director of the Community College Research Center and the National Center for Postsecondary Research, both housed at Teachers College. An economist specializing in education, labor economics, and econometrics, Mr. Bailey has recently analyzed student access and success at community colleges, with a particular focus on the experiences of low-income and minority students. In June 2010, Secretary of Education Arne Duncan appointed Mr. Bailey chairperson of the Committee on Measures of Student Success, which will develop recommendations for community colleges to comply with completion-rate disclosure requirements under the Higher Education Opportunity Act. In 1996, with support from the Alfred P. Sloan Foundation, Mr. Bailey established the Community College Research Center (CCRC) at Teachers College, which conducts a large portfolio of qualitative and quantitative research based on both fieldwork at colleges and analysis of national- and state-level datasets. The findings of much of CCRC's work are found in his most recent book, *Defending the Community College Equity Agenda* (Johns Hopkins University Press, 2006).

ELAINE DELOTT BAKER is senior counsel to the vice president for community outreach at the Community College of Denver and director of its accelerated remediation programs, FastStart@CCD and College Connection. She was principal investigator of the Colorado Community College System's Lumina Initiative for Performance and director of its Ready for College grant. Ms. Baker's current interests are the successful transition of low-skilled youth and adults to postsecondary education and training, the challenges of scaling innovation, and the interplay of policy and practice in postsecondary reform. She is a frequent presenter at national forums, webinars, and conferences on issues of acceleration, contextualization, and workforce development.

Her recent publications include *Technology Solutions for Developmental Math* (Bill and Melinda Gates Foundation, 2008), *Calculating the Productivity of Innovation* (Ford Foundation, 2009), and *Contextual Teaching and Learning* (Bay Area Workforce Collaborative and the California Community College System, 2009). Ms. Baker serves on the advisory boards of the National College Transition Network and the GED Testing Service and consults with numerous foundations, intermediaries, and public interest groups.

ERIC BETTINGER is an active researcher in the economics of higher education at Stanford University. His research is quantitative and uses statistical techniques to identify causal relationships between components in higher education and student outcomes. In recent years, he has published several articles focusing on the role of remediation in higher education. Mr. Bettinger has also published articles about the effects of need-based financial aid on student retention. Using statistical tools and exploiting "natural experiments," his research suggests that need-based awards significantly improve students' likelihood of persisting in higher education after the first year. In other work, Mr. Bettinger has studied the role of adjunct faculty and other faculty characteristics in student outcomes. He has conducted randomized interventions to examine the factors that impact student success in primary and secondary school, and he helped conduct research on educational voucher programs in Colombia and the United States. Currently, Mr. Bettinger is involved in evaluating a randomized experiment that streamlines the financial-aid application process for low-income families in the United States.

BRIAN BOSWORTH is the founder and president of FutureWorks, a private consulting and public policy research firm based in Seattle, Washington, that focuses on postsecondary education and regional economic development. Before establishing FutureWorks in 1999, Mr. Bosworth spent more than a decade in international development assistance work in Latin America and 12 years as an executive leader in state-based economic growth programs in the United States. He also worked as an independent consultant with several state and regional economic development groups. FutureWorks offers policy research and development and consulting services on regional economic development, with a particular focus on issues of equity, sustainable growth, and skill development. Mr. Bosworth has directed several projects designing new approaches to regional workforce education and postsecondary education. These projects typically have involved research, policy analysis and development, and implementation engagement with development practitioners and educators. FutureWorks is now working with national and state organizations to develop and implement strategies to increase postsecondary completion and labor market success for low-income youth and working adults.

MATTHEW M. CHINGOS is a fellow in the Brown Center on Education Policy at the Brookings Institution, a postdoctoral fellow at the Program on Education Policy and Governance at Harvard University, and a research associate and project manager at the Andrew W. Mellon Foundation. He studies education politics, economics, and policy at both the K–12 and postsecondary levels. Mr. Chingos's first book is *Crossing the Finish Line: Completing College at America's Public Universities* (Princeton University Press, 2009, with William G. Bowen and Michael S. McPherson). His current research examines teacher labor markets, class-size reduction policies, citizen perceptions of school quality, online learning, and the college choices of low-income students.

ARTHUR M. HAUPTMAN has been an independent public policy consultant specializing in higher education finance issues since 1981. An internationally recognized expert, he has written extensively on student financial aid, fee setting at public and private institutions, and the public funding of institutions in the United States and around the world. A consistent theme of his work is that public policies are more effective when these three key elements of higher education financing are linked systematically. In the United States, Mr. Hauptman has consulted with many federal and state agencies as well as higher education associations and institutions. He played key roles in developing the rationale for a number of federal programs, including direct student loans, income-contingent repayment, GEARUP, and tuition tax credits. For states, he has argued for countercyclical policies to address the adverse effects of recessions, tying public-sector tuition fees to general income growth rather than costs, and paying institutions on the basis of their performance. Internationally, he has consulted with the governments or funding bodies in more than two dozen industrialized and developing countries to develop financing strategies for tertiary education.

DIANE AUER JONES is currently the vice president for external and regulatory affairs at Career Education Corporation. Trained as a molecular biologist, Ms. Jones spent the first 13 years of her career working as a laboratory researcher and community college biology professor before moving to a career in public policy, which began during her term as a program director at the National Science Foundation. From there she moved to Capitol Hill, where she was first a professional staffer and then acting staff director for the Research Subcommittee of the House Committee on Science. She spent several years as Princeton University's director of government affairs but returned to government as deputy to the associate director for science in the White House Office of Science and Technology Policy. Ms. Jones was then nominated by the president and confirmed by the Senate to serve as the assistant secretary for postsecondary education at the Department of Education. She has a deep interest in preserving the integrity and rich diversity of the American system of higher education, while also improving access and success for those students who have been underserved by traditional institutions and educational pathways.

ANDREW P. KELLY is a research fellow in education policy studies at the American Enterprise Institute and a doctoral candidate in political science at the University of California–Berkeley. He oversees the higher education work of AEI's education policy department. His research focuses on higher education accountability, congressional policymaking, and political behavior. As a graduate student, Mr. Kelly was a National Science Foundation interdisciplinary training fellow and graduate student instructor. Previously, he was a research assistant at AEI, where his work focused on the preparation of school leaders, collective bargaining in public schools, and the politics of education. His research has appeared in *Teachers College Record, Educational Policy, Policy Studies Journal, Education Next, Education Week, Insider Higher Ed*, and various edited volumes.

BRIDGET TERRY LONG is a professor of education and economics at the Harvard University Graduate School of Education. Her work focuses on college access and choice, factors that influence student outcomes, and the behavior of postsecondary institutions. Past projects examine the effects of financial aid programs, the impact of postsecondary remediation on degree completion, and the influence of class size and faculty characteristics on student persistence. Current projects include an aid simplification experiment, analysis of the growing gender gap in college enrollment, examination of institutional admissions policies, and continued research on the impact of financial aid. She is a faculty research associate of the National Bureau of Economic Research (NBER) and research affiliate of the National Center for Postsecondary Research (NCPR). She has also served as a visiting scholar with the New England Public Policy Center at the Boston Federal Reserve Bank. She received the National Academy of Education / Spencer Postdoctoral Fellowship and has been awarded numerous research grants from organizations, including the Bill and Melinda Gates Foundation, the National Science Foundation, the Lumina Foundation for Education, and the Ford Foundation. In July 2005, the *Chronicle of Higher Education* featured her as one of the "new voices" in higher education; and in 2008, the National Association of Student Financial Aid Administrators (NASFAA) awarded her the Robert P. Huff Golden Quill Award for excellence in research and published works on student financial assistance.

GERI HOCKFIELD MALANDRA was appointed provost of Kaplan University in September 2010. Previously, she founded and was principal of Malandra Consulting LLC, a company created to assist higher education leaders and connect stakeholders in developing and implementing outcomes-focused management, accountability, and policy initiatives. She served as senior vice president for leadership, membership, and policy research for the American Council on Education. Before this, Ms. Malandra was vice chancellor for strategic management for the 15-campus University of Texas System, where she led the development of its 10-year strategic plan, its first comprehensive accountability and performance reports, and a system-wide academic leadership institute. She also served as executive vice chancellor *ad interim* for academic affairs, overseeing the work of the nine universities. Her public service includes an appointment by Secretary of Education Margaret Spellings to serve as a member and vice chair of the National Advisory Committee on Institutional Quality and Integrity. At the University of Minnesota, as associate vice provost, Ms. Malan-

dra led the development of Minnesota's first comprehensive accountability reporting system, as well as policy initiatives and legislative
reports on issues related to accountability, accreditation, academic
program review, and planning issues. At Minnesota, she held earlier
management and policy positions focused on faculty and research development and organizational improvement in the College of Liberal
Arts and the College of Continuing Education.

RICHARD PETRICK served on the Ohio Board of Regents in a number
of leadership roles for 20 years, including serving as budget director
and associate vice chancellor for finance. He retired from the Regents
in August 2010 as vice chancellor for finance and data management.
Before joining the Regents, he worked for the Ohio General Assembly as an education finance analyst and division chief for the non-
partisan Legislative Budget Office. Over the past ten years, Mr. Petrick
has focused much of his work on developing and implementing
performance-based subsidy and financial-aid programs, improving
efficiency and productivity, and raising revenue for agency and campus operations through grants and interagency and interstate initiatives. He has been a frequent contributor to national, regional, and
state higher education initiatives, serving as a participant, presenter,
or moderator at the State Higher Education Executive Officers and
Midwest Higher Education Compact professional development and
policy-planning conferences, as well as contributing to many state,
campus, and private initiatives, such as the Aspen Institute.

JOSIPA ROKSA is assistant professor of sociology at the University of
Virginia, with a courtesy appointment in the Curry School of Education. She is also a faculty affiliate at the Center for Advanced Study
of Teaching and Learning and the Virginia Education Science Training Program. Ms. Roksa's research examines social stratification in
educational and labor market outcomes, with a focus on higher education. She is particularly interested in understanding how families
transmit advantages to their children, how interactions between the
educational system and the labor market produce unequal patterns
of individual attainment, and whether and how much students are
learning in higher education. Ms. Roksa is currently conducting studies examining how young adults' transitions into work, marriage, and
parenthood explain socioeconomic and racial or ethnic inequalities

in college completion and subsequent labor market outcomes. With Richard Arum, she is the author of *Academically Adrift: Limited Learning on College Campuses* (University of Chicago Press, 2011).

MARK SCHNEIDER is a visiting scholar at the American Enterprise Institute and a vice president at the American Institutes for Research, based in Washington, DC. He served as the U.S. commissioner of education statistics from 2005 to 2008 and a deputy commissioner in the National Center for Education Research from 2004 to 2005. He is also a distinguished professor emeritus of political science at the State University of New York–Stony Brook. Mr. Schneider is the author of numerous articles and books on education policy. His most recent book is *Higher Education Accountability* (Palgrave, December 2010). He also wrote *Charter Schools: Hope or Hype?* (Princeton University Press, 2007) and *Choosing Schools* (Princeton University Press, 2000), which won the Policy Study Organization's Aaron Wildavsky Best Book Award. His current work focuses on accountability in higher education and charter schools.

Page numbers in italics refer to figures, tables, and charts.

African American students *(cont.)*
  in the labor force, 105
  participation rate, 248, 249, 262
  remediation, 175
Alliance for Excellent Education, 179
American Community Survey (ACS),
    111, 112
American Council for Education (ACE),
    215
American Public University, 304
American Reinvestment and Recovery
    Act (ARRA), 228
Apprenticeship Advisory Council, 130
apprenticeship programs
  Ability to Benefit students, 133
  academic credit, 146, 147
  accreditation of, 144, 149, 150
  barriers to access, 10, 144
  benefits of, 10, 128–29, 148
  challenges to, 132
  compensation during, 127, 129, 133,
    141–42, 143, 148
  completion rate of, 130, 132, 133
  cost of, 146, 148
  defined, 127–28
  earning potential from, 141–42
  employee-employer relationship, 133,
    147
  expansion of, 6–7, 127, 132–34
  field industries, 131–32
  financial aid, 145–46
  and for-profit partnerships, 146–48
  green energy jobs, 132
  health care jobs, 132
  incentives for participation, 145–46
  journeyperson, 134, 143
  and kinesthetic learners, 126–27, 128
  lack of information about, 130–31, 144
  legislation of, 129–30
  need for, 143, 148, 149, 150
  in non-U.S. countries, 127–28, 139
  and Obama policy goals, 296
  outcome tracking, 134
  potential earnings, 143
  and practical learning/application,
    127, 128–29, 150
  pretraining for, 132
  public perception of, 141, 143–44
  registration of, 131–32, 149
  role models and mentors, 128

selective admission to, 133
sponsors of, 130, 131, 133, 150–52
standards of, 129, 130, 133–34, 146,
    148, 150
student evaluations, 146
in Switzerland, 127–28
tax incentives for, 146, 149, 150
time-based approach, 130, 134
See also Swiss Apprenticeship Model
Arizona General Education Curriculum
    (AGEC), 213–14
Arkansas Department of Higher Educa-
    tion, 179
Arum, Richard, 307
Asker, Eric H., 162
Assessment of Skills for Successful
    Entry and Transfer (ASSET), 178
ASSIST (Articulation System Stimu-
    lating Interinstitutional Student
    Transfer), 211
associate's degrees
  admission into baccalaureate pro-
    grams, 211, 212–13
  African American students, 85, 106,
    115
  attainment rate, 7, 23, *24*, 29, 30, 38,
    39, 42, 49, 74–75, 76, 77, *78*, 79, 80,
    103–4, 109, 110, 225
  cost of, 111
  earning potential, 82, 114, 120, 296
  and financial aid, 187
  graduation rate, 3, 83, 84
  and health care–related programs,
    109
  Hispanic students, 85, 106, 115
  and labor market need, 114, 120, 142,
    143, 294, 296
  longitudinal tracking, 84, *85*
  and nontraditional students, 305
  number conferred, 77–79
  policy design, 7, 42, 73, 77
  white students, 106, 115
attainment rate
  ability to reach Obama initiative, 5, 6,
    8, 17, *28*, 34–37, 39–40, 105, 293,
    294–95, 296
  academic preparedness, 18, 54,
    64–65, 227
  by age, 20–21, 21–22, *22*, 24–25, *25*,
    30–31, *49*

Mokher, Christine, 81
multi-institutional attendance
    bachelor's degree attainment, 203–5
    credit portability, 205, 206–10,
        216–17
    excess credits, 208–9
    increase in, 202–3
    time to degree, 206
Murray, Charles, 39
Mustard, David, 160

Natalicio, Diana, 250, 251, 256, 257,
    260–61
National Apprenticeship Act of 1937
    (Fitzgerald Act), 129
National Center for Academic Transfor-
    mation (NCAT), 192, 300
National Center for Education Statistics
    (NCES), 105, 112, 113, 119, 144, 176
National Center for Higher Education
    Management Systems (NCHEMS),
    29, 75, 104–5, 271, 288
National Center on Public Policy and
    Higher Education, 31
National Defense Education Act of
    1958, 37
National Education Longitudinal Study
    (NELS), 3, 53, 76, 80, 83, 112
National Governors Association (NGA),
    31, 37, 306
National Longitudinal Study of 1972,
    3, 112
National Student Clearinghouse, 64
A Nation at Risk, 22
Nicholson-Goodman, Jo Victoria, 239
No Child Left Behind (NCLB), 35
nontraditional students
    academic preparedness, 126
    accumulation of debt, 310
    certificate programs, 115, 116
    and degree attainment, 218
    and development courses, 177
    full-time employment, 216, 302
    increase in, 218, 298, 310
    need-based aid, 160
    omitted from outcome measure-
        ments, 257, 305
    online course delivery, 299
    and unexpected hardships, 167–68
Nora, Amaury, 162

Obama, Barack
    additional initiative proposals, 41
    address to Congress (February 2009),
        1, 27, 48, 104–5, 201
Obama administration
    and Access and Completion Fund,
        6, 41
    and Closing the Gap initiative goals,
        246–47
Obama administration education
    initiative
    achievement feasibility, 8, 12, 35–37,
        39–40, 48, 49, 102, 105, 294,
        295–96
    attainment gap, 75
    attainment rate, 24–25, 25, 27–31, 28,
        32, 73–74, 102, 293
    certificate program exclusion, 30
    certificates counted as degrees, 77, 83
    compared to past reform efforts,
        37–38
    completion goal, 11, 17, 75, 76, 201
    degree production increase, 74, 294
    effectiveness of, 17, 34–35, 38–39
    emphasis on community colleges, 9, 76
    exclusion of older students, 30
    goal assessment, 294–96
    international comparisons, 75
    measurement differentiation, 30
    and minority students, 246
    policy development, 29–30
    and population growth, 73
    as realistic goal, 17, 35–37, 38
    regain U.S. position, 24, 30, 48
    shift to completion emphasis, 1, 31–34
    total degree production, 73
    See also completion agenda
Occupational Outlook Handbook (U.S.
    Department of Commerce), 142–43
Office of Apprenticeships, 129, 144, 149
Office of Institutional Research, 229
Office of Vocational and Adult Educa-
    tion (OVAE), 226, 233, 239
Ohio Board of Regents, 12, 176, 270,
    273, 274
Ohio College Opportunity Grant
    (OCOG), 168
Ohio higher education reform, 87
    community college reform, 272–73
    and faculty effectiveness, 56

Ohio higher education reform *(cont.)*
  Governor's Commission, 281
  Higher Education Funding Commission, 274–76
  influence of states, 11
  Managing for the Future Task Force, 272–73
  need-based aid policy, 164–65
  Ohio College Opportunity Grant (OCOG), 168
  Ohio Instruction Grant (OIG), 168
  outcomes-based funding, 12, 269
  performance-based funding, 7, 12
  Securing the Future report, 273, 274
  and Strickland policy changes, 283–84
  TANF Educational Awards Program, 282–83, *283*, 288
Ohio Instruction Grant (OIG), 168
online course delivery
  attainment rate, 299, 303
  barrier reduction, 60
  completion rate, 61
  cost of, 60, 300
  effectiveness of, 59–60
  enrollment increases, 80–81, 299–300
  for-profit institutions, 299
  growth of, 299
  increased productivity, 59, 60
  nontraditional learners, 299
  Open Learning Initiative, 59
  PLA credits, 216
  program design, 60, 300–301
  quality of, 61, 300
  remediation programs, 60
  self-paced, 60–61
  transfer between campuses, 60
Opening Doors initiative (MDRC), 57–58
Opening Doors Program (Louisiana), 166
Open Learning Initiative (Carnegie Mellon University), 59, 300
Oreopoulos, Philip, 167
Organisation for Economic Co-operation and Development (OECD), 4
outcomes-based funding
  Access Challenge program, 271, *275*, 276–77, 279, 280, 282
  at-risk students, *275*, 278, 279–80, *285*, 286

course completion, 282, *283*, *285*, 286
data collection system, 269, 270–71, 276
degree/certificate completion, 279–80, 282, 286–87
enrollment-based formula, 276, 279, 280, 281–82, 284, 286
evaluation of, 288
and financial aid, 282–83, 286
funding formula, 271, 284, 289–90
goals of, 278–79
Jobs Challenge program, *275*, 276, 278, 279, 280
participation by policymakers, 269
Research Challenge program, 271, 274, 275, *275*, 276, 278, 279, 280, 281, 288
School Success Challenge program, *275*
selective admissions policies, 286
Selective Excellence program, 271, 272, 287, 288
stakeholder participation, 269, 276, 287, 288–89
state funding for, 269, 276, *277*, 278
subsidy allocations, 270–71
Success Challenge program, *275*, 276, 278, 279–80
Technology Challenge program, *275*
time to degree, 279–80
tuition costs, 276–77, 280
See also performance-based funding
OVAE grants, 226, 233, 239

Palameta, Boris, 166–67
Paredes, Raymund A., 251, 253, 255, 256, 258, 260, 261, 262, 264
participation rate
  and African American students, 248
  and attainment rate, 32
  community college, 19–20
  financial aid, 20
  and Hispanic students, 249
  measure of higher education, 17, 18, 19, 21
  U.S. standing, 19, *19*
Pennington, Hilary, 27
performance-based funding
  conditional support of, 166
  increased use of, 286
  in Louisiana, 32–33